Kwaku Boamah's well-researched and careful study of texts and the history of martyrdom in the African context breaks new ground, bringing home to those interested in African Christianity a dimension of the life of the church that we have often overlooked. The church was birthed within a history of pain, suffering, persecution, and martyrdom. The faith has survived because of the courage of our martyrs. "The blood of the martyrs is seed of the church," Tertullian is quoted to have said. Here in this volume Boamah has espoused the meaning of this statement for those who want to understand the contextual significance of the church fathers for our times. This is educative, illuminating, and engaging in the same breath!

J. Kwabena Asamoah-Gyadu, PhD
President & Baëta-Grau Professor of African Christianity and Pentecostalism,
Trinity Theological Seminary, Legon, Ghana

The early Christians presented themselves as familiar with occasional persecution, suffering, sickness, and death. Two recent and unrelated phenomena have brought the question of the Christian relationship to persecution and suffering into question. Radicalizing a traditional scholarly position, some scholars question whether it is appropriate to maintain that the Roman authorities persecuted the Christians; and some preachers claim that true Christians should claim a life of prosperity without suffering and sorrow. Through a meticulous and systematic comparison of early Christian martyr texts and apologetic literature, Boamah provides a balanced appraisal of how Christians viewed and responded to persecution. The memory of this provides an antidote to the so-called prosperity gospel. Some modern scholars have argued that it has detrimental effects for Christians to remember persecution, while some "prosperity" preachers claim that it is dangerous for Christians to acknowledge that they are suffering. Boamah's book shows that such approaches ignore historic and contemporary realities and have negative ethical consequences.

Jakob Engberg, PhD
Associate Professor of Church History and Practical Theology,
Aarhus University, Denmark

Kwaku Boamah, in this study, challenges the prosperity gospel as a Christian expression of faith from a historical perspective. Exploring the martyr and apologetic texts of the persecution and martyrdom of the early Christians, he draws attention to two main issues. First, from a methodological perspective, the complementarity of the two genres of texts in examining hostilities against Christians in the Roman empire; second, martyrdom as an inescapable feature of Christian witness. Furthermore, with examples from Ghana, he illustrates how establishing the Christian faith in Ghana has martyrdom features. His conclusion suggests that there can be no Christianity without sacrifice and suffering, contrary to the stance of prosperity gospel preachers.

This work is a good read for students and scholars of the Christian religion, religious leaders, and researchers in religious studies. I recommend it to all.

George Ossom-Batsa, PhD
Associate Professor of Biblical Studies and Mission,
University of Ghana, Legon

At the present time it is of vital importance to emphasize and reemphasize the impact of North African Christianity during the first five hundred years of Christian history. The period produced a munificence of great theologians and churchmen from Tertullian to Augustine. Dr. Boamah's study investigates, through a critical examination of the extant texts, the effects and consequences of persecution and martyrdom up to the close of the third century. The author proceeds to investigate some theological relationships and contrasts between the early African theologies of persecution and the prosperity theology widely fashionable in contemporary African revivalist theology, which appears to be in part responsible for the dynamic growth of Christianity across the African continent. The author identifies some of the persecutions of Christians that have occurred on the African continent during the nineteenth and twentieth centuries and offers a critical discussion of how these incidents have been interpreted. This masterly work is a must-read for both those interested in the history of persecution during the period of the early church and of the contemporary progress of Christianity on the African continent.

James C. Thomas, PhD
Associate Professor, Department for the Study of Religions,
University of Ghana, Legon

The Cross or Prosperity Gospel

Persecution and Martyrdom in the Early Church

Kwaku Boamah

© 2022 Kwaku Boamah

Published 2022 by Langham Academic (Previously Langham Monographs)
An imprint of Langham Publishing
www.langhampublishing.org

Langham Publishing and its imprints are a ministry of Langham Partnership

Langham Partnership
PO Box 296, Carlisle, Cumbria, CA3 9WZ, UK
www.langham.org

ISBNs:
978-1-83973-535-6 Print
978-1-83973-675-9 ePub
978-1-83973-677-3 PDF

Kwaku Boamah has asserted his right under the Copyright, Designs and Patents Act, 1988 to be identified as the Author of this work.

All rights reserved. No part of this publication may be reproduced, stored in a retrieval system or transmitted, in any form or by any means, electronic, mechanical, photocopying, recording or otherwise, without the prior written permission of the publisher or the Copyright Licensing Agency.

Requests to reuse content from Langham Publishing are processed through PLSclear. Please visit www.plsclear.com to complete your request.

Scripture quotations marked (NKJV) are from the New King James Version (NKJV). Copyright © 1982 by Thomas Nelson, Inc. Used by permission. All rights reserved.

Scripture quotations marked (RSV) are from Revised Standard Version of the Bible, copyright © 1946, 1952, and 1971 National Council of the Churches of Christ in the United States of America. Used by permission. All rights reserved.

Scripture quotations marked (Berean Study Bible) are taken from The Holy Bible, Berean Study Bible, BSB. Copyright ©2016, 2020 by Bible Hub. Used by Permission. All Rights Reserved Worldwide.

British Library Cataloguing-in-Publication Data
A catalogue record for this book is available from the British Library

ISBN: 978-1-83973-535-6

Cover & Book Design: projectluz.com

Langham Partnership actively supports theological dialogue and an author's right to publish but does not necessarily endorse the views and opinions set forth here or in works referenced within this publication, nor can we guarantee technical and grammatical correctness. Langham Partnership does not accept any responsibility or liability to persons or property as a consequence of the reading, use or interpretation of its published content.

To the many who have suffered and died for the cross
as well as those who keep on suffering today and
are ready to die for the course of the gospel.

Also to Hon. Prof. Ato Essuman and family, my parents
(Mr. and Mrs. Appiah Kubi and Mr. and Mrs. Adueni-Kuffo),
siblings, mentors, supervisors, friends and most of all my
wife (Mrs. Catherine Boamah) including our boys (Polycarp
Appiah-Kubi Boamah and Tertullian Boahen Boamah)

Contents

Preface xi

Chapter One 1
Christian Reception in Indigenous Cultures
    Scholarship on Persecution and Martyrdom 6
        The Roman Religiosity 7
        Nature of the Persecution and Martyrdom – Martyr Texts 8
        Studies on the Apologetic Texts 15
        Apologetic Texts and Martyr Texts 23
        Suffering in Christianity Today 25
    Period and Selected Texts Used 28
    Approaches 31
    Contributions 35
    Going Forward 36

Chapter Two 37
The Ghanaian Example of the Persecution and Martyrdom
    Emergence of Christianity in Africa 39
        Traditional African Response to Christianity 41
        European Missionaries 45
        African Agents 48
    Conclusion 53

Chapter Three 55
They Killed Us – Martyr Texts
    The Origin and Purpose of the Martyr Texts 56
    Background of Martyr Narratives 58
        Martyrdom of Polycarp 59
        Martyrdom of Justin and Companions 60
        Scillitan Martyrs 62
        Martyrdom of Perpetua 64
    Narrative and Protocol Forms Compared 65
        Narrative Martyr Texts 66
        Protocol Martyr Texts 82
        Similarities and Differences 89
    Conclusion 94

Chapter Four 95
"You Killed Us" – Apologetic Texts
    Submission Status of Apologies 96

  Purpose And Audience 99
  Background of the Apologetic Texts 100
   Justin Martyr 101
   Tatian the Assyrian 104
   Tertullian..107
  Internal Comparison of the Apologetic Texts.......................115
   Apologetic Texts to Authorities (Apologies)................115
   Apologies to the Public 127
   Similarities and Differences..135
  Submission Status 142
  Conclusion...145

Chapter Five 147
 A Two Genre Sources Approaches and Reception by the Authorities –
 Martyr and Apologetic Texts
  Fusion of the Martyr and Apologetic Texts...........................149
   Similarities 149
   Nuances...152
   Differences 154
  Submission Status of the Apologetic Texts 155
  Conclusion...159

Chapter Six 161
 Epilogue
  Purpose and Audience of the Martyr and Apologetic Texts............163
  Findings – Martyr and Apologetic Texts Compared 164
   The Usefulness of Apologetic Texts...............................164
   Submission Status of the Apologetic Texts 166
   The Texts and Contemporary Ghanaian Christianity................169
  Lessons for Contemporary Ghanaian Christianity 170
   Recording History 171
   Communalism/Solidarity..173
   Recount History to the Generations 175
   The Courage of the Martyrs 176
   Restrain over Reaction 177
  Commendations 177
  Future Studies..179
  Conclusion...179

Bibliography..183

Index 193

List of Tables

Table 1.1 Ancient sources with their date of writing 30
Table 3.1 Polemic attacks in the apologetic texts 143

Preface

Expressions present in music, sermons, and lifestyles of some contemporary Ghanaian preachers suggest that once people decide to follow Christ, they will not face predicaments such as sickness, barrenness, and pain. However, a look at Christian history demonstrates that there is no Christianity without a cross; in essence, suffering is part of the Christian tradition and theology. It is important therefore to recollect, reflect and learn from the history of the early Christians and the coming of Christianity to Ghana how contemporary Ghanaian Christians can deal with the question of suffering. The history of the early church shows that Christians were subjected to persecutions and martyrdoms at the hands of the Romans. The character of these persecutions and the motives of the persecutors are "classic" issues that have been debated over the centuries in ancient history, theology, religious studies, classical philology, and legal history. Traditionally, most studies on the persecution and martyrdom of the early Christians in the Roman Empire have used the martyr narratives and pagan texts as sources, while references to apologetic literature are found only sparingly. In the martyr-texts, the Christian authors projected images of the persecutions and presented these images to their Christian readers in order to console them and help them make sense of suffering. Similarly, contemporary apologetic texts projected images of suffering and persecution. However, little is noted of scholars who have attempted to compare the contemporary images projected in these two types of texts, and no one has done so systematically. It is debated in scholarship whether the apologists were defending against "real" accusations raised by the outsiders or whether they invented accusations as a pretext for promoting their ideas. Additionally, many scholars have claimed that the apologies addressed to authorities were not intended for submissions to their addressees. How do the martyr and apologetic texts corroborate, supplement, or contradict each other concerning the images of the persecution and martyrdom of the early Christians? What do the two types of texts promote? This question is best addressed through a systematic comparison of the martyr and apologetic sources.

The motivation for this book is: to examine the image of the persecution and martyrdom of the early Christians as portrayed in the martyr and apologetic texts as well as the relevance of these texts to Ghanaian Christianity. It is, therefore, pertinent to ask what image of the persecution and martyrdom of the early Christians is promoted in the martyr and apologetic texts including the relevance of the engagements of these texts to Ghanaian Christianity. The research objectives are segmented as:

1. *To weigh against each other, the portrait of the hostilities presented in the apologetic texts as corroborative, supplementary, or contradictive to the martyr narratives.* In this case, when the two genres of texts are compared internally and externally, how do they show different foci or significant overlaps, nuances, and/or contradictions?
2. *To establish the submission status of the apologies.* To determine this, the research question shall be: What features of the texts after the comparisons may suggest the apologies were intended for submission or otherwise?
3. *To explore some examples of persecution and martyrdom in Ghanaian Christian history especially during the missionary period.* To contextualize the discussion, the research asks, are there similarities to be found between the plight of the early Christians in the Roman Empire and those in the Ghanaian missionary period?
4. *To assess lessons from the martyr and apologetic texts that are relevant today for helping Ghanaian Christians deal with present sufferings.* It is imperative to eventually address how the Ghanaian Christians should respond to suffering based on reflections from the martyr and apologetic texts.

The comparison is relevant because the two types of texts emerge as different Christian responses to the hostilities against the early Christians in the Roman Empire. Both kinds of texts emerged as crisis literature, born out of the persecutions and martyrdom, from the same geographical area and written during the same decade. The two types of texts were however addressed to different audiences; the martyr-texts implicitly or explicitly to Christian readers, and the apologetic texts to outsiders (Roman magistrates or emperors, on one hand, and the general public on the other). Based on this, my thesis is that a detailed agreement in the image projected by the two types of texts would suggest that both kinds of texts do reflect the actual character of the persecutions; but at the same time, it would also suggest that the addressing of the apologetic texts to outsiders was a literary "fiction" since the authors found no need to target their addressees. Conversely, if there is little agreement in the image projected, this suggests that images of persecution and martyrdom were constructed at liberty by the authors and fashioned to serve different rhetoric and ideological purposes aimed at specific inside and outside audiences. The "balance" is struck if the study reveals a general agreement in the image projected by the two types of texts with some detailed differences that can be argued, are based on the authors' consideration of their respective audiences. If such a general agreement with detailed changes is found, it will arguably show that the image projected is generally accurate, and it will show that the two types of texts were intended for different audiences. Two distinct periods, but each of them formative and challenging and therefore on some level comparable (in the sense that they may be fruitfully compared with a view to both differences and similarities), will be studied. The main effort is devoted to a study of texts written in the mid-second to early third centuries of the Roman Empire. For comparison with the missionary period of the Ghanaian church history, how persecution and martyrdom in this period are presented is also studied.

The main purpose of this study is to systematically compare the early Christian martyr-literature to the early Christian apologetic literature to investigate if these sources corroborate, supplement, or even contradict their pictures of the character of the persecutions and the motives of the persecutors. Furthermore, it aims to discuss the submission status of the apologetic texts, i.e. if those texts that were addressed to emperors and magistrates were intended for submission. I, therefore, will survey the picture of the persecution and martyrdom of the early Christians as portrayed in the martyr and apologetic texts, discuss texts presenting an image of persecution and martyrdom in the missionary history of Ghana, and also present the relevance of the martyr and apologetic texts to Ghanaian Christianity.

The objectives of this book are attained through a systematic comparison of the texts both internally (i.e. martyr texts are compared to martyr texts and apologetic texts are compared to apologetic texts) and externally (martyr texts are compared to apologetic texts) to identify the similarities and differences in the image they project of the persecutions, the persecutors, and their motives. The texts are analyzed through the literary-critical method to study the rhetorical features of persuasions by focusing on the speakers, audience, context, and the discourse of the texts. In this way, the texts are each divided into two different subcategories and compared internally and externally at three levels that I have termed harmony, synthesis, and fusion. The objective is to find out if the two classes of texts when compared corroborate, supplement, or even contradict each other. These methods also help to scientifically determine the submission status of the apologetic texts to their addressees especially the authorities. Given these methods, the internal and external comparisons show that the apologetic texts are useful sources for the study of the persecution and martyrdom of the early church. More importantly, the methods employed show that even though there are some nuances (pointing to different audiences) between the texts, the two types of accounts do not contradict but rather provide evidence to support each other. Additionally, regarding the submission status of the apologies, it is argued that those apologies that were addressed to the authorities were intended for submission. This conclusion is based on the nuances in the internal comparison within the apologetic texts and the external comparison with the martyr texts. The subject of persecution and martyrdom is also an African story where there are examples of hostilities, especially from the missionary era. Both historical contexts offer some lessons and perspectives for the contemporary African Christians who may go through suffering, but who have recently encountered a prosperity gospel out of tune with the roots of Christianity (also in Ghana).

This project contributes to academic studies in many respects. The novelty in the methods, sources, and contextualization of the African examples, breaks new ground in the studies of the persecution and martyrdom of Christians. The study offers a paradigm shift in academia where scholars are encouraged to use both genres of texts to explore the hostilities against the Christians because the texts lend credence and complement one another.

The methods adopted in this book scientifically suggest that the texts were intended to receive the attention of their addressees. Moreover, it is clear from the research that the subject of the persecution and martyrdom is very relevant to Africa. This study is a novel attempt to compare the early beginnings of Christianity in Roman and African contexts.

CHAPTER ONE

Christian Reception in Indigenous Cultures

Christian faith is often portrayed today in the churches and on the media as offering its members predicament-free lives because all troubles are "rolled away."[1] This idea is reflected in the theme of many Christian evangelistic crusades such as "Jesus is the Answer" indicating that any person who becomes a Christian finds answers to all the questions of life such as hunger, ill-health, poverty among others. This idea is common in African gospel music. Many gospel songs today paint a flowery picture of Christianity where a person may be in abject poverty but upon becoming Christian experiences total transformation and begins to enjoy great affluence. An example of popular Ghanaian gospel music in this light is that of Patience Nyarko entitled "Obi nyani mi" translated as "someone should wake me up" based on Psalm 126 where the music video characterizes a roadside mechanic whose fortune is turned around and is now living in a big mansion with many servants and posh cars after he became a Christian. He thinks he must be dreaming since he finds this unbelievable. Another one of such songs is by Christiana Love titled "W'agye me" meaning "He (God) has saved me" in which a man who was suffering a lot of predicaments (sickness, hunger, etc.) and rejected by all, is later transformed by God. Christiana Love has another song titled "hyebre sesafo" meaning "destiny changer" where in the music video, a young man lost his job as a taxi driver, and because he could not pay rent, also lost his apartment. In his dreams, he is chased by demons and loses his only son in

---

1. Boamah, "Persecution and Martyrdom," 32.

a hit-and-run car accident but the video indicates that a "few months after God's intervention," he is totally transformed with much wealth. What is even more worrying is the evolution of "celebrity pastors"; pastors especially of charismatic churches display their wealth by way of what they wear and exhibit their flamboyant cars and buildings to show how well God has blessed them, using their affluence as a standard of being Christian. In Ghana, a respectable charismatic pastor, Archbishop Nicholas Duncan-Williams is noted to have said at the ordination of new pastors that "As a Christian, you should wear the best of clothing, drive expensive cars, and live in comfortable houses so that the glory of God could be seen in your life because the God you worship is very expensive."[2] To this extent, the contemporary Ghanaian Christian expression, due to its affinity to the prosperity theology, has little space for suffering.

However, it is imperative to pause and ask, in the light of these features of Christian expression in the eyes of the public, "What is the place of the cross in Christian expression today?" This inquiry is crucial because it can be argued that Christianity the world over and through the centuries has been born out of the blood and sweat of first-generation Christians especially and that this continues in successive generations. When Jesus began the Christian movement, he had to die, the early apostles died because of their faith and the situation was not any different when the message of the cross was presented in Africa. The church today must therefore learn from the examples of the early church in handling issues of suffering as a result of their faith.

The early church suffered various degrees of hostilities because of their faith in establishing the church; therefore Tertullian emphasizes "the blood of Christians is seed."[3] This statement affirms the fact that Christianity was born out of the blood of the first Christians. Jesus also suggests that in this world the Christian will certainly suffer:

> If the world hates you, you know that it hated me before *it hated you* (italics mine). If you were of the world, the world would love its own. Yet because you are not of the world, but I chose you out of the world, therefore the world hates you. Remember the word that I said to you, "A servant is not greater than his

---

2. GhanaWeb, "I'm Expensive Pastor."
3. Tertullian, *Apology De Spectaculis*, 13.

master." If they persecuted me, they will also persecute you. If they kept my word, they will keep yours also.⁴

It is consequently in this light that this work seeks to affirm the reality that the theme of suffering because of one's faith is not not merely a historical artifact but a contemporary reality. The subject of the persecution and martyrdom is not only a second–fourth century paradigm but continues even today and is an African reality. This work explores the subject of the persecution and martyrdom of the early Christians as well as examples of such hostilities in African church history during the missionary era, including some reflections for the contemporary African Christian.

In the event of the persecution and martyrdom of the early Christians, they resorted to writing texts which included the martyr and apologetic texts. This implies that the martyr and apologetic texts are both crises literature influenced by the same context. However, traditional scholarship has generally favored the martyr narratives on the subject of the persecution and martyrdom of the Christians against the apologetic texts. Most scholarship so far on the subject of the persecution and martyrdom of the early Christians have depended on the martyr narratives with virtually no reference to the apologetic texts. The apologetic and martyr texts introduce the different reactions of Christians to the charges against them, therefore; a systematic comparison is not only necessary but crucial. Jakob Engberg has called for a comparative study between the martyr and apologetic texts for a better appreciation of the nature of the hostilities against the Christians.⁵ The apologetic texts, compared to the martyr texts, are not often used for exploration of the persecution and martyrdom of the Christians. Although Ste. Croix and a few scholars have made scattered references to famous passages from a few apologetic texts,⁶ there have been no systematic and comparative studies of the hostilities that emerge in the martyr texts with those that emerge from a study of the apologetic texts. When such a study is commenced, it may potentially corroborate or supplement and even contradict the picture that emerges from the martyr accounts regarding the nature of the persecution.

---

4. John 15:18–20, NKJV.
5. Engberg, "Truth Begs No Favours," 181.
6. Ste. Croix, "Why Were the Early Christians?" 9, 23.

Additionally, the apologetic texts that were addressed to Roman authorities have generated debate among scholars. Whereas some scholars argue that addressing the texts to the Roman authorities was only a literary device, intended to heighten interest in the text through the employment of such prominent addressees,[7] others also suggest that the writing of small books on different issues to emperors and magistrates was one of the standard forms of communication in the governing structure of the Roman Empire.[8] It is hence desirable to establish the submission status of such apologetic texts.

The ancient Christian ideals of suffering for the faith and responding to accusations are not peculiar to the early church. This tradition continues to inspire in the modern-day African church, where Christians still face persecution and violent deaths. In Ghana, there are similar examples of hostilities against missionaries especially during the missionary era which are comparable to the plight of the early Christians in the Roman Empire. There are examples like the case of a Presbyterian local agent, Samuel Otu,[9] disruption of the activities of Augustinian Catholic Fathers in 1576 at Komenda and Efutu[10] as well as two Presbyterian maidens at Mamfe.[11] Consequently, this book explores the subject of the persecution and martyrdom as an African story. Although the concept of Christians facing some socio-economic losses because of their faith is still prevalent today in Ghana and other parts of the world, some preachers and expressions of Christian faith today make it seem that Christianity is devoid of suffering. This comes in large measure from the propagation of the prosperity gospel mainly started by a section of Pentecostal and charismatic ministries.[12] These preachers tell their congregations that a Christian should not fall sick, lose their job, be unemployed, or live in poverty. Traditional Christian accounts of the suffering of the just from the passion narratives of Christ in the Gospels,[13] the accounts of Paul and the apostles'

---

7. Jacobsen, "Apologetics and Apologies," 13–17.

8. Engberg, "Condemnation, Criticism and Consternation," 201–3.

9. Sanneh, *West African Christianity*, 115; Agyemang, *Ghana's First Christian Martyr*; Presbyterian Church of Ghana, *Brief Biography*.

10. Debrunner, *History of Christianity in Ghana*, 27; Witgen, *Gold Coast Mission History*, 20–25; Sanneh, *West African Christianity*, 26–27.

11. Theophilus, *Mamfe: Missionary Report*, 15.2.

12. Heuser, "Religio-Scapes of Prosperity," 17–24.

13. Matthew 27:26–66; Mark 13:15–47; Luke 23:24–56; John 19:16–42.

tribulations in Acts,[14] and the early Christian martyr texts highlight how such prosperity-teaching is out of touch with texts and traditions that are fundamental to Christianity in both its global and African context.[15] Even today, such sufferings are still ongoing years after the establishment of the faith. It is therefore imperative to enquire: What can the Ghanaian Christians today learn from how the early Christians faced these similar hostilities in their times?

This book examines important aspects of how the early Christians reacted to hostilities against them. Specifically, it investigates and compares how the early Christians presented the character of the persecution, the identity of the persecutors, and the motives of the opponents in two types of early Christian literature, the apologetic and martyr texts. The study focuses on the mid-second to early third centuries as well as the Christian missionary era in Ghana. This focus is motivated both by the pragmatic need to limit the work to what is manageable and by the fact that the two types of texts investigated emerged from the same period. It is hoped that such a study will pave the way for a more informed debate on the persecution and martyrdom of the Christians as such – a debate that takes the apologetic texts into greater account and analyzes them more systematically. Additionally, the study reflects on the strategies of the early church in dealing with the sufferings they faced as evident from the texts to help Ghanaian Christians deal with current predicaments and sufferings. This is to assess if and how the responses to suffering, persecution, and martyrdom in the early Christian apologetic texts and martyr texts along with the memory of suffering, persecution, and martyrdom in the missionary age in Africa may have relevance for African Christianity in today's age.

I have observed from scholarship that most scholars have tried to answer questions on how and why the Christians were persecuted and martyred, largely based on the martyr texts. Sherwin-White, for instance, raises questions against Ste. Croix for using the apologetic texts to address issues related to the persecution and martyrdom of Christians,[16] thereby suggesting that

---

14. Acts 12; 2 Corinthians 11:16–33.

15. Oden, *How Africa Shaped*, 117.

16. Sherwin-White, "Early Persecutions and Roman," 207–12; Ste. Croix, "Why Were the Early Christians?" 23.

the apologetic texts are not useful for understanding the persecution and martyrdom of the early Christians. The reliance on martyr texts alone has left a gap in regard to the usefulness of the apologetic texts which also show a vital response of Christians to the hostilities. This approach has resulted in an unsystematic discussion of the trustworthiness of the different kinds of sources, which have raised some questions such as: Were the apologies ever forwarded to the emperors or governors they were addressed to? Do the apologetic texts reflect "real" knowledge of the issues raised by outsiders? In light of these issues, I seek to investigate how these genres of texts from the same context corroborate, supplement, or even contradict each other on the subject of persecution and martyrdom. Furthermore, from a contemporary Ghanaian perspective where Christian expression is quite emotional due to the prosperity theology, I compare the two beginnings of the church in the Roman and Ghanaian missionary contexts and draw out reflections for the Ghanaian Christian today in dealing with current predicaments.

Scholarship on Persecution and Martyrdom

Since this work is a continuation of what is already there in scholarship, it is important to evaluate what scholars have done already. Generally, scholarship so far has focussed on the following questions: Why were the Romans hostile to the early Christians? Who was involved in the persecution and martyrdom of the Christians? On what legal basis were the Christians persecuted and martyred? These and many more questions have been engaged by scholars on the persecution and martyrdom of the early Christians in the Roman Empire.

The review of existing literature in this section has two main parts; first, a review of existing scholarly research on the hostilities against the early Christians, and second, the section on Ghanaian Christian expression will review studies on the prosperity gospel especially in Africa. The review on prosperity theology is important because many Ghanaian Christians profess a Christianity without the cross. To assemble what scholars have done concerning the hostilities against the early church, scholarly engagement on the context of the Roman Empire is evaluated to affirm some of the conditions that gave rise to the hostilities against Christians. Furthermore, scholarly positions on persecution and martyrdom based largely on the use of the martyr texts and texts written by outsiders on the Christians are presented.

Moreover, scholarly debates with regard to the addressees of the apologetic texts, as well as some of the charges against the Christians in these texts are explored. Besides, scholarly investigations into a possible relationship between the martyr and apologetic texts are also scrutinized. In general, the literature review in this part emphasizes the usefulness of both types of texts in determining the plight of the early Christians in the Roman Empire.

From the African viewpoint, the review tries to trace the emergence of the prosperity gospel in Africa. Both parts of the literature review confirm a research gap in scholarly discoveries regarding the hostilities against the early Christians due to the unsystematic application of the apologetic texts. The review of literature on the prosperity gospel shows the gap in Ghanaian Christian expression where many Christians live the Christian experience without a history; a suffering-free faith, which demonstrates the relevance of the persecution and martyrdom of the early Christians to African Christianity.

The Roman Religiosity

Scholarship on the context of the Roman Empire affirms that the Romans were very particular in their religion, though they were polytheistic.[17] Very often, their reaction to foreign religion wavered between reception and rejection. For example, Mary Beard, Joseph North, and Simon Price suggest that the Romans' polytheistic nature allowed them to import Magna Mater[18] into the Roman pantheon of gods when they perceived a need for her help during the war in the third century BC. However, their suspicious nature toward other religions caused them to modify some aspects of such imported gods to help them situate the gods in the Roman worldview.[19] They had concepts for accepted religiosity – "*religio*" which honors the gods and "*superstitio*" which dishonored or wronged the gods.[20] A religion that is seen as a threat to the political, moral, social, and economic fabric of the Roman society is

---

17. Engberg, *Impulsore Chresto*, 70–71.

18. Beard, North, and Price, *Religions of Rome*, 80. Magna Mater was from Asia Minor and was also called Cybele.

19. Beard, North, and Price, 212. When Magna Mater was transported to Rome, there were major modifications to suit the Roman context when it was introduced such as the changing of name among others. Furthermore, Roman polytheism does not suggest an all-embracing attitude toward any religious practice.

20. Beard, North, and Price, 215–19; Bediako, *Theology and Identity*, 21–29.

suppressed because it is *superstitio*.[21] Christianity was seen as a foreign religion and therefore, until around the fourth century, many Christians suffered all forms of oppression and even death.[22] The persecution and martyrdom of the early Christians took place in both Rome and the provinces of the Roman Empire.

Why were the Christians persecuted? What motivated the Roman authorities and the general public in opposing Christianity? What were the Christians accused of and on what legal grounds were the Christians persecuted? These questions are to an extent answered in traditional scholarship based mainly on the martyr texts and on texts written by pagan authors about the Christians. However, a systematic comparison of the martyr texts and apologetic texts should help to ascertain whether it will be productive in the future to make systematic and comprehensive use of the apologetic texts when studying the persecution and martyrdom of the Christians.[23] Nonetheless, it is imperative to know what scholars have identified so far on the persecution and martyrdom of the early Christians in their predominant use of the martyr texts and the pagan texts written about the Christians.

Nature of the Persecution and Martyrdom – Martyr Texts

Persecution and martyrdom in this book embody the hostilities meted out to Christians from the early second century to about the mid-third century. Persecution of the early Christians in the Roman Empire took the form of mockery and torture including other uncomfortable actions because of their professed faith. Martyrdom, on the other hand, based on its Greek etymology implies dying as a result of a person's devotion and witness.[24] John S. Pobee argues that "a martyr is a zealous devotee of God, who is willing and able to undergo suffering because of his deep-rooted conviction that the Almighty God is the ultimate authority and ruler of the world who alone matters."[25] The thin line therefore between persecution and martyrdom is that where persecution leads to death it becomes martyrdom.

---

21. This included cults like the cult of Bacchus which was suppressed in 186 BC because of perceived sexual and moral depravity. Beard, North, and Price, 95–99.

22. Beard, North, and Price, 365–66.

23. What is meant by external and internal comparison will be explained below.

24. Pobee, *Persecution and Martyrdom*, 24.

25. Pobee, 34.

I have earlier argued that there cannot be discussions about persecution or martyrdom without discussing the authority behind it.[26] In the Acts of the Apostles, there are instances of popular hostility without any authority involved (Acts 14:19–20; 19:21–41) as well as instances where local non-Roman authorities such as Jewish authorities, provincial governors, and Roman client kings are involved. Again, in the martyrdom of Perpetua and her companions, where regional Roman authorities were involved, the magistrate ruled that the condemned Christians should be executed on the birthday of the emperor believing it would please the emperor to have them killed.[27] Another instance can be extracted from the Acts of the Apostles where Paul was stoned and assumed to be dead but later got up and continued his work (Acts 14:19–28). This incident makes the distinction between persecution and martyrdom quite difficult. In the eyes of those who stoned him, Paul was dead (martyred) but to the disciples, he was just stoned and did not die (persecuted).

It is therefore not easy to give a precise definition or draw a clear-cut distinction between persecution and martyrdom. However, to a large extent persecution does not necessarily lead to death – but martyrdom relates to death as a result of a person's belief. Owing to a belief in the sanctity of life, people do not find pleasure in murder, so we often find the unending aggression of the Roman authorities toward the early Christians difficult to understand. It is therefore crucial to pose a few questions in this section. How well did the non-Christians know the Christian sect? Why were the non-Christians hostile? The actions of the oppressors could be attributed to their perception of the Christian faith and practices. It is therefore appropriate to try to assess the perceptions of the non-Christians based on Christian and non-Christian texts in circulation around the period.

Allegations and Charges

The persecution and martyrdom of the early Christians were influenced by several accusations and motives.[28] Some of the accusations found in the martyr narratives included the Christians being ungodly, superstitious, and

---

26. Boamah, *Magic and Obstinacy*, 17, 44–46.
27. *Martyrdom of Perpetua* 16:3.
28. Sherwin-White, "Early Persecutions and Roman," 207–12; Ste. Croix, "Why Were the Early Christians?" 6–38; Ste. Croix, "A Rejoinder," 28–33; Walsh, "On Christian Atheism," 255–77.

immoral; the narratives also reveal misconceptions about Christian doctrines and practices, and many other motives.[29] The name "Christian" was indeed a major charge against the Christians because it implied all kinds of social vices.[30] The word Christian was associated with abominable practices such as cannibalism and incest.[31]

Concluding the discussions on the charges against the Christians in scholarly writings thus far, the arguments can be put into two groups: monocausal and multicausal theorists. Some scholars believe that the persecution and martyrdom of the Christians were based on multiple allegations while others believe that the Christian charge was based on a single allegation. Those who belong to the single allegation theory include Ste. Croix, Janssen, and Sherwin-White. Ste. Croix believes that the charge of "ungodliness" finds expression through the centuries.[32] For him, the charge of ungodliness is tied to the charge of *superstitio* because the ungodliness of the Christians gave rise to their being described as *superstitio*. This position affirms Janssen's position that the ultimate charge of *superstitio* encouraged the non-Christians in their actions.[33] Furthermore, Ste. Croix argues strongly that the Christians were persecuted not for what they did but for what they did not do, suggesting that the Christians were persecuted and martyred because they did not pray to the Roman gods – making them ungodly.

Although Sherwin-White believes in the monocausal theory, he asserts that it is dispensational.[34] Thus in each dispensation, there is only one charge against the Christians. He contends on evidence that up until the second century, the reason for the persecution and martyrdom was influenced by a perception of "immoral acts" by the Christians which included incest and cannibalism. Yet, further in a transitionary period between the second and mid-second century, the charge changed to "Christian obstinacy." During this period, hostility toward Christians was fuelled by their disregard or

---

29. Engberg, *Impulsore Chresto*, 187–201; Janssen, "'Superstitio' and the Persecution," 131–59; Sherwin-White, "Early Persecutions and Roman," 772–87; Ste. Croix, "Why Were the Early Christians?" 6–38; Walsh, 255–77.

30. Benko, *Pagan Rome*, 1–29.

31. Benko, *Pagan Rome*, 54–74; Walsh, "On Christian Atheism," 264–67; Engberg, *Impulsore Chresto*, 187–91; Sherwin-White, "Why Were the Early Christians?" 23–24.

32. Ste. Croix, "Why Were the Early Christians?" 6–38.

33. Janssen, "'Superstitio' and the Persecution," 131–59.

34. Sherwin-White, "Early Persecutions and Roman," 772–87.

stubbornness toward the authorities. Sherwin-White further argues that after the mid-second century, the reason for the hostilities shifted to the perception of the "ungodliness" of the Christians.

The second category of scholars who believe in multiple charges includes Walsh, Benko, and Engberg.[35] Walsh on his part argues strongly against the monocausal theory but agrees with Sherwin-White's assertion that after the mid-second century, ungodliness was the main charge.[36] However, he further adds that accusations of Christian immorality such as debauchery equally played an important role in persecution and martyrdom. Benko, on his part, argues that the main charges against the Christians were immorality, cannibalism, and their name.[37] There was a cluster of reasons which gave room for the hostilities against the Christians. Engberg believes that the monocausal argument cannot stand and thereby acknowledges that there were smaller charges embedded in the major charges.[38] He argues that the most important charges were those of *superstitio* and ungodliness. For instance, an ungodly person who does not honor and respect the gods is also likely to be obstinate to authorities or parents, as well as show a lack of respect for the laws and norms of the society. Engberg's position is based on both Christian and non-Christian texts. *Superstitio* is prominent in pagan texts while the Christian texts project the charge of ungodliness. Given Engberg's position, it is clear that the charges were related in many respects where one charge is related to the others. All these arguments make it clear that the charges of ungodliness, *superstitio*, name, obstinacy, and magic can be seen as very important in the persecution and martyrdom of the early Christians.

Because of the research objectives, this work investigates a catalogue of the charges raised in the martyr and apologetic texts. These charges are compared to show a comprehensive picture of the charges levelled against the early Christians according to the Christian texts. This book also includes an investigation and comparison of how the Christians defended themselves against the charges and misconceptions levelled against them. Meanwhile, scholars have also enquired into the legal basis for the persecution and martyrdom of

---

35. Walsh, "On Christian Atheism," 256–62; Benko, *Pagan Rome*, 10–11; Engberg, *Impulsore Chresto*, 187–201.

36. Walsh, 261.

37. Benko, *Pagan Rome*, 1–24.

38. Engberg, *Impulsore Chresto*, 173–76.

the early Christians as presented in the two types of Christian texts, which will be discussed below.

Legal Basis of the Persecution and Martyrdom

The legality of the persecution and martyrdom of the early Christians has been discussed among scholars over the years.[39] The main questions have been: Was there any specific law against the Christians? What judicial procedure did the Christians face? The real question is whether there was a specific law against the Christians or Christianity. These questions are based on the premise that the hostility against the Christians was intensive, not just in Rome but even in other parts of the empire. Furthermore, apart from the authorities of the Roman Empire, other national assets such as the soldiers, colosseum, and amphitheatre etc. could not have been employed if there was no general acceptable basis for their use in the empire or province.[40] These questions have given rise to several schools of thought.

Sherwin-White, Ste. Croix, and Barnes do not agree that there was a specific law banning Christianity in the Roman Empire.[41] On the other hand, those who favor the specific law such as Keresztes put forward a very important question based on Pliny's decision to have the "faithful" Christian confessors put to death.[42] Keresztes argues that unlike the Christians, the Bacchanals, Druids, and Isis, were referred to as "other superstitions"; hence the Christians were punished differently from the others. The others were punished for particular vices, unlike the Christians who were punished based on the charge of their being Christians.[43] Why then were the Christians opposed, especially if there was no specific legislation against them?

Sherwin-White surveys the various positions of scholars concerning the Roman attitude toward Christians (up until the third century and the Great Persecutions).[44] Two schools of thought maintain that the Christians were

---

39. Sherwin-White, "Early Persecutions and Roman," 199–213; Sherwin-White, "Why Were the Early Christians?" 23–27; Sherwin-White, *Letters of Pliny*, 691–712; Ste. Croix, "Why Were the Early Christians?" 28–33; Barnes, "Legislation against the Christians," 32–50.

40. Boamah, *Magic and Obstinacy*, 44–45.

41. Sherwin-White, "Early Persecutions and Roman," 207–12; Ste. Croix, "Why Were the Early Christians?" 6–38; Barnes, "Legislation against the Christians," 32–50.

42. Keresztes, "Paul and the Christian Church," 278.

43. Keresztes, 284.

44. Sherwin-White, "Early Persecutions and Roman," 199.

prosecuted simply for being Christians (the *nomen*) – within these schools of thought, there are different theories regarding the underlying motives for the hostility toward Christianity. One of these ideologies, ascribing to the general law theory, maintains that this practice was based on a general law against Christianity.[45] Another school of thought maintains that no such law existed or was required – the practice for persecuting Christians simply had its legal foundation in the power and legal rights of Roman magistrates to enforce order and set up trials.[46] The third school of thought holds that Christians were not suppressed for being Christians, but only for specific crimes that they were believed to have committed.[47]

The general law school led by Callawaert and most French and Belgian scholars maintains that there was a law in the empire against Christianity. This school of thought holds that this law may have been enacted either by Nero or Domitian. However, scholars like Sherwin-White do not find enough evidence in support of the general law theory. Sherwin-White rather finds evidence of laws restraining the practice of Christianity only in Rome and not in the other provinces.[48] Ste. Croix also argues that there were no general edicts, not even "Tertullian's notorious reference to an '*Institutum Neronianum*' is evidence of this. Ste. Croix accepts that after AD 117, Trajan's rescripts were published and served as a guideline for (some) governors as a precedent, although it stresses that there were no general edicts.[49]

The second school of thought, supported by Theodor Mommsen, is called the "*coercitio*" theory. Mommsen argues that the legal basis of the persecution was the Roman governors' interest to preserve peace and order in their provinces. The "*jus coercitio*" theory implies that the legal basis for the persecution against Christians had no reference to a specific law. Generally, most historians have supported the theory originally posted by Mommsen – that the Roman governors had the supreme power in their respective provinces to act without reference to any specific legislation but rather as they best saw fit. Sherwin-White, for example, agrees with this theory and substantiates

---

45. Sherwin-White, 201–2.
46. Sherwin-White, 202.
47. Sherwin-White, 199.
48. Sherwin-White, 202–03.
49. Ste. Croix, "Why Were the Early Christians?" 14.

this by adding that the sources do not give enough evidence for the "general law-theory," and that those sources which could support this theory are only explaining persecutions restricted to Rome and do not include the situation in the provinces. Sherwin-White argues that enforcement of law often depended primarily on private initiative. He demonstrates that the evidence conclusively shows that the Christians faced not police-like action, but a formal legal process called *cognitio extra ordinem*.[50] It is a judicial process where the governor plays the dual roles of an interrogator (examiner of the case) and a judge.

Conrat is one of the proponents of the third school of thought on the legal basis of the persecution and martyrdom of the early Christians. This school of thought holds that the Christians were charged based on anti-social acts that were prohibited by the Romans. The Christians were dealt with based on what the Romans called *scelera* (sin or crime), *flagitia*, and *contumacia*.[51] Sherwin-White agrees with Last's solution that only part of the Christians behavior was criminal and therefore forbidden (and suppressed). The development of this theory not only combines the two former positions but also avoids the pitfalls in which they find themselves. On a general level, Ste. Croix agrees with Sherwin-White but attempts to prove him wrong on one very important point, namely Pliny's shift from *flagiatia*-accusations to *contumacia*-accusations.[52] Ste. Croix – regarding martyr reports – points to the *contumacia* as being the stubbornness in confessing three times that they were Christians,[53] and not as political obstinacy.

In summary, Sherwin-White posits that there were no centrally coordinated persecutions of the Christians in the first centuries and that the policy was to deal with the cases individually, based on "real" offences like *flagitia* and *contumacia*. Ste. Croix, like Sherwin-White and many other recent scholars (such as Engberg), maintain that there was no law specifically directed against the Christians.[54] However, Ste. Croix disagrees with Sherwin-White on the motive of the hostilities against the Christians. The most important

---

50. Sherwin-White, "Early Persecutions and Roman," 205–08.
51. Sherwin-White, 210–12.
52. Ste. Croix, "Why Were the Early Christians?" 18.
53. Ste. Croix, 19.
54. Ste. Croix, 8–9.

reason, according to Ste. Croix, is that the authorities and the general public considered the Christians to be atheists who by their actions would invoke the anger of the gods and destroy the good relationship that existed between the society and the gods.[55] Engberg, though not too interested in the legal basis, argues that based on (an experienced lawyer) Pliny's doubt, there may not have been a specific law against the Christians.[56] This makes the attempt to understand the reasons why the Christians were persecuted and martyred relevant. To achieve this task, all the possible sources including the apologetic texts must be employed. In this case, therefore, the martyr and apologetic texts cannot be overlooked if this exploration will be worthwhile to all. Consequently, it is prudent to turn attention to what scholars have been discussing with regard to the apologetic texts which are useful for a deeper understanding of this issue.

Studies on the Apologetic Texts

The apologetic texts, in general, have received great attention from scholars though they are rarely systematically analyzed as compared to other kinds of sources in studies that seek to understand the persecution and martyrdom of the Christians. In this section, scholarly discussions regarding the apologetic genre and content as well as the audience or addressees, and the charges and the apologists' response are presented to better understand the picture the Christians painted of the persecutions and their persecutors.

Genre and Content of the Apologetic Texts

Many scholars have given great attention to the definition of the apologetic texts. The second century is described as a period in which Christian apologetic writing flourished.[57] It is crucial to define what makes up the genre of materials in this category of texts; however, Anders Klostergaard Petersen laments the neglect of a definition of the apologetic genre by scholars in recent times.[58] He identifies that recent scholars have given up the attempt to find a critical definition because earlier efforts have proven futile. In this regard,

---

55. Ste. Croix, 24.
56. Engberg, *Impulsore Chresto*, 174.
57. Alexander, "Acts of the Apostles," 15.
58. Petersen, "Diversity of Apologetics," 17–23.

he holds that scholars need to have a clear understanding of what "genre" is when trying to understand the apologetic genre. He argues that the unsuccessful attempts at defining the apologetic genre are because of a lack of a clear universal understanding of "genre." To be successful, the genre should encompass content, form, and characteristics that differentiate it from other groups of texts.[59]

Jacobsen agrees with Petersen by stating that genre should not only be about form but also the content and intention of the text.[60] Petersen is quick to caution that the genre should not be seen as static but rather dynamic.[61] Influenced by Fowler, he suggests that "every literary work changes the genre it relates to … by conformity, variation, innovation, or antagonism."[62] He, therefore, holds that apologetic texts should be seen as a complex breed of texts which has the aim to create an identity for its in-group members.[63] Edwards, Goodman, Price, and Rowland, borrowing from Conte, maintain that a "genre should not be seen as a mechanical receipt-book for the production of text, but rather as a discursive form capable of constructing a coherent model of the world in its image."[64] The idea of apologetics as a mark of identity of a group of people is shared by many other scholars. Jacobsen, for instance, cites Kahlos in support of Petersen's emphasis on the role of apologetic texts as a tool of identity creation.[65] The apologetic text, therefore, helps to create their "otherliness" from other social and religious groups.

In a similar light, Price equally posits that apologetics is about the creation and maintenance of boundaries.[66] It is noteworthy that almost all scholars, including Petersen, Jacobsen, Young, Price, Cameron etc., maintain that it is not possible to define the apologetic genre.[67] Jacobsen supports Cameron's proposal that we define the category as an "apologetic method" where apology

---

59. Petersen, 32.
60. Jacobsen, "Apologetics and Apologies," 20.
61. Petersen, "Diversity of Apologetics," 33.
62. Petersen, 33.
63. Petersen, 16.
64. Edward et al., "Introduction: Apologetics," 2.
65. Jacobsen, "Apologetics and Apologies," 9.
66. Price, "Latin Christian Apologetics," 105.
67. Jacobsen, "Apologetics and Apologies," 18; Petersen, "Diversity of Apologetics," 33; Price, 113.

(defense) is used as a strategy or a method of argument.[68] Young attempts to stress the oral aspect of apology by stating that the apologetic genre takes the form of a "letter" but has a content "of defence" and assumes the model of a law court presentation.[69] Jacobsen and many others support the idea that apologetics can be oral or can be written when a physical presence is impossible.[70]

In light of these discussions, the motivation of an apologetic text is important to scholars because the motivation is likely to influence the content, genre, and strategy for the writing. Ulrich contributes to this discussion by identifying three factors for the rise of the apologetic texts.[71] The first reason for the apologetic texts, according to Ulrich, is that the early Christians believed they possessed certain absolute truths of life. The idea of absolute truth is crucial for Christianity to show its uniqueness from other religions in the Greco-Roman empire. This truth fundamentally questioned the saving ability of other religions. The second reason identified by Ulrich is that the apologists needed to clear misconceptions against Christianity by non-Christians, and the third reason is, martyrdom was an important factor. According to Ulrich, the authors argue against the charges levelled against the Christians and they try to point to absurdities or anomalies in the procedures employed by the authorities in trials against Christians. This third reason for the composition of apologetic texts as identified by Ulrich resonates with me.

Jacobsen suggests that the apologetic texts cannot be defined by genre or addressee but on the basis and content of the text.[72] In agreement, Petersen, like many other scholars, proposes that the content of an apologetic text must have an element of defense.[73] Petersen cites Anaximense who maintains that the defense must either prove their innocence, or admit their guilt but prove they are backed by law and are therefore not guilty, or seek forgiveness.[74] Jacobsen argues against Petersen and remarks that his analysis of submitting

---

68. Jacobsen, 19.
69. Young, "Greek Apologists," 91.
70. Jacobsen, "Apologetics and Apologies," 5.
71. Ulrich, "Apologists and Apologetics," 1–7.
72. Jacobsen, "Apologetics and Apologies," 21.
73. Petersen, "Diversity of Apologetics," 27-31.
74. Petersen, "Diversity of Apologetics", 36

defense as a definitive mark of an apologetic text is too fluid[75] since every text has an element of defense. He adds that it is the intensity of the defense that makes it possible to classify the text as apologetic.[76] To Jacobsen, the defense is to answer some labelled attacks, which may be explicit or implicit (real or imagined).[77] In agreement with other scholars such as Geffcken, Seeberg, Harnack, and Adams, Jacobsen posits that apologetic texts have a double intention, that is, to defend and explain. The explanation is important because the Christians were a small group of people in the early Roman world, whose faith many non-Christians did not know about. This ignorance on the part of the non-Christians led to speculations, and therefore there was a need to explain to the public who the Christians were and what they believed in.[78]

Ulrich argues that this explanation is crucial because the non-Christians in some ways could not even differentiate between Christianity and Judaism.[79] He uses examples from Tacitus's erroneous thought of Christianity as "*chrestoi-virtuous*" from *chrestoi*, meaning kind. These words do not have the same etymology; *christoi* implies *anointed*, but *chrestoi* is a moral term. Pliny also thought that the Christians were a political organization.[80] Bediako further affirms that the distinction between the Jews and Christians gave room for the persecution and martyrdom of the Christians.[81] While the Jews were seen as a nation, the Christians were perceived as a sect. Apologetics, therefore, refute negative thoughts toward them by stating a defense and painting a positive picture of themselves via explanation. Petersen disagrees with Edwards, Goodman, Price, and Rowland in their exclusion of polemics from the components of an apologetic text.[82] He posits that polemics may be an aggressive way to defend oneself against charges. However, Edwards, Goodman, Price, and Rowland maintain that polemics may not necessarily be used to defend a previous charge by the oppressor.[83]

---

75. Jacobsen, 12.
76. Jacobsen, 12.
77. Jacobsen, 5.
78. Jacobsen, 8.
79. Ulrich, "Apologists and Apologetics," 4.
80. Wilken, *Christians as the Romans Saw*, 15–25.
81. Bediako, *Theology and Identity*, 15.
82. Petersen, "Diversity of Apologetics," 30.
83. Edward et al., "Introduction: Apologetics," 1.

Price also tries to distinguish between polemics and apologetics by stating that polemics attack without showing any positive views while apologetics address out-group members by correcting misconceptions to present a positive view.[84] Ulrich who also believes apologetics may include polemics maintains that "All such polemics from the apologists should be understood in an eschatological context with the addressees."[85] The arguments here show that polemics may be very important in an apologetic text. To this end, Jacobsen argues that the content of the apologetic style has four main argumentative strategies.[86] In the first place, the apologists adopt an ironic rhetorical approach. Second, they equate Christianity to the best Greek traditions like philosophy. Third, they cite examples from converted "Greeks" to Christianity and finally, they reject negative charges and advance positive explanations of Christianity. All these strategies are adopted to strongly foster the defensive elements in these apologetic texts.

It follows from the discussions that there are no accepted boundaries for the texts called apologetics. Scholars have found their efforts to determine this boundary unsuccessful because the various texts that make up this category are diverse. However, almost all scholars agree that an apologetic text must be predominantly defensive in its approach. The obvious questions to ask at this stage are, what do they defend and to whom were these defenses directed.

Addressees and Audience of the Apologetic Texts

A major feature of apologetic texts which makes them similar to letters is that they have addressees.[87] However, apologetic texts differ from letters in terms of the predominant defense content. Apologetic texts written by Christians are usually addressed to emperors, magistrates, or the pagan public. The addressee of an apologetic text may in theory differ from or be identical with (to various degrees overlap with) the intended audience of the text (who, the author expects, will read the text) and the actual audience (who in reality read the text).

---

84. Price, "Latin Christian Apologetics," 106.
85. Ulrich, "Apologists and Apologetics," 21.
86. Jacobsen, "Main Topics in Early Christian,", 102–6.
87. Young, "Greek Apologists," 91.

The questions of the relationship between addressees and intended audiences of the apologetic texts have received much attention from scholars. Interestingly, Jacobsen argues that identification of the addressees of the apologetic text cannot help in identifying the genre of the apologetic text.[88] His argument is grounded on the premise that the explicit addressees of the apologetic texts should not lead scholars into wrongly thinking that they were the only intended audience of the text – the intended audience might be wider or even different from the addressees. Jacobsen argues that although in most cases, the explicit addressees of the texts might either be emperors and governors or those in authority, the intended audience was in most cases, in-group members.[89] This position is a departure from earlier scholars like G. Kruger and B. Altaner, who maintained that based on the apology of Justin, the explicit addressees of the apologies were the intended readers – the emperors.[90] Ulrich, like Jacobsen and many other recent scholars, caution that scholarship does not simply presume that the addressees were also the (only) intended readers of the texts.[91] To Ulrich, the apologies also imply a "self-justification about Christianity's identity",[92] therefore, the Christians themselves were also intended readers of these texts.

To these recent scholars, the function of these texts is to equip Christians with arguments to be able to withstand anti-Christian arguments against them. Price agrees with this position that apologetic texts were meant to strengthen the Christian faith and to equip the Christians against the non-Christians.[93] So the Christians, who were often the intended readers, found the apologetic texts more useful than the explicit addressees. This argument supports Ulrich who states that "the apologists aimed to establish the Christian faith as a legitimate *religio* in the Ciceronian sense and present it as a sensible religion or philosophy."[94] Thus, the authors of these apologetic texts had the Christians in mind when elaborating their works. Petersen agrees with this position by suggesting that although the text is addressed

---

88. Jacobsen, "Apologetics and Apologies," 17.
89. Jacobsen, 16.
90. Jacobsen, 14–15.
91. Ulrich, "Apologists and Apologetics," 28–29.
92. Ulrich, 29.
93. Price, "Latin Christian Apologetics," 105–6.
94. Ulrich, "Apologists and Apologetics," 17.

to non-Christians, it "predominantly" has the Christians as its target.[95] For him, the apologies have an "important internal function" not only against external opponents but even more internal ramifications.[96]

Jacobsen identifies three audiences and the aims for targeting them.[97] In the first place, he suggests that the target of the apologists was the Roman authorities, intending to defend the Christian faith against the charges which were fuelling the persecution and martyrdom of the Christians. Second, the texts targeted the Greco-Roman public to convert them to Christianity. Finally, Jacobsen believes the apologetic texts were written with a strong Christian orientation to build the faith of the Christians by encouraging them to hold on to what they believed.

Relative to the discussions on the addressees and the intended audiences of the apologetic texts, it is concluded that the explicit addressees of these texts were not the only intended readers of the texts. Recent scholarship posits that these texts were equally intended for Christians to use, though they were addressed to outsiders. Notwithstanding, scholars are divided on the submission status of the apologies. Some are of the view that the explicit address is but a literary tool to gain attention and that the texts were not intended to be submitted to the explicit addressees. Others hold that it was a standard practice to write such treaties to the emperors and hence they were intended to be submitted.[98] These arguments are made but without strong proof. It is in this regard that this book presents evidence to give credence to the idea that the authors of the apologetic texts intended those in authority to read their texts.

Charges in the Apologetic Texts

If the apologetic texts can be useful to the discourse on the hostilities against the Christians and indeed if they were written to defend a case, then it is necessary to know what they found worth defending. This is important because scholars such as Jacobsen and Engberg agree that the tag of an apology is to defend and therefore the perceived misconception must be evident in the

---

95. Petersen, "Diversity of Apologetics," 26.
96. Petersen, 27.
97. Jacobsen, "Main Topics," 106–8.
98. Jacobsen, 107.

apologetic text.⁹⁹ Scholarship has not been blind to this fact in the apologetic literature. Most of these charges have already been discussed by scholars who used the martyr texts to understand the persecution of the Christians, so attention was given to examine the charges presented in the apologetic texts in comparison to and possibly to contrast what was found in the martyr texts.

The focus was on the possibility of using both martyr and apologetic texts to understand how the Christians in the two types of texts presented their opponents and the positions of their opponents. There are further implications beyond this book for understanding the phenomena of persecution and martyrdom on a broader basis of comparing what is found in the apologetic texts, the martyr texts, and in pagan literature about the Christians. It is important to note that many scholars argue that there is the possibility that the charges the apologists deal with may be fabrications and not real.¹⁰⁰ However, others such as Engberg disagree with this school of thought because the setting and time of the writing of the apologetic texts were the same as that of the martyr texts, thus the writers "dealt with real accusation, real opponents, real persecution and not just papyri or parchment-tigers."¹⁰¹

Ulrich identifies charges such as ritual murder, cannibalism, cultic promiscuity including incest, obstinacy, and stupidity by worshipping a donkey, and the most important charge at the time, the charge of atheism.¹⁰² Young also identifies with the charges of the name "Christian" and atheism based on the apology of Justin as well as the charge of idolatry in Tatian's work.¹⁰³ Jacobsen on his part categorizes the charges under political, religious, and ethical headings.¹⁰⁴ Politically, the Christians were charged for being a disorderly group who met in secret places and did not partake in the emperor worship. Religiously, the main charge was atheism because the Christians were professing a new religious movement and refused to worship the traditional deities. The Romans liked things that were linked to antiquity *(the mos maiorum)*¹⁰⁵ but the Christians dissociated from such things. This caused

---

99. Jacobsen, "Apologetics and Apologies," 5–8; Engberg, "Truth Begs No Favours," 178.
100. Engberg, 178.
101. Engberg, 208.
102. Ulrich, "Apologists and Apologetics," 13–16.
103. Young, "Greek Apologists," 82–85.
104. Jacobsen, "Main Topics," 85–101.
105. Jacobsen, 95.

them to be perceived as a new movement without any affiliation with antiquity and hence, they were not considered as an organization that could be allowed to thrive. Ethically, the Christians' meetings in secret places were perceived by non-Christians as intended for engaging in cannibalism (the Eucharist) and incest by kissing one another with a holy kiss even though they called each other "brother or sister."

It is important to stress at this point that there are similarities between the charges identified in the martyr and apologetic texts. Most importantly, it affirms Sherwin-White and Ste. Croix's position that in the second century, the charge of atheism was often pronounced since it gave enough reasons for the persecution and martyrdom of the Christians. This study does not only stress these similarities but also the nuances in the charges and their mode of presentation in the apologetic and martyr texts.

Apologetic Texts and Martyr Texts

This book aims to compare how the martyr texts and apologetic texts present the character of the persecution, present their opponents, and the charges and allegations of these opponents. Earlier scholars who primarily engaged in studying the persecution of the early Christians have not systematically compared the two types of texts and have tended to discuss the martyr texts more than the apologetic texts. In the exchanges between Sherwin-White and Ste. Croix, Ste. Croix uses some apologetic texts to advance his arguments but in response, Sherwin-White questions Ste. Croix for using the apologies.[106] It is thus obvious that Sherwin-White and other scholars view the apologetic texts as not credible sources in the debate on the persecution and martyrdom of the Christians. Judith Lieu also argues against Edward, Goodman, and Price with regard to their book titled *Apologetics in the Roman Empire: Pagans, Jews, and Christians*. She asserts that the work has no essay on the martyr accounts and only four references in the index.[107] Lieu identifies some perceived differences between the apologetic and the martyr texts. She relates this to the phrase "what has Athens to do with Jerusalem?"[108] where Athens is seen as a place of reasoning and a representative of the apologetic

---

106. Sherwin-White, "Why Were the Early Christians?" 23.
107. Lieu, "Audience of Apologetics," 207.
108. Lieu, 205.

texts while Jerusalem is related to faith and synonymous with the martyr texts. Again, others believe that the apologies have an explicit audience but the martyr texts do not.[109]

However, Lieu argues that the account of the martyrdoms of Polycarp, Perpetua, and her companions as well as those in Lyon were written in the form of letters to some churches, hence her assertion that they have an explicit audience. The crux of her argument seeks to show the great similarities between the two classes of texts.[110] She argues that both texts cannot be defined in terms of genre and both are written with the Christians in mind which Engberg agrees with.[111] She further suggests that these texts were both written in the same crisis period, hence the belief that this serves as a propelling force of the persecutions and martyrdoms. In effect, Lieu drives home the point that both texts influence and depend on each other.[112] She mentions that the protocol martyr narrative types are like the apologies, while Justin's apology uses some martyr narratives too. These similarities as projected by Lieu are important developments that draw the attention of scholars to the possibility of using these texts together to unveil a comprehensive picture of the plight of the Christians in the second and third centuries.

It is in this light that Engberg calls for the systematic approach in the combination of the two classes of texts to understand the persecution and martyrdom of the early Christians.[113] He tries to show the way on a soft level by using several martyr and apologetic texts to evaluate these assertions. In the end, he shows that it is possible to use these two classes of texts for a better understanding of the persecution and martyrdom of the early Christians.

This book identifies with Engberg's call but goes even further to do not just an external comparison but two levels of internal comparisons. The uniqueness of this book is found in sources, methodology, and research questions. In terms of sources, Engberg uses apologetic texts addressed only to the emperors but this book does not only use those addressed to the authorities but also those addressed to the non-Christian public. The apologist

---

109. Lieu, 206.
110. Lieu, 206–10.
111. Lieu, 207–9; Engberg, "Truth Begs No Favours," 184–85.
112. Lieu, 207–11.
113. Engberg, "Truth Begs No Favours," 181.

Tertullian, for example, addressed one of his apologetic works to the pagan public and another to the governors. Another apologist Justin Martyr wrote two apologies to an emperor whereas his student Tatian wrote to the public. The other novelty in this study is the methodology employed: a systematic comparison. The systematic comparison compares the two types of texts "internally" within each class of texts before carrying out an "external" comparison between martyr texts and apologetic texts. Engberg compares the apologies to the martyr narratives (external comparison) but has, in contrast to this work, not conducted "internal" comparisons of the two types of texts. Finally, the questions pursued in this book do not focus on the character of the persecution, the identity of the persecutors, and their motives, but rather on how these aspects are presented in the two types of texts. This comparison will potentially be relevant for later studies of persecution and martyrdom.

Suffering in Christianity Today

I Peter 5:10 says, "And the God of all grace, who called you to his eternal glory in Christ, after you have suffered a little while, will himself restore you and make you strong, firm and steadfast." This verse shows a strong relationship between Christianity and suffering as well as an encouragement to endure pain as a result of one's faith. However, the emergence of the Neo-Pentecostal theology of Kenneth Hagin in the 1960s introduced some shifts.[114] What is interesting is that when Pentecostalism began Pentecostals were poor and spoke against wealth.[115] However, this soon changed due to trade and world economic movements.[116]

The prosperity theology is sometimes called *name it and claim it; Faith Formula Theology, Faith Equals Fortune Message; Holistic Gospel; Health and Wealth Gospel*.[117] It stresses the positive confession of faith for breakthroughs in all aspects of life and holds that poverty is a curse.[118] Pastors of the prosperity gospel messages use extravagant means of travel including private jets while adorning themselves with luxurious garbs. Their chapels (cathedrals)

---

114. Lee, "Prosperity Theology," 227.
115. Lee, 227.
116. Lee, 227.
117. Kwateng-Yeboah, *Social Effect of Prosperity Gospel*, 56.
118. Lee, "Prosperity Theology," 228; Asamoah-Gyadu, *Contemporary Pentecostal Christianity*, 89.

use state of the art technology, thrilling worship forms, and liberal dressing of members.[119] During their worship services, they emphasize financial giving and seed or covenant sowing[120] including donating cars, houses, etc.[121] It is important to assess how the prosperity gospel evolved in Africa.

Prosperity Gospel in Africa

Kwateng-Yeboah suggests that the spread of the prosperity message to Africa is quite difficult to trace. Meanwhile, some scholars, including Paul Gifford maintain it entered Africa from North America. However, Matthew Ojo, Asamoah-Gyadu, and others hold a strong position that the Africans' worldview, evident by their cultural practices, constantly seeks prosperity.[122] The conditions that gave rise to the birth of the prosperity gospel in North America were prevailing in Africa too which influenced the theology when it emerged. Benson Idahosa who was trained by Kenneth Hagin is noted to have been the progenitor of the prosperity gospel in Africa.[123] Idahosa also affected people like Mensa Otabil, Nicholas Duncan Williams, and many others through his Bible School and visits to African countries for crusades and leadership seminars.

Additionally, the role of David Oyedepo of the Living Faith World Outreach or Winners Chapel cannot be overemphasized in the spread of the prosperity gospel in Africa.[124] He had four private jets, houses in Britain and the US, including a publishing company where he published his numerous books for sale. At one time, he was estimated to be worth US$ 150 million.[125] He was influenced by Kenneth Hagin's books and television programs.[126] Within sixteen years of his ministry, Oyedepo had planted thirty-

---

119. Lee, "Prosperity Theology," 231.
120. Asamoah-Gyadu, *Contemporary Pentecostal Christianity*, 79.
121. Asamoah-Gyadu, 91.
122. Kwateng-Yeboah, *Social Effect of Prosperity Gospel*, 56; Asamoah-Gyadu, 79.
123. Kwateng-Yeboah, 58.
124. Kwateng-Yeboah, 59.
125. Kwateng-Yeboah, 59.
126. Gifford, "Prosperity Theology of David," 84; Oyedepo mentions Gloria Copeland as his role model and adds that he slept on Kenneth Copeland's bed. Oyedepo also claims that he had a vision of God telling him that a baton has been passed on from Kenneth Hagin to him. Kwateng-Yeboah, 58.

eight branches in various African countries.[127] He, like Kenneth Hagin, emphasized faith, testimonies, and quoting of Scriptures.[128]

Prosperity Gospel in Ghana

The Ghanaian Christian landscape has not been free from the ideals of the prosperity gospel in diverse ways. Idahosa is often credited with the influx of the prosperity gospel in Ghana because he is deemed to have trained preachers like Nicholas Duncan Williams and Mensa Otabil.[129] These other preachers also trained the likes of Dag-Heward Mills, Ampiah Kwofie, Sam Korankye-Ankrah, and Eastwood Anaba who in turn trained many other neo-prophetic persons such as Elisha Salifu Amoako and Isaac Owusu Bempah. Duncan Williams, in the 1980s, used the television as well as other means to trumpet the prosperity gospel while arguing that God wants his people to be rich and have the best of lives. Asamoah-Gyadu recalls that Duncan Williams preached that Jesus wore a designer cloth because his garment was seamless, also adding that on his crucifixion, the soldiers needed to cast lots to own the garment.[130] He was captured to have remarked in 2011 that:

> "No matter how rich you are in my church, I will not allow you to intimidate me with your wealth because you cannot even buy the perfume I use not to talk of the attire I wear," he told the congregation at the church located at Abrepo … "As a Christian, you should wear the best of clothing, drive in expensive cars, and live in comfortable houses so that the glory of God could be seen in your life because the God you worship is very expensive."[131]

These comments are a reflection of how he lives, his theology, and most of all the kind of training he is giving to his followers. In effect, he does not understand why a Christian should suffer in any way. It is however interesting that his compatriot Mensa Otabil, though trained by the same person, discounts excessive wealth although he also attracts the elites of the society

---

127. Kwateng-Yeboah, 59.
128. Gifford, "Prosperity Theology of David," 85–99.
129. Kwateng-Yeboah, *Social Effect of Prosperity Gospel*, 59–60.
130. Asamoah-Gyadu, *African Charismatics*, 205; Kwateng-Yeboah, 59.
131. GhanaWeb, "I'm Expensive."

and has some important holdings in the country.[132] Asamoah-Gyadu observes that these preachers interpret the cross to mean God has taken away humanity's shame and hence the Christian has to live comfortably.[133] These Christians have no place for suffering and persecution in their understanding of the Christian faith and hence the change in the wedding vow from "for better for worse" to "for better for best."[134] Some biblical passages they often use in prayer and preaching are 3 John 2; Phil 4:1–7; Luke 6:38; John 10:10; Deut 8:18.[135] The relevance of these sufferings to the early Christians and Christians today, especially those in Ghana will be evaluated.

The review of the existing literature has shown the interests of various scholars concerning the persecution and martyrdom of the early Christians as well as the question of suffering in Christianity, especially the development of the prosperity gospel. The discussions by the various scholars have created schools and positions all intending to appreciate these phenomena in Christian development. There is, however, a gap related to the trustworthiness of the various sources used to understand the plight of the Christians in the Roman Empire from the time of Nero to the period of Constantine. It is therefore prudent to systematically compare the various reactions which led to the writing of the martyr and apologetic texts by the Christians. A systematic comparison will lead to a corroboration, supplementing, or even contradiction of the images of the persecution and martyrdom as portrayed by these two classes of texts.

Period and Selected Texts Used

This book consists of two main contexts: the early Roman mid-second to early third centuries (specifically between AD 150–212) and the modern missionary Ghanaian period. The mid-second to early third century period was chosen because it includes the period of systematic and widespread nature of the hostilities and again it marks the development of the texts used in this book. There were more systematic persecutions in AD 250, 257–260, and

---

132. Kwateng-Yeboah, *Social Effect of Prosperity Gospel*, 5
133. Gyadu, *Contemporary Pentecostal Christianity*, 105–6.
134. Gyadu, 107–10.
135. Kwateng-Yeboah, *Social Effect of Prosperity Gospel*, 56.

303–311/313. But these were "untypically" harsh and also untypical because they were initiated by the emperors. However, the period AD 150–212 was a period where the intensity and character of the persecutions were "typical" which followed quite similar patterns.

Thus, apart from a need to limit this work, the period is influenced by the primary texts as boundaries of the study. *Apologeticum*, Tertullian's most famous apologetic work, is argued to have been written in Carthage around AD 197. His other work, *Ad Nationes*, is maintained to have been written in the same year. Some scholars maintain that *Ad Nationes* formed the draft for the writing of the *Apologeticum*; which means that they were both written in the latter part of the second century. Tertullian's address to Scapula is dated to AD 212. On the other hand, the first and second apologetic texts of Justin Martyr are dated between AD 150 and 157 based on reference to Felix as a recent prefect of Egypt. It is generally believed that the *Second Apology* was originally part of the larger *First Apology*. Furthermore, Tatian's work *Ad Graecos* is equally believed to have been written around the second century too. He addresses the Greeks on the pain the Christians were suffering for being Christians in the Greco-Roman world.

The apologetic texts are compared to the following martyr narratives which were all written in the second or third century AD: "The Martyrdom of Polycarp" is a contemporary letter written in AD 155 by the Christians in Smyrna and addressed to other Christians in Asia Minor describing the martyrdom of Bishop Polycarp and other martyrs. Meanwhile, the text of the martyrdom of Justin and his companions is largely dated to AD 165. Furthermore, Scillitan Martyrs is a martyr text written around AD 180 in a form that resembles a Roman court protocol. Scholars have often debated whether such a protocol was used as a source by a Christian author. Finally, the *Martyrdom of Perpetua*, a compound text, was explicitly written to edify Christians, consisting of passages written by an editor and passages written by two of the martyrs in prison. These narratives are chosen because they are connected to the apologies both geographically and with regard to time. Robert Grant claims, for example, that Justin's apology was written in response to the Martyrdom of Polycarp[136] because it makes a lot of reference to burn-

---

136. Grant, *Greek Apologists of the Second Century*, 3, 53–54.

ing by fire. This suggests that they may have both been written under similar conditions in chronology and geography.

These texts were read in their original languages, Latin and Greek, along with their modern translations in English. Below is a table of the primary texts used in this book which indicates their form or style of writing and their addressing forms as well as their dates:[137]

Table 1.1 Ancient sources with their date of writing

Text	Subgenre of Text	Date
Justin, *First Apology*	Apologies[138]	150
Martyrdom of Polycarp	Narrative account[139]	155
Justin, *Second Apology*	Apologies	157
Martyrdom of Justin and His Companions	Protocol account[140]	165
Acts of the Scillitan Martyrs	Protocol account	180
Tertullian, *Apologeticum*	Apologies	197
Tertullian, *Ad Nationes*	Apologetic	197
Tatian, *Ad Graecos*	Apologetic	2nd Century
Martyrdom of Perpetua and Felicitas	Narrative account	208
Tertullian, *Ad Scapulam*	Apologies	212

---

137. For the purpose of this work, the accounts of the martyrs referenced are the translation of Herbert Musurillo. Justin's *First and Second Apologies* are Leslie William Bernard's translation. Molly Whittaker's edited translation of Tatian's *Oratio Ad Graecos* is used. Tertullian's *Apologeticum* was read in T. R. Glover's translation and Alexander Roberts and James Donaldson's for *Ad Naiones*. Rudolph Arbesmann's translation of Tertullian's address to Scpula is used.

138. Engberg has suggested that the apologetic texts written to Roman authorities should be called apologies while the others addressed to the general public should be called apologetic. Engberg, "From among You," 51.

139. These are martyr narrative accounts written in the form of a story.

140. These martyr narrative forms are written in the form of courtroom proceedings where there are questions and answers.

Approaches

This book adopts the literary critical approach following the rhetorical critical analysis of George Kennedy. The rhetorical analysis helps to develop elements that are compared in a systematic comparative method in addressing the objectives of the study. The literary critical approach proves helpful in the discussion of the rhetorical style of the texts.[141] The study is textual and, therefore, it is essential to understand the authorship, language, historical setting, and content of the text.[142]

George Kennedy suggests that the writer of a text has a purpose which he/she hopes to accomplish through the text.[143] Hayes and Holladay show that literary criticism and rhetorical criticism are highly related since both of them are aimed at persuasion.[144] Tate argues that rhetorical criticism is concerned with communication between the author and reader, looking at the strategies employed to influence the reader.[145] Scholars such as Kennedy, Hayes, and Holladay as well as Tate maintain that ancient rhetoric was greatly influenced by Aristotle's persuasive styles.[146] These strategies include *ethos* which is the character of the speaker, *pathos* which refers to the feeling and reaction of the audience, and finally *logos* which is the logic or the discourse of the text. To this extent, rhetorical studies look at the invention, thus, the planning of the text, arrangement, and order of the text and style in terms of the method; these three are often present in written forms, while the oral forms are built on the memory (preparation) and delivery is concerned with the voice and gestures.

Because of this, Kennedy suggests that every rhetorical study must consider four items for persuasion: the speaker or writer, audience, discourse, and the context or occasion.[147] The speaker or writer of the texts must be identified because the identity of the author influences what is written or

---

141. Hayes and Holladay, *Biblical Exegesis*, 73–82; Krentz, *Historical Critical Method*, 30–32.

142. Hayes and Holladay, *Biblical Exegesis*, 73.

143. Kennedy, *New Testament Interpretation*, 3.

144. Hayes and Holladay, *Biblical Exegesis*, 74.

145. Tate, *Biblical Interpretation*, 285.

146. Kennedy, *New Testament Interpretation*, 15; Hayes and Holladay, *Biblical Exegesis*, 74–75; Tate, 285.

147. Kennedy, 15.

spoken. An appreciation of the audience (both implied and implicit) helps to identify the purpose or perlocutionary effect of the texts among other things. The discourse of a text is mainly the content, issues raised, and how they are presented. Therefore, a discourse analysis helps to know what the author of the text seeks to say and how it is said to elicit the needed effect on the audience. An understanding of the context or the occasion of a text unravels the push factor of a text. Thus, what necessitated the writing or the speech of a text? This is very important because the choice of words, the imagery used, and the structure of the texts are to a large extent influenced by the push factor. These four elements guided the study of the texts to present a comprehensive picture of the persecution and martyrdom of the early Christians using the martyr and apologetic texts.

The systematic comparative method focuses on historical similarities as well as differences between the two sets of texts.[148] The method is grounded on Paden's perspective that a comparative method looks out for resemblance and contrast between various components. The comparison method, therefore, focuses on similarities and differences based on comparative elements that come out from the literary-critical approach. This method is applied at two levels: internally and externally. Internally, the martyr texts are subdivided into subgenre based on the form or style of writing and evaluated within to bring out a comprehensive picture of the hostilities depicted by martyr texts. The martyr texts subdivision is possible because some of the martyr texts are narrative in character (e.g. *Martyrdom of Polycarp* and the *Martyrdom of Perpetua*) while others follow a court protocol style (e.g. *Scillitan Martyrs* as well as the *Martyrdom of Justin and His Companions*). The authors of these two subgenres within the group of martyr texts may have a reason for adopting the style they adopted. This implies the formation of the texts may dictate the content and features of the sub-genre. The content of the two subgenres dictated by the style of the text may lead to some possible similarities and differences between the two divisions, which are analyzed internally. The internal comparison helps to highlight similarities and differences between these subgenres. This comparison shows a coherent picture of the persecution and martyrdom of the Christians illustrated by the martyr texts.

---

148. Paden, "Comparative Religion," 225.

In like manner, the apologetic texts, based on the differentiation of the addressees, are divided into two: those addressed to authorities (described as apologies)[149] and those addressed to the general public.[150] The *First* and *Second Apology* of Justin Martyr are addressed to Emperor Antoninus Pius whereas, his student Tatian wrote *Ad Graecos* to the Greek public. Tertullian wrote two apologies, *Apologeticum* and *Ad Scapulam*, which were addressed to authorities, and an apologetic text *Ad Nationes*, addressed to the general public. It is interesting to study the issues raised in texts addressed to the authorities and texts addressed to the public separately. It is also necessary to know if both Justin and Tatian present the issues in the same manner despite the difference in addressees. Furthermore, does Tertullian change his style and content when writing to authorities as compared to when he writes to the general public? Such comparisons provide insights into the intentions that prompted the writing of the texts and informs the debate on the question of whether or not the formal addressees were also (part of) the intended audiences for the texts.

It is anticipated that a petition to the authorities should follow a particular form and content besides containing fewer polemics (since the apologetics are a petition or an appeal) unlike the martyr texts, which are often written to encourage surviving Christians. Although the context of the texts is influenced by the hostilities against the Christians, the motivations for the two texts (martyr and apologetic) are different, and hence the style, rhetoric, and content are expected to be different. It is even more interesting that some scholars believe Tertullian is the editor of the account of the martyrdom of Perpetua and her companions.[151] The external comparison helps to answer the questions of the book in three broad ways. In the first place, a radical difference will mean not reflecting a common context, which is to suggest that the apologetic texts are not useful on the subject of the persecution and martyrdom of the early Christians. In the second place, if the analyses show a close similarity, it will mean the texts were not aimed at different audiences implying that the apologies were not intended for submission after all. A third position may show a coherent similarity with nuanced differences to reflect the same context but

---

149. Engberg, "From among You," 51.
150. Engberg, 51.
151. Boamah, *Magic and Obstinacy*, 23, note 56.

described with different aims and audiences in mind. This reveals that the apologetic texts are useful on the subject of the persecution and martyrdom of the early Christians and even more importantly, that the apologies were at the very least intended for submission to their addressees.

The two kinds of texts, martyr and apologetic, are therefore compared systematically on three levels. First, where the martyr texts and the apologetic texts are compared internally, the result is labeled "harmony" (even if potentially, the comparison reveals more differences than similarities). Second, the two subgroups in the two categories of texts are compared with each other. The result of this comparison is labeled "synthesis" (again even if potentially the comparison will reveal more differences than similarities). The harmonized and synchronized versions are both designated to be comparisons at the "internal" level since martyr texts are compared to martyr texts and apologetic texts to apologetic texts. On the third level, where martyr texts are compared to apologetic texts externally, the result is labeled "fusion" (again even if potentially the comparison will reveal more differences than similarities). None of these words carry any theological implication and are chosen simply to make it clear which of the three levels of comparison are discussed.

On the other hand, the study compares the early church period to the Ghanaian missionary era since they both mark the early beginnings of Christianity in a new context. The two contexts show the beginnings of Christianity in an already established socioreligious environment. In doing this, therefore, the study identifies examples of European and African missionaries facing persecution and martyrdom in Ghana during the missionary era. These examples of similar characters with the plight of the early Christians in the Roman context will signify the role of suffering in Christian expression. In the light of the similar context of suffering in both the early Roman and Ghanaian missionary contexts, reflections from the martyr and apologetic texts will be drawn to help the contemporary Ghanaian Christian in dealing with suffering because of their faith. The lessons drawn from these texts will help Christians today deal with the challenges they face. Since the contexts are similar, lessons from how the early church was able to endure the predicaments of their time would help contemporary Christians today put up with the same.

The literary critical approach following the rhetorical critical model of Kennedy helps to create the comparative categories for the broad comparative elements such as the accounts, actions, accusations, argumentation strategies, and themes. These elements are used to measure to what extent they corroborate, supplement, or contradict each other. Furthermore, the two beginning contexts of Christianity in the Roman and Ghanaian contexts are also compared to identify examples of persecutions and martyrdoms as well as lessons drawn from the martyr and apologetic texts for the contemporary Ghanaian Christians.

Contributions

This book contributes to knowledge on how the Christians in two types of contemporary texts perceive and present the persecutions they were subjected to in the Roman Empire. Little attention has been paid to the systematic comparison of sources in the study of the persecution and martyrdom of the early Christians, therefore this book evaluates the trustworthiness of the sources. The study further has a direct bearing on the discussion of the submission status of the apologetic texts to their addressees and more indirect ramifications for the study of how and why the Christians were being persecuted. The internal comparisons within the martyr texts and the apologetic texts as against the external comparison of the martyr and apologetic texts provide a new path in the study of the persecution and martyrdom of the early Christians.

Furthermore, I show the usefulness of the apologetic texts to the study of the persecution and martyrdom of the early Christians. So far, in the study of this phenomenon, only relatively scattered or unsystematic references have been made to the apologetic texts. I demonstrate that the apologetic texts are equally very relevant to understanding the phenomena of persecution and martyrdom.

Finally, the Ghanaian perspective shows the relevance of the subject of persecution and martyrdom of the early Christians to Africa as a whole using the Ghanaian examples. Many Ghanaian Christians seem to profess a Christianity devoid of suffering; but from the example of the early Christians, it is argued that suffering forms a part of the Christian calling. The examples of hostilities in African Christian history from the missionary era affirm the fact that the subject of the persecution and martyrdom of the early Christians is also an African story. The novelty here again is what the Christians today and especially the African Christians can learn from the example of the early church in dealing with contemporary suffering.

Going Forward

This book is organized into six chapters. The first chapter has discussed the background issues, which introduced the subject of the persecution and martyrdom of the early Christians to create the context of the book. The second chapter situates the subject of the persecution and martyrdom of the early Christians in the Ghanaian context, especially from the missionary period. This part, though modern, seeks to show the relevance of the subject of persecution and martyrdom in Ghana by especially bringing out examples of sufferings and deaths of Christians for the purpose of the Christian faith.

The third and fourth chapters investigate internally, the martyr and apologetic texts exclusively. These two classes of texts are therefore divided into two: based on the writing forms (martyr texts) and their addressees (apologetic texts). The comparisons aim to bring out the similarities and differences to see if they internally corroborate, supplement, or even contradict each other. The fifth chapter compares the two genres of texts. The apologetic texts are placed side by side with the martyr texts to find similarities and differences in order to demonstrate if they corroborate, supplement, or contradict each other. This external comparison invariably helps address the submission status of the apologies to their addressees, especially those addressed to the authorities.

The final chapter addresses the objectives of the research, arrived at by a discussion of the issues based on the research objectives and questions thus raised. The chapter further draws a few lessons the Ghanaian Christians can learn from these accounts in dealing with contemporary sufferings. In the end, some recommendations, based on the findings are suggested for further studies and application.

CHAPTER TWO

The Ghanaian Example of the Persecution and Martyrdom

A part of the Ghanaian national pledge says, "I promise to hold in high esteem, our heritage, won for us, through the blood and toil of our fathers" which recounts the history of the founding of the nation as emanating from the "blood and toils" of the founding fathers.[1] In like manner, the inception of the church in Ghana, like the example of the early Christians, was through the "blood and toils" of the first Christians. The phenomena of persecution and martyrdom of the Christians is not only an event of history but also a contemporary reality.[2] Many Christians around the world, including Africans, still face persecution and martyrdom in various forms. Langdon Gilkey asserts that "suffering represents a universally shared experience, but still one always received, experienced and understood it in a particular way."[3] Therefore, the subject of suffering for various reasons including as a result of faith is shared by all humans irrespective of geography or time. However, the challenge is that it is understood differently by different people especially in terms of the reasons why. In the African context, Thomas Oden maintains that the persecution and martyrdom are in respect to the Christian concept of "the communion of saints."[4] Therefore in the third century, the Romans persecuted and martyred the early Christians; whereas in the seventh century,

---

1. "National Pledge", see: https://ghanahighcommissionuk.com/anthempledge.aspx.
2. Boamah, "Apologetic and Martyr Texts," 48.
3. Gilkey, "Christian Understanding of Suffering," 50.
4. Oden, *How Africa Shaped*, 117.

the Arabs invaded Christian territories and in the nineteenth century, colonial powers scrambled for Africa; and today, jihadist sects are wrestling for control.[5]

Although the modern trends of persecution and martyrdom are quite different from what happened to the early Christians in the second and third centuries in Rome, the underlying motivation and sufferings of the Christians remain the same, irrespective of the time and place. The motivation of the Romans against the Christians was predominantly to protect the social, political, and religious worldview of the time and place. Today, many Christians face forms of hostilities aimed at forcing them to uphold the general sociocultural dynamics of the setting within which they find themselves.

This chapter focuses on some Ghanaian examples to show the relevance of the subject of the persecution and martyrdom among Christians today. Africa, due to the global shift in the Christian movement to the global south, has become one of the major homes of Christianity.[6] Since the subjects of persecution and martyrdom are all engaging phenomena in Christian history, it is greatly significant to trace their elements to a place from where Christianity in the world today gains its strength. In doing this, the study seeks to demonstrate the level of continuity of Christian history spanning the second century to the modern era (Rome to Africa-Ghana). This chapter discusses examples of persecution and martyrdom in Ghana from the missionary era, which included both the European and African missionaries. Just as it was necessary to understand the context of the early church in the Roman Empire, so it is needful to understand the history of the beginnings of the Christian faith in Ghana. Furthermore, the chapter builds bridges from the Roman second-third centuries to the modern Ghanaian context by drawing lessons from the martyr and apologetic texts. The lessons are intended to help the Ghanaian Christian in dealing with the hostilities of contemporary times.

---

5. Oden, *How Africa Shaped*, 117.

6. Walls, *Missionary Movement in Christian History*, 79–110; Walls, *Cross-Cultural Process*, 117–19; Bediako, *Jesus in Africa*, 3–7.

Emergence of Christianity in Africa

The history of the church in Africa is traced from biblical times, especially the time of Jesus's earthly ministry.[7] In the first instance, when Jesus was born and needed to be kept safe from the cruelty of King Herod, the spirit of God directed his earthly parents to an African country, Egypt (Matthew 2:13–15). Additionally, on the day of Pentecost, which marked the birth of the church, the people gathered included Egyptians and Libyans who were Africans but could hear the disciples speak in their native languages (Acts 2:10). What is more, the apostle Philip was led by the Spirit to leave the large congregation he was ministering to in order to minister to a lonely African from Ethiopia, a eunuch in the desert (Acts 8:26–40). This eunuch has been identified as Judich,[8] and was believed to have come from Meroe, serving Queen Candace.[9] By Judich's efforts, there grew a flourishing Christian kingdom in the upper Nile valley for centuries. Historically, it is suggested that John Mark, who wrote the Gospel of Mark visited Egypt while apostle Thomas travelled through Egypt to India where he was martyred.[10] These and many other examples from the Bible and other Christian sources show that the gospel of Christ is not alien to Africans.

Christianity in the western part of Africa was largely introduced by Catholic Portuguese Christians during their economic exploration under the leadership of Don Diego D'Azambuja who landed at Elmina, a place in the then Gold Coast (now Ghana) on 19 January 1482.[11] These first Portuguese explorers, on landing ashore, acquired a piece of land from the king of Elmina, Nana Kwamena Ansah, whose name they recorded as Caramansa. They celebrated the first mass and later erected the image of St. Anthony, which was later corrupted by the indigenes as a god by the name Nana Antona. This first missionary effort did not yield many converts and is sometimes described as a failure especially because the Portuguese were more interested in economic activities than missionary efforts. Sanneh describes this period

---

7. Sanneh, *West African Christianity*, 1–4.
8. Sanneh, 3.
9. Sanneh. 3.
10. Sanneh, 4.
11. Debrunner, *History of Christianity*, 16–19; Witgen, *Gold Coast Mission History*, 1–8; Sanneh, *West African Christianity*, 22; Essamuah, *Genuinely Ghanaian*, 2.

as the incubation period.[12] The second wave of the missionary effort can be described as the period of the chaplaincy. This was the period of colonization when European explorers who came to Africa had chaplains on board to take care of the spiritual needs of the Europeans. These chaplains sometimes extended their duties to the local people especially "mulatto" children. This period was also plagued by some setbacks such as finance, misconduct of the merchants, health, conflicts, and language challenges. The third stage of the European missionary enterprise, which was more systematic and comprehensive, can be described as the period of the missionary groups. During this period, many of the religious organizations in Europe and America began to send missionary teams to evangelize the people and plant their denominational congregations in Africa. There were groups like the Society for the Propagation of the Gospel (SPG), Augustinian priests, Caucasian priests, Dominicans, Wesleyan Missionary Society, Basel Mission Society, Breman Mission, and many other missionary groups.[13]

This phase of the missionary enterprise used education, translation, health, economic empowerment, and other strategies to plant churches in Africa. One of the most important strategies of the Society for the Propagation of the Gospel was advocated by CMS secretary Henry Venn known as the three "selfs."[14] He advocated that Africans themselves should lead the African churches (self-governing). Again, the Africans should lead the evangelization process (self-propagation) and the Africans must be made to generate funds to run the African church (self-financing). This and many other strategies adopted by these missionary groups engaged the Africans in the missionary efforts as interpreters, translators, preachers, and sometimes even missionaries. The collaboration between the European and African agents was necessary because the Europeans were frequently affected by malaria. Many of the European missionaries died barely six months after arriving, therefore the African agents did most of the evangelical works, while some were sent to Europe to be trained and brought back, and others were trained in Africa for the local people.

---

12. Sanneh, *West African Christianity*, 20.
13. Agbeti, *West African Church History*, 11–102; Sanneh, 26–34.
14. Agbeti, 28–29.

Traditional African Response to Christianity

It is crucial to examine the response of the indigenous African people, especially the authorities, toward the emergence of Christianity on African soil. The importance of this investigation is born out of the fact that generally, the presence of a new religion in the face of an established religion is likely to be met with some resistance. Although it is said that African traditional religion is elastic and accommodative, it resisted the presence and growth of Christianity in Africa just as the Romans did.

African traditional religion worshippers, like the Romans, resisted Christianity during the missionary days because they wanted to preserve their relationship with the gods for the safety of their society. In most cases, the traditional priests fuelled such feelings against the missionaries because the presence of the Christians could anger the gods thereby bringing some calamities on the people. For instance, Freeman is deemed to have recorded in his diary that "since my arrival in Ashanti, the fetish men seem to have taken the alarm a day or two back. The Twissah fetish men said that the town was in danger of being destroyed by fire and that they must make fetish to ward off the danger."[15] The idea of securing the safety of the society by pleasing the traditional gods, therefore, affected the reception of the Christian faith by the populace. In Fomena, the people were not ready to accept the Christian faith because it would mean abandoning the traditional religion. Birtwhistle, therefore, remarks: "they said they were afraid that trouble would come to their nation if they neglected their fetish days and observed the Christian Sunday."[16] The idea of the safety of society guaranteed a cordial relationship between the people and the gods and was very important to the Africans.

It is even more interesting that in most cases, the chiefs were rather more receptive to the missionaries than the priests because of which the people agitated. This was a prominent trait during Freeman's mission where chiefs were often receptive but they did not easily accept the faith because they believed "this might have a disruptive effect on the State."[17] Sanneh, for instance, explains that one of the important reasons why Nana Kwamena Ansah

---

15. Ekem, *Priesthood in Context*, 93.
16. Birtwhistle, *Thomas Birch Freeman*, 35.
17. Birtwhistle, 62.

could not accept Christianity was that as a chief, he needed to preside over the religious ceremonies of his people so he could not become a Christian.[18]

In Mamfe-Akuapem, Christians could not visit a Christian woman who was unconscious due to child labor because her condition was blamed on her family's decision to become Christians.[19] As a purification rite, twelve sheep were slaughtered and her husband was asked to carry the thirteenth sheep to the shrine while confessing that he had brought this calamity from the gods on his wife because they became Christians. The man refused to do this because it was against his newfound faith.

Again, the Northern German Missionary Society (Bremen) was prevented from entering the hinterland of Anlo because it was the preserve of the gods and therefore the people were prevented from hearing the gospel.[20] Dorvlo remarks, "there was the feeling that Christianity was a strange and rival religion that would take the people away from the indigenous religion and destroy the customs that bound them together as one."[21] This implies that people saw Christianity as disruptive of their social network, customs, and traditions. In one instance, the people are even said to have blamed the king for some mishap as a result of the presence of the Christians in Anlo. These accusations resonate with the situation of the early church.[22] The Christians were often blamed for any misfortune in a foreign land and this is evident in the comparison with the Roman Empire context. The 150th anniversary brochure on the history of the Evangelical Presbyterian Church in Anyako recounts a similar situation in 1857, where the lack of rains was blamed on the presence of the Christians.[23] The arrival of rains fortunately saved the Christians from being beaten and evicted.

Theophilous Opoku, an early African pastor in Mamfe reports some incidence of conflicts between the Christians and the traditional authority.[24]

---

18. Sanneh, *West African Christianity*, 24.
19. Ekem, *Priesthood in Context*, 81–82.
20. Dorvlo, "Contributions of German Missionary," 125.
21. Dorvlo, 126.
22. Tertullian, "Ad Nationes," 8.
23. Evangelical Presbyterian Church Anyako (Bremen Mission), *150th Anniversary Celebration Brochure*, 15–16.
24. Opoku, *Mamfe Missionary Report*, 1891; Sill, *Encounters in Quest*, 236–41; Dankwa, "'Shameless Maidens,'" 104–16.

He recounts that around 1868, the significant growth of Christianity in the Mamfe community led to conflicts between Christians and the traditional people. He writes that in 1869, the conflicts, owing to the increasing numbers of Christians in Mamfe, led to an announcement by the local authority that nobody should become Christian. Anybody who disobeyed would be made to pay one hundred "heads" of cowries (which was predominantly used as means of exchange at the time) which are still valued as $34 today.[25] If a child became a Christian, his/her parents would be responsible. This situation in Mamfe was quite similar to the plight of the early Christians in the Roman Empire, although in the Roman Empire scholarship cannot affirm that there was any specific law against the Christians. Thus, it can be seen that just as in the Roman Empire, owing to the rise of Christianity in Mamfe, attempts were made to stop the growth of the faith in foreign lands.

It was during the period of attempt by the Mamfe traditional council to curtail Christian growth that two young maidens faced the anger of the people of Mamfe. Yaa Kade was believed to be fourteen or fifteen years of age and was later christened Wilhelmina. Gyamea was about eighteen years old and was christened Maria. These two maidens decided to become Christians at a time when all the people of Mamfe had been banned by the Mamfe traditional authority from becoming Christians and refused to bow to pressure to recant. Opoku recounts that

> the parents and relatives of our dear heroines with hard entreaties and in tears constantly begged these their daughters to yield and deny the faith they have professed, but were always met with the same answer from the girls: "If they choose to kill us, we are not afraid to die in this plight."[26]

The Christians in Mamfe saw the actions of these maidens as heroic just as the early Christians saw the martyrs as heroic (as identified in chapter three under the sub-heading, Identity of the Martyrs). The role of their relatives is very similar to that of the role played by the relatives of Perpetua and her companions. Additionally, the resilience of these ladies resembles the steadfastness of the early Christians which has been described as obstinacy. They

---

25. Sill, 237.
26. Opoku, *Mamfe Missionary Report*, 1891.

showed no fear of death should they be killed because they defied orders not to become Christians just as the early martyrs, according to the texts, were not afraid of death.

Given their obstinacy and unpreparedness to recant, they were threatened that they would be sold into slavery among other threats to get them to denounce their faith. Additionally, woods, clubs, cutlasses, swords as well as spears, and war songs were used to push them to renounce the Christian faith. Kade is recorded to have remarked, "it will give me no shame for having become a slave for Christ's sake, but I will rather glory and rejoice in it."[27] Gyamea also pointed out that "for timid and simple girls as we are, it is disagreeable for us to be put in logs, though, but still this will never deter us and induce us to deny our Lord, whom we love and for the sake of that love, we have given ourselves to."[28] This statement resembles the words of Polycarp.[29] To this end, when the people saw that the maidens would not recant, they were held in stocks (made from heavy blocks of wood) and starved for some days. They were shaved by the local priestess and their bald heads washed with water from the shrine of Topere to nullify their baptism into Christianity. They were fortunately saved by the governor who heard about their plight.[30]

Their stubborn witness paid off and soon after, many others responded to the call of the gospel and the town of Mamfe was won for the Lord. This story is similar to the stories of the early Christians like Perpetua, Felicity, Justin Martyr, Polycarp, and the many other Christians who died because of their faith, making the subject of the persecution and martyrdom of the Christians an African story.

In general, it is concluded that the response of traditional religion to Christianity was quite hostile. Many of the missionaries, just like the early Christians, suffered a great deal at the hands of the local people especially the traditional priests. The main motivation for such actions was largely to preserve the peace between the people and the gods as well as to ensure the safety of the society.

---

27. Sill, *Encounters in Quest*, 238.
28. Sill, 238.
29. Martyrdom of Polycarp, 9:3.
30. Sill, *Encounters in Quest*, 239.

In all of these efforts of evangelizing the African continent, the missionaries, both Europeans and Africans faced occasions of hostilities. They faced several persecutions and many others were martyred by natural causes or human efforts. The purpose of this section is to identify some of the hostilities against both European and African missionaries in their quest to plant the church in Africa especially their first entry into the western part of Africa in 1471 to the third period of the missionary groups around 1760.

European Missionaries

It is rather interesting that the European and American missionaries who came to Africa and Ghana knew very well that they might die and yet, they still accepted the challenge of leaving their comfort zones. To many of the missionaries, Africa was the "white man's grave,"[31] yet they were willing to go there. Dunwell, for instance, registered his fears when Captain Potter informed him and other crew members on the ship that brought him that among other things, the Fantes themselves could even poison his food.[32] Many of them did not survive for long and they died owing to natural issues such as the weather and malaria or due to human hostilities.[33] It is recorded that the Methodist mission sent thirty-two European missionaries within ten years but fifteen of them died before spending even eight months, while apart from Freeman, Brooking, and the Allens, the others could not survive two years.[34] This section, therefore, highlights a few examples from the records of some of the missionary groups who worked in Ghana and Africa.

Since the Portuguese explorers could not make expected evangelistic gains, the king of Portugal called on the Order of the Hermits of St. Augustine, who sent five Fathers in 1572 and made some important gains even among chiefs and their households.[35] The work of the Fathers in sharing faith among the people increased the number of Christians, especially among royal households. This angered the youth of Efutu and Komenda leading to some vandalism. The youth destroyed the church and some of the sacramental objects and

---

31. Essamuah, *Genuinely Ghanaian*, 11.
32. Bartels, *Roots of Ghana Methodism*, 12–13.
33. Bartels, 5.
34. Birtwhistle, *Thomas Birch Freeman*, 55.
35. Witgen, *Gold Coast Mission History*, 23–24; Debrunner, *History of Christianity in Ghana*, 33–34; Sanneh, *West African Christianity*, 26–28.

killed (martyred) four out of the five Augustinian priests; the only survivor escaped martyrdom because he was not at the station at the time of the attack.

Again, the activities of the Basel Mission also faced some natural martyrdom where three missionaries were sent on 13 March, 1832 but by July, two of them had already died leaving only Andrew Riis.[36] They died as a result of malaria and the temperate weather, however, Riis was saved because he moved to Akropong, where the weather was more conducive and he was ably assisted by a traditional herbalist who gave him some ritual baths and herbs to drink. Riis did not abandon the mission but carried the ministry to other places like Aburi and Kwahu.[37] Although he did not win many converts, he was not discouraged by the delayed response to his message. Sanneh records that Riis won his first convert in Akropong after twenty years of ministry, and in Aburi, his first convert was after eight years of work.[38] It is significant that he won over Mohenu, a traditional priest who later adopted the name Paul and became a missionary.[39] The missionaries' resilience, vision, and fortitude in the face of persecution in a foreign land and culture offer important lessons for Ghanaian Christians.

Another Basel missionary who, in the face of great challenges, stood firm for the propagation of the gospel was Frederick Augustus Ramseyer who entered the endangered environment of the Ashantis in 1896 and three years later, in 1899, established a mission.[40] However, some riots destroyed the mission built by Ramseyer and he narrowly escaped death but three people died as a result of the riots including Samuel Otu who is described as the first Ghanaian martyr by the Presbyterian Church of Ghana.[41] Despite these developments, Ramseyer is believed to have returned to rebuild the mission in December 1901, and by 1914, he had founded twenty congregations with eight hundred converts and seventeen schools in the Ashanti land.[42]

---

36. Agbeti, *West African Church History*, 62–64; Bartels, *Roots of Ghana Methodism*, 5.

37. Debrunner, *History of Christianity in Ghana*, 99–100.

38. Debrunner, 27; Witgen, *Gold Coast Mission History*, 20–25; Sanneh, *West African Christianity*, 115.

39. Sanneh, 113.

40. Sanneh, 114–15.

41. Sanneh, 115; Agyemang, *Ghana's First Christian Martyr*, 7–22; Presbyterian Church of Ghana, *Brief Biography*, 2.

42. Sanneh, 115.

The Wesleyan Methodist Missionary Society also faced some examples of hostilities similar to the plight of the early Christians in the Roman Empire. The first Methodist missionary was Joseph Rhodes Dunwell, a twenty-seven-year-old lay preacher who arrived on 1 January 1835.[43] Bartels recounts from Dunwell's diary how afraid he was but still agreed to come to a foreign country to spread the gospel.[44] Dunwell laid some strong foundations for the already existing group of Christians who had requested Bibles but also got a missionary along with the Bibles.[45] However, his life span on the continent was short; he lived for only six months, dying on 24 June 1835. This did not deter the missionaries. After fifteen months, Rev. George Wrigley and his wife Harriet Wrigley were sent. Due to the good work done by the African agents who handled the church after the demise of Dunwell, there was the need to send more missionaries to help the Wrigleys. Therefore Rev. and Mrs. Peter Harrop arrived on 15 January 1837 to help with the missionary work. Unfortunately, Mrs. Harrop died three weeks after her arrival. Rev. Harrop and Mrs. Harriet Wrigley also died three days after Mrs. Harrop's death on 8 February 1837, leaving only Rev. George Wrigley who also died within nine months.[46] The Wrigleys expanded the missionary activities to Anomabu, Dixcove, Abura, Dunkwa, and Dominasi.[47] It was after them that Thomas Birch Freeman, whose mother was English and father African, was sent to work from 1838 to 1890. The belief was that he could resist the weather and malaria because he had African blood.[48]

Like the Basel and Catholic missionaries, the works of the Methodist missionaries were sometimes met with resistance and riots from the community. There were disturbances and persecution of the Christians in Obidan and Anomabo.[49] The greatest opposition against the Wesleyan Methodist Society was encountered in their attempt to propagate the gospel to the people of

---

43. Bartels, *Roots of Ghana Methodism*, 12–14; Sanneh, *West African Christianity*, 119; Agbeti, *West African Church History*, 55; Essamuah, *Genuinely Ghanaian*, 10.

44. Bartels, *Roots of Ghana Methodism*, 13.

45. Agbeti, *West African Church History,* 55–56; Bartels, 11.

46. Debrunner, *History of Christianity in Ghana*, 96–99; Essamuah, *Genuinely Ghanaian*, 11; Bartels, *Roots of Ghana Methodism,* 12–75.

47. Bartels, 20–28; Sanneh, *West African Christianity,* 118; Agbeti, *West African Church History*, 55.

48. Sanneh, 120–23; Bartels, 28–131.

49. Bartels, 56–59.

Kumasi and its environs who are often described as "warlike."[50] They met fierce resistance but the missionaries did not give up and Freeman was eventually very successful not just in the Fante lands but Kumasi, Accra, Nigeria, and other parts of the Western African territories.[51] Birtwhistle cites from Freeman's journal how nervous he was but found solace in the hymn "My life, my blood, I here present, If for Thy truth they may be spent."[52] Freeman suffered a lot of things such as walking long distances through the rains and sleeping in structures that would not be given to pigs[53] and described his life as being in "one incessant whirl"[54] When his wife died, he wrote in his journal that "but now she is removed into the eternal world, and is now I trust in the enjoyment of a martyr's crown."[55] These missionaries gave up everything and left their countries, not knowing what was awaiting them in these foreign lands; they agreed to go, even when others had died painfully, for the sake of the gospel.

In general, the faith, obstinacy, resilience, and fortitude of these European missionaries in the spread of the gospel in Ghana and Africa as a whole, deserve commendation. They stood firm in the face of great opposition, leaving the comfort of their countries for the sake of the gospel and some of them died in defense of their faith. They complement the Christians' history of persecution and martyrdom in the African church history by their pains and glories. However, they were not the only ones who suffered. Many of their African counterparts who complemented their efforts as interpreters, hosts, and companions, equally suffered a great deal, thereby being examples of the persecution and martyrdom in African church history.

African Agents

The history of the church in Africa will not be complete without the sufferings of the many African agents who through toil, sweat, tears, blood, and life established the church. These Africans fit into Tertullian's truism that "the blood

---

50. Birtwhistle, *Thomas Birch Freeman*, 20–26.
51. Sanneh, *West African Christianity*, 122–23; Agbeti, *West African Church History*, 56–57.
52. Birtwhistle, *Thomas Birch Freeman*, 5.
53. Birtwhistle, 44–54.
54. Birtwhistle, 55.
55. Birtwhistle, 10.

of Christians is seed."⁵⁶ There were many Africans who complemented the efforts of the Europeans and in some cases initiated the establishment of the church amidst the loss of property, dignity, family, and even life. Birtwhistle, for instance, recounts Freeman's interpreter at Dominasi whose foot was cut while bathing by an oyster shell which made him lame.⁵⁷ Although this was an accident, he suffered this fate for the gospel. Many more Africans have equally suffered in the missionary enterprise on the African soil. This section exemplifies some of the cases of African agents who suffered different types of persecution and martyrdom for the sake of the gospel and Christianity in Africa.

In Ghana, a Presbyterian catechist, Samuel Otu, was martyred in 1900 because he was seen as a spy for the Europeans given that he was a Christian.⁵⁸ Samuel Otu was originally from Larteh in the eastern region but as a missionary, Ramseyer posted him to Techimantia.⁵⁹ However, owing to mistrust between the Asantes and the British colonial authorities, all missionaries were expelled from the Ashanti towns.

Otu's martyrdom fits very well into the account of the early Christian martyrs in many ways. In the first place, like the account of the martyrdom of Polycarp, he was betrayed by gossip. When the announcement was made to halt the activities of the allies of the Europeans, Samuel Otu and his family refused to leave the Asante land because they were consumed by the missionary work. Someone, therefore, is said to have given a report that Nana Kofi Kuma was hiding "a clerk who was also a spy for the British at Techimantia."⁶⁰ This is similar to the plight of Polycarp who was in hiding but someone betrayed him by informing the authorities of his location and even though he got to know and was encouraged to escape, he resisted and was arrested.⁶¹ Additionally, Samuel Otu, just like Polycarp, prayed and his prayer shows his willingness to die for the cause of the gospel. This prayer resembles what Jesus prayed before his crucifixion: "Lord thy will be done,

---

56. Tertullian, *Apologeticum*, 50:13.
57. Birtwhistle, *Thomas Birch Freeman*, 30.
58. Agyemang, *Ghana's First Christian Martyr*, 9–17; Presbyterian Church of Ghana, *Brief Biography*, 2–4.
59. Sanneh, *West African Christianity*, 119; Agbeti, *West African Church History*, 54–55.
60. Presbyterian Church of Ghana, *Brief Biography*, 2.
61. Martyrdom of Polycarp, 6.

not ours."[62] His use of "ours" shows he was not alone and indeed he was with his wife who had prayed ahead of him for salvation based on the biblical examples of Daniel and the Israelites in Egypt. In the end, his wife encouraged him with these words:

> As I have been warning you, they will arrest us. You know we came here to preach the Word of God, not to do our private business. We came here to preach the Word of God unto men's salvation. But if you are arrested and killed you will be counted worthy of your Lord's commendation as a martyr of Jesus and His Cross. Fear not; harm to the flesh is painful to any person but the spirit prevails over the pains of the human body.[63]

These words show the sufferings they were facing were nothing new to them, but that they anticipated that such a plight would come their way. They were just like the early Christian martyrs who showed their resolve and positive perspectives for death because of the cross of God.

Furthermore, the charge for Otu's martyrdom resembles what the early Christians faced. Although his case was more political than religious, it was a pure situation of allegiance. He was killed because he was seen as a spy of the British colonial authority, owing to his attire which gave him an identity that brought into question his allegiance as an African.[64] He was seen as a spy since the Asantes and the British were at war and their allies including missionaries were expected to vacate the Ashanti land. This was because the Asantes believed that allies such as missionaries irrespective of race may leak some information from the Asantes to the British. The question of allegiance made the Roman authorities demand the martyrs to pray using the *genius* of the emperor. Therefore, since Samuel Otu's allegiance was questionable to the Asantes, like the early Christians, he was killed because of his faith.

Even more importantly, some of the things Otu suffered together with his wife were a replica of the situation of the early Christians. His wife recounts that:

---

62. Agyemang, *Ghana's First Christian Martyr*, 17.
63. Agyemang.
64. Presbyterian Church of Ghana, *Brief Biography*, 2–3.

> Here my husband was ordered to put his hands on the sticks after being asked to take off his coat, he was bound tightly to the sticks with rope. I was also put in fetters on my ankles … My husband was placed trussed in the stock or sticks, unable to move his hands or legs on Thursday and Friday but he was removed from the stock on Saturday.[65]

After his execution too, his wife was also stripped naked to find out if she was hiding valuable things in her clothes and later her hair was shaved.[66] These harsh treatments given to Samuel Otu and his wife by the traditional authority in Techimantia for the sake of the gospel represent the pains, sweat, and blood of Africans for the gospel in Ghana reminiscent of the plight of the early Christians in the Roman Empire. The Presbyterian Church of Ghana has honored him today with a church named after him and a statue erected on the church compound at Techimantia for the courage shown in the defense of his faith. He is described as the first Ghanaian martyr.

An additional example of Africans who lost privileges, suffered, and gave up their lives for the sake of the gospel in Africa is William de-Graft. In the history of the Methodist church in Ghana the pains of William de-Graft cannot be overemphasized with regard to the persecutions he suffered. Owing to his convictions in regard to biblical interpretations, de-Graft formed a Bible Band, sometimes called the "Meeting" to study the word of God together.[67] He insisted that when the Bible was read as an English textbook, it should be interpreted. Because of his insistence on Bible interpretation in school, he was dismissed together with some of his friends from the castle school. Due to this disagreement with Joseph Smith (the headteacher of the school) regarding the interpretation of the Bible, the governor of the Gold Coast at the time ordered him to be whipped and dismissed from the school. Given his dismissal, he could not be employed and his dream of working with the government as a clerk on completion of his education was destroyed.[68] It was due to the loss of job opportunities as a result of his faith that motivated him to seek greener pastures at Dixcove where he met Captain Potter, a Christian

---

65. Agyemang, *Ghana's First Christian Martyr*, 16–17.
66. Agyemang, 19.
67. Bartels, *Roots of Ghana Methodism*, 8.
68. Agbeti, *West African Church History*, 55; Bartels, 8–10.

ship owner. Dunwell then requested Bibles for the Bible Band which ended up sending a missionary, Joseph Rhodes Dunwell to the Gold Coast. Essamuah remarks that

> the differences in biblical hermeneutics between the two factions within the Fante Bible Band mirrored in the large society between the chiefly class and the new educated elite, were to lead to the persecution of de-Graft who fell into disfavor with the current governor who was friendlier with Smith, probably because the latter was more compliant. De-Graft was briefly imprisoned and deported from Cape Coast, then resettled at Dixcove.[69]

According to Essamuah, de-Graft faced imprisonment and deportation. However, other sources affirm that de-Graft was beaten and imprisoned along with some other followers but his deportation may not be substantiated as suggested by Essamuah. Birtwhistle and Bartels agree that de-Graft left for Dixcove because of economic reasons since he could never secure a job in any government setup.[70] Again, if he was deported or excommunicated from Cape Coast, he could not attend the meetings of the "Meeting or Bible Club." Instead, it can be argued that he had to forsake his dreams of working with the government service for the sake of the gospel; he sacrificed his future for the gospel. Some of the early Christians suffered hostilities of imprisonment, beating, loss of privileges, and many others for the sake of the gospel of Christ as demonstrated in the case of William de-Graft.

In general, it can strongly be argued that Africans have had their fair share of the persecution and martyrdom, which characterized the development of the Christian faith from the early first century. During the missionary periods, some Africans suffered torture and death due to their Christian faith. Persecution and martyrdom are equally an African story. It is also important to stress that the account of Christian persecution and martyrdom is not only a historical occurrence but a continuous one even in contemporary society. Even today, many Christians suffer various forms of hostilities and death as a result of their faith. Looking forward, it is vital to deal with how the African and Ghanaian Christians should conceptualize the hostilities they face today.

---

69. Essamuah, *Genuinely Ghanaian*, 10.
70. Birtwhistle, *Thomas Birch Freeman*, 2; Bartels, *Roots of Ghana Methodism*, 8–10.

This conceptualization can best be concluded if Christians today can draw lessons from the early church examples. It is always true that it is wise to learn from people who have come from a place a person is about to travel to. Therefore, the way the early church contained the hostilities against them can help the church today in dealing with its current predicaments of hostilities.

Conclusion

The story of the persecution and martyrdom of the early Christians is certainly an African story. Many Christians suffer various levels of discomfort as a result of their faith. In all of these, the resilience and capacity of the early church, similar to the examples of the early African missionaries, are relevant today. The hymnist lauds this point in the lines:

> *Faith of our fathers, living still*
> *In spite of dungeon, fire and sword,*
> *O how our hearts beat high with joy*
> *Whene'er we hear that glorious word*
> *Faith of our fathers'! Holy faith!*
> *We will be true to thee till death.*[71]

Christians today can learn from these examples and strategies adopted by the early Christians in dealing with the hostilities against them and this can be a study ground for Christians all over the world. Therefore, their histories serve as learning opportunities for suffering Christians today since the Christians see martyrdom as a baptismal faith that involves participation in the death and resurrection of Christ.[72] Hence, if this is the way their master Jesus went, the subjects need to follow the same path.

The examples of hostilities against the early Christians are largely captured in two main genres of texts from antiquity; the martyr and apologetic texts.[73] Scholarship on the subject of the persecution and martyrdom has largely depended on the martyr texts with very scanty attention to the apologetic texts as a useful source to understanding this phenomenon. However, this

---

71. Fredrick William Faber, "Faith of our Fathers".
72. Oden, *How Africa Shaped the Christian Mind*, 119.
73. Boamah, "Apologetic and Martyr Text," 32.

work argues that the two genres of texts are both engineered by the subject of persecution and martyrdom. Whereas the martyr texts were written by Christians to a largely Christian audience, the apologetic texts were written by Christians to the largely non-Christian audience with both explaining something about the hostilities. To demonstrate the usefulness of the apologetic texts in filling some gaps in the image of the hostilities when the martyr texts are used alone, this work compares the two genres of texts in a rather systematic way in the following chapters for a comprehensive appreciation of the phenomena in the Roman Empire. Not only that, the comparison helps to address the possible or otherwise reception of those non-Christians who are addressed by the apologists.

CHAPTER THREE

They Killed Us – Martyr Texts

The persecution and martyrdom of the early Christians in the Roman Empire have occupied the attention of scholars over the past decades and even centuries. A major category of texts which reflect these hostilities against the Christians is the martyr texts. These genres of texts are largely written to Christian audiences with an interest in the non-Christians. The authors therefore largely suggest to the Christian audience that they (Christians) are killed by the non-Christians, therefore the title "They Killed Us."

These texts capture a whole range of the aspects of oppression against the early Christians. Many Christian martyr texts offer descriptions of how the early Christians were persecuted. There is a general consensus among scholars that most of these texts were written in late antiquity or the early Middle Ages long after the end of the persecutions and that only a few of the accounts were contemporary with the persecutions.[1] Adolf von Harnack contributed extensively to scholarship by classifying contemporary accounts from the later accounts.[2]

For the purposes of this book, this chapter compares a division of the martyr texts based on the style of writing to show the similarities and differences in how they describe the persecutions and find out if the account in one form corroborates, supplements, or contradicts the other. This internal systematic comparison will focus on the extent to which the two subcategories of the martyr texts present similar or different "picture(s)" of the persecution and martyrdom of the early Christians. Such a comparison is relevant

---

1. Musurillo, *Acts of the Christian Martyrs*, xi–xii.
2. Musurillo, xi; Barnes, "Legislation against the Christians," 509.

in itself but has a further ramification for establishing the trustworthiness or the picture(s) that these texts paint of the hostilities, the opponents, and their motives. If the two kinds of texts present significantly overlapping pictures, then their accounts are corroborative and/or supplementary to each other but if they present largely different "pictures," then they may not be very good sources for understanding the phenomena of the persecution and martyrdom of the Christians.

The martyr texts can be categorized into two. The first category, labeled narrative martyr texts (*Martyrdom of Polycarp* and *Martyrdom of Perpetua and Companions*), are written in the form of stories that describe some of the events that occurred during the persecution and martyrdom of the Christians. The second category, labeled protocol martyr texts (*Martyrdom of Justin and His Companions* as well as the *Scillitan Martyrs*), are in the form of court protocols focusing on the dialogue between the judge (emperor or governors) and the martyrs.

In this chapter, the martyr texts are compared internally.[3] First, one subgroup of martyr texts, the narrative martyr texts, are compared at a harmony level. Second, in the other subgroup of martyr texts, the protocol texts are equally compared to reach harmony. Third, the two harmonies are compared to get a synthesis of the comparative levels adopted in this work.

The Origin and Purpose of the Martyr Texts

Early Christians took to writing in the heat of the hostilities against them. Some of these texts were written by the martyrs themselves and eyewitnesses or later Christians who knew about the hostilities. The writing of martyr texts was not only during the time of the hostilities but sometimes even at a later time. Scholars including Edward Gibbon, Thierry Ruinart, Adolf von Harnack, and Musurillo have been engaged in setting out texts that were written before the end of the hostilities (contemporary), and those that were written later (near-contemporary).[4] Barnes affirms that the four texts that are

---

3. For a description of the terms internal, external, harmony, synchrony and fusion, see above under approaches.

4. Musurillo, *Acts of the Christian Martyrs*, xi–xii.

analyzed in this book were all written by contemporary authors.[5] The account of the *Martyrdom of Perpetua* was written by two of the martyrs themselves during their time in prison and an editor who provided the framework with the introduction and conclusion; the *Martyrdom of Polycarp* was documented as a letter from the eyewitnesses to other Christians abroad. It is difficult to determine the authors of the account of the *Martyrdom of Justin and His Companions* and the *Scillitan Martyrs* but according to Barnes, they are both near-contemporary texts.[6]

Following Kennedy's rhetorical critical model, the persuasive objectives of the texts based on the context or occasion of the discourse of the texts with attention on the author and audience are adopted. In analyzing the perlocutionary effect of the texts, two main questions are therefore evaluated. First, what stimulated the authors to write these texts? This question explores the prevailing sociopolitical and religious circumstances that led to the authors writing these accounts. Second, what did the authors seek to achieve by writing these texts? It is imperative to note that the authors of these texts did not write for pleasure, but had a serious end in view. These questions are important to attain the purpose of the study.

The account of the persecution and martyrdom of the early Christians as presented by the martyr texts indicates three factors and purposes for writing these texts. First, the authors sought to encourage Christians.[7] There was a great need to encourage Christians not to give up in the face of the hostilities. To this extent, the explicit audience to the text was the Christians, who needed to be encouraged. Second, owing to the confusion regarding the identity of the Christians especially in distinguishing them from the Jews, the authors of these texts wanted to define the Christians' identity.[8] Wilken remarks that the confusion of the identity of the Christians is evident in Galen's misconception: "It is curious that Galen, writing in the middle of the second-century lumps together Jews and Christians."[9] This confusion was widespread in the Roman Empire as Lynch affirms, "during its first three or four decades, Christianity

---

5. Barnes, "Pre-Decian Act Martyrs," 509–31.
6. Barnes, 509–31.
7. Engberg, "Martyrdom and Persecution," 95; Stark, *Rise of Christianity*, 163–89.
8. Lieu, "Audience of Apologetics," 218–21; Wilken, *Christians as the Romans Saw*, 113.
9. Lieu, 218–21.

was a sect within Judaism."[10] In the light of this motive of defining Christian identity, it is clear that the authors had non-Christians in mind as the implied audience of the text. This was an important target for the authors because when the non-Christians (who are usually the plaintiff and perpetrators of the hostilities) had a clear appreciation of who the Christians were, they might be attracted to the Christian faith. Consequently, the texts were also an evangelistic tool, no wonder Tertullian remarks that the "blood of the martyrs is seed." Third, the authors of the martyr texts wanted the martyrs to be remembered as part of Christian history.[11] Some of the accounts, therefore, include specific dates and sometimes even time of the executions for remembrance and celebration. Frend argues that "churches had their roll of honour of martyrs whose 'birthdays' (*natalicia*) were celebrated each year"[12] which is similarly affirmed by Hartog.[13]

It is without a doubt that here too it is evident the authors were writing to the Christians. In essence, therefore, the writers of the martyr texts (narratives and protocol) intended their texts to be read by both Christians (to encourage them and record their history) as well as the non-Christians (to construct the Christians' identity).

Background of Martyr Narratives

There is no doubt that the writing of texts is often born out of circumstances around the authors and audience. Two of the texts analyzed in this study were written from an African context, thus the *Martyrdom of Perpetua* and the Acts of the *Scillitan Martyrs* show that Africa has been part of the Christian history from its cradle. In using Kennedy's model, a discussion of the background of the texts in this section brings out the general feature of the texts, authorship, and the context of the texts.

---

10. Lynch, *Early Christianity*, 82.
11. Hartog, *Polycarp's* Epistle, 166.
12. Frend, *Martyrdom in the Early Church*, 257.
13. Hartog, *Polycarp's* Epistle, 166.

Martyrdom of Polycarp

Polycarp, which means fruitfulness or productivity, was a common slave name especially in the second century.[14] However, the Polycarp in this account was a bishop of Smyrna in the second century and a companion of St. John,[15] one of the apostles of Christ. According to Tertullian and Eusebius, Polycarp's appointment as bishop was by apostle John and analogous to the ordination of Clement in Rome by the apostle Peter.[16] Polycarp's connection with apostle John is asserted by Irenaeus, Tertullian, and Jerome among many other early church fathers.[17] Koester describes him as "the most significant ecclesiastical leader," and Pervo says that "if historians of Christian origin could be granted one interview with a personage of the period 100–150, Polycarp would be the choice of many."[18] Hartog tells us that Ignatius described Polycarp as someone with a "godly mind," "blameless face," and a person who has a great "desire for the truth."[19] Hartog also gives Eusebius's description of Polycarp "as an 'apostolic man' and a 'true and good shepherd'".[20] Polycarp, according to the account, was the twelfth to be martyred in Smyrna on 23 February at 2 p.m.[21]

Hartog remarks that

> few early Christian works "have exercised a greater fascination" than Mart. Pol., and few can match "its moving pathos and edifying effect." Mart. Pol. builds a distinctive image of Polycarp as both "a distinguished teacher" and "an eminent martyr." He was "an apostolic and prophetic teacher… and bishop of the catholic church."[22]

The account of his martyrdom is to a large extent modelled on the account of the crucifixion of Christ.[23] Hartog even pushes the imitation of Christ in

---

14. Hartog, note 1.
15. Musurillo, *Acts of the Christian Martyrs*, xiii.
16. Hartog, *Polycarp's* Epistle, 4.
17. Hartog, 11.
18. Hartog, 1.
19. Hartog, 2.
20. Hartog, 4.
21. Martyrdom of Polycarp, 20–21.
22. Hartog, *Polycarp's* Epistle, 165.
23. He was betrayed, arrested by a local magistrate called Herod, rode on a donkey, prayed before his arrest, etc.

the *Martyrdom of Polycarp* to further look into christological elements which are far-reaching in the text as well.[24]

Although many of the martyr narratives were written later after the incidence of the martyrdom, scholars consider the *Martyrdom of Polycarp* as one of the few accounts which were written soon after the martyrdom.[25] Almost all scholars agree that Polycarp was martyred in the second half of the second century at age eighty-six.[26] However, the precise date is debated. Hartog recounts and foretells that "the date has been the subject of controversy for nearly three centuries, and it would be hazardous to say that the last word on the question has been spoken."[27] The dating of the martyrdom of Polycarp is influenced by two main extracts: chapter 21 of the account of the martyrdom names L. Statius Quadratus as the Consul Ordinaries; and Eusebius's discussion of Polycarp's martyrdom right after mentioning the successor of Marcus Aurelius.[28] H. Von Campenhausen favors 166–7 but a majority of scholars including Musurillo suggest 155–6. Meanwhile, T. D. Barnes supports 156–7 but has no problem with 157–8 or even 158–9.[29] Some scholars have also suggested a dating of the martyrdom to 176–7 but this position has not been given much attention.[30] Overall, Engberg tries to cover the arguments by giving a window of 155–59; Hartog convincingly pushes it further to 155–61.[31]

Martyrdom of Justin and Companions

Although the exact date for the martyrdom of Justin and companions is not certain, scholars generally agree it may have occurred around 165.[32] The account recounts the killings of seven Christians including Justin in Rome in the presence of the urban Prefect Iunius Rusticus during the time of Emperor

---

24. Hartog, "Christology of the Martyrdom," 141–47.
25. Engberg, "Truth Begs No Favours," 183. However, Moss disagrees strongly with this position and argues that the account was not likely to have been recorded in the same year of the incident since the text uses future tense verb forms. Moss, "On the Dating of Polycarp," 54; Hartog, *Polycarp's* Epistle, 182.
26. Musurillo, *Acts of the Christian Martyrs*, xiii; Engberg, *Impulsore Chresto*, 62; Hartog, 9.
27. Hartog, 200.
28. Hartog, 192–200; Musurillo, *Acts of the Christian Martyrs*, xiii.
29. Musurillo, xiii, Hartog, 195.
30. Hartog, 191.
31. Engberg, "Truth Begs No Favours," 184; Hartog, 200.
32. Musurillo, *Acts of the Christian Martyrs*, xviii; Engberg, 184.

Marcus Aurelius.[33] Rusticus was a Roman urban prefect from 163 to around 168, who had a great influence on Marcus Aurelius's Stoic thoughts.[34]

Musurillo suggests that shortly before Justin's arrest, Justin had a "bitter debate with a Cynic philosopher named Crescens"[35] which may have served as the immediate reason for his arrest with his companions.[36] Justin is said to have been martyred along with his companions: Charito, Charition, Evelpistus, Hierax, Paeon, and Liberian. It is not certain if these companions were converted to Christianity by Justin since they did not answer that question directly;[37] Hierax responded that he had been a Christian for a long time thus suggesting he was not converted by Justin, and Evelpistus admitted he listened to Justin's preaching.[38] However, Musurillo argues strongly that they were probably associated with Justin's school in Rome where an earlier martyr, Ptolemaeus, had some connections.[39]

The authenticity and usefulness of these accounts have captured the attention of many scholarly investigations. There are six manuscripts with three different recensions.[40] All three recensions are in Greek[41] and the oldest known and mostly used recension is called the Vulgate version from around the eighth century. The second recension, which is the Paris manuscript, is longer and is from about the ninth century and the final recension is called the Jerusalem manuscript from the twelfth century. Following Musurillo's classification, the shorter recension, the Paris manuscript, is referred to as A; the longer recension which is known as the middle recension and suggests the Vulgate version is referred to as B and the third recension, the Jerusalem manuscript is referred to as C.[42] Bisbee, in discussing the relationship between the three recensions, cites Lazzita who maintains:

---

33. Musurillo, xviii.
34. Musurillo, 43, note 1.
35. Musurillo, xviii.
36. The personality of Justin will be discussed alongside his apology in the next chapter.
37. Martyrdom of Justin and Companions (recensions A and B) 4.5.
38. Martyrdom of Justin and Companions, 4.7.
39. Musurillo, *Acts of the Christian Martyrs*, xix.
40. Bisbee, "Acts of Justin Martyr," 129.
41. Musurillo, *Acts of the Christian Martyrs*, xviii.
42. Musurillo, xix.

The First text (rec. A), the most ancient, goes back to a period of peace, as one may conclude from the beginning, but which could also be placed, and probably is placed before the conclusion of the persecutions; the second text (rec. B), a reworking of the first, is probably of the fourth century; the third text (rec. C) is later, perhaps much later even than the fourth century.[43]

Meanwhile, Musurillo also holds that,

> Although the relationship between the shorter and the middle versions is still not completely clear, it would seem more likely that the middle version does indeed derive from the tradition of the shorter one, which modifies the speeches of Justin and omits the reference to the burial of the martyrs' bodies.[44]

Therefore, Lazzati is bold to suggest that the Paris manuscript is the original, based on the principle of the "most ancient text, and is the briefest with a minimal literary elaboration." Musurillo does not agree with this principle particularly in attribution to these texts.[45] Bisbee had also tried to establish that recension B is not from A but other sources by adopting form-critical studies of the texts looking at the introductory formulae, the body of the trial, the judgment announced, and the conclusion of the texts.[46] In light of the issues regarding the authenticity of the account of the martyrdom of Justin and his companions, I will use the three recensions because I follow Musurillo's work and the three may have some emphases which may be useful to the study.

Scillitan Martyrs

This account is described as the earliest document from the African and Latin Church.[47] It recounts the martyrdom of twelve African Christians who lived in Scillinear Carthage which was near modern-day Tunis.

---

43. Bisbee, "Acts of Justin Martyr," 300.
44. Musurillo, *Acts of the Christian Martyrs*, xviii.
45. Chadwick, xix.
46. Bisbee, "Acts of Justin Martyr," 129–57.
47. Musurillo, *Acts of the Christian Martyrs*, xxii.

There are twelve Christians in this document, seven men (Speratus, Nartzalus, Cittinus, Veturius, Felix, Aquilinus, and Laetanius) and five women (Donata, Vestia, Secunda, Januaria, and Generosa).[48] Speratus may have been the representative of the group as he spoke more than the others. Five others responded only once and they were silent throughout the account until the judgment was given and their names were listed. It is argued that since they were very enthusiastic and expressed a lot of joy for their sentencing, they were likely to be young Christians with Speratus as their teacher. This position is strongly supported by Philip Carrington who states that "the record reminds us of the Acts of the Martyrdom of Justin and his companions in Rome, so that Speratus with his simple answers and his New Testament books may have been a teacher like Justin witnessing his faith to his pupils."[49] Frend similarly shows the relationship between the accounts of the Scillitan martyrs and the *Martyrdom of Perpetua*.[50]

The characters' names suggest humble origin, but compared to this it is striking, as Mussurillo observes, that the proconsul did not humiliate or torture them but killed them by beheading them as though they were Roman citizens.[51] Frend, influenced by Tertullian's *Ad Scapulam* 3.4, suggests that the first proconsul to be hostile to the Christians in this region was Vigellus Saturninus who executed four Christians at Madaura on 4 July 180.[52] Philip Carrington suggests that Saturninus became hostile to the Christians only four or five weeks after he joined office.[53] The proconsul is believed to have turned against these twelve named young Christians on 17 July 180.[54] This date is strongly supported by many other scholars including Musurillo,[55] Andrew Rutherfurd,[56] and Engberg.[57]

---

48. Frend, *Martyrdom and Persecution*, 313.
49. Carrington, *Early Christian Church*, 292.
50. Frend, *Martyrdom and Persecution*, 313.
51. Musurillo, *Acts of the Christian Martyrs*, xxii.
52. Frend, *Martyrdom and Persecution*, 313; Carrington, *Christian Church*, 291.
53. Carrington, 290.
54. Frend, *Martyrdom and Persecution*, 313.
55. Musurillo, *Acts of the Christian Martyrs*, xxii.
56. Rutherfurd, *Passion of the Scillitan Martyrs*, 283.
57. Engberg, "Truth Begs No Favours," 184.

A major debate around the text is on distinguishing the original language. There are three versions in Latin and one in Greek.[58] Andrew Rutherfurd suggests that the texts have suffered various corruptions due to translations and transcription to and from Greek and Latin. However, most scholars use the Latin version from Armitage Robinson collected from the ninth century in the British Museum, which is the shortest account in circulation.[59]

The Scillitan Martyrs account is of great significance due to the context and the form it assumes. The context of this account is the Roman African province which drives home the point that Africa has been a central part of the Christian story from the earliest existence of Christianity. This area covered North African coastal regions around present-day Tunisia, Algeria, and Libya. More importantly in line with the objectives of this work, the form of the text is very significant. As Frend identifies, it is written in the same form and style as the protocols from contemporary Roman courtroom proceedings. This makes the account quite dramatic, although subtly avoiding all graphic descriptions of violence, which may be found more in the narrative martyr texts.

Martyrdom of Perpetua

The *Martyrdom of Perpetua* recounts the martyrdom of six individuals; two women and four men.[60] Five of them were catechumens and the sixth was their teacher, Saturus.[61] Two of them, Rovocatus and Felicity, were probably slaves or people of low status (*humiliores*) since they have names (*cognomina*) that indicate this.[62] Hoffmann suggests that since they were paired, these slaves were likely to be couples, with Felicity in her final stage of pregnancy.[63] Two of the other catechumens, Saturinus and Secundulus, were not identified as slaves but were again only called in the narrative by their *cognomina*; Hoffmann suggests that they may have been freedmen. Their identification in the passage as adolescents suggests that they would not have been above

---

58. Musurillo, *Acts of the Christian Martyrs*, xxiii.

59. Rutherfurd, *Passion of the Scillitan Martyrs*, 283; Musurillo, *Acts of the Christian Martyrs*, xxiii.

60. Heffernan, *Passion of Perpetua and Felicity*, 18.

61. Heffernan, 19.

62. Heffernan; most slave names in Africa at the time ended in – *atus*.

63. Heffernan.

sixteen years. Hoffmann argues that they most likely lived together in the same household under one master who was likely to be Perpetua's father.[64]

In contrast to all other characters in the narrative including the Roman governor, who were called only by one of their names, the account mentions that Perpetua was also called Vibia. This name is of a Roman North African origin, from a prominent family in the middle of the first century with some military influence.[65] Vibia Perpetua was a young lady of about twenty-two years[66] who was from an elitist family and well catered for, described in the text as *honestenata* (good family and upbringing, born well or respectably born).[67] The account tells the reader that Perpetua, also a catechumen, was newly married and with a young baby.[68] Hoffmann suggests that Perpetua's father was likely to be in his early forties and a pagan but her mother was most likely a Christian.[69] The suggestion that her mother was likely to be a Christian stems from the fact that she is not mentioned by name. Her identity may have been hidden so she could live and take care of Perpetua's baby.[70] This argument is supported because if her identity was made known, it would be possible for some members of the public to report her to be included for martyrdom. Though predominantly narrative, the style of this account has some protocol contents.

Narrative and Protocol Forms Compared

The internal comparison of the narrative and protocol forms of the martyr texts, in this section, seeks to identify if the two classes of texts corroborate, supplement, or contradict each other. If this comparison brings out a single image of the persecution based on these texts, then their accounts are corroborated but if not then, the accounts will need some other verification.

The comparative elements are developed largely from the review of existing literature and the rhetorical critical approach. Using the existing scholarly

---

64. Heffernan, 21.
65. Heffernan, 21.
66. *Martyrdom of Perpetua*, 2.
67. *Martyrdom of Perpetua*, 2:1; Heffernan, *Passion of Perpetua and Felicity*, 21.
68. *Martyrdom of Perpetua*, 2:1–3.
69. Heffernan, *Passion of Perpetua and Felicity*, 22–23.
70. Heffernan, 20.

discussions on many of the issues, we will do a comparison of these two forms to identify their similarities and differences. The background analysis of the texts based on Kennedy's model of the speaker, audience, discourse, and context[71] has also influenced the creation of these comparative elements where they are compared systematically to show their convergence and divergence within and between the genre of the texts. In all, eleven elements are identified as the basis of the comparison based on the literature review and the rhetorical critical approach, which are: storyline, the character of martyrs, identity of persecutors, legal procedure, charges and allegations, motives, demands, the form of suffering, polemics, defense, and apology including their peculiarities.

In light of this method, the main comparative elements are grouped into three. The first three elements seek to compare how the accounts are presented and also the identity of the characters in the text. They are designated as "account," which describes the nature of the account. This category, therefore, includes the comparison of the following; storyline, the identity of the martyrs, and identity of the persecutors.

The second category, labeled "accusations," compares the legal process adopted and the accusations that were leveled against the Christians, the motivation of the persecutors' action as well as the demand from the authorities to appease the gods. The comparative elements include legal procedure, charges, and allegations, motives as well as demands.

The final category of elements of comparison is captured under "action," which focuses attention on the features of the account. It encompasses the form of suffering, polemics, defense, and apology including their peculiarities.

Narrative Martyr Texts

This section presents the harmonized picture of the narrative martyr accounts. The harmony of the texts will be in two categories – where the first part will harmonize the account of the *Martyrdom of Polycarp* to the account of the *Martyrdom of Perpetua and Felicity*, bringing out their similarities and differences. The other part harmonizes the account of the martyrdom of *Justin and His Companions* as well as the *Scillitan Martyrs* by stressing their similarities and differences, and also based on the comparative elements.

---

71. Kennedy, *New Testament Interpretation*, 15.

These two harmonized versions are then synchronized using the comparative elements to equally bring out their similarities and differences. This means that based on the comparative elements, the subsequent section will analyze the synchronized version of the two accounts regarding the persecution and martyrdom of the Christians. The analysis is derived based on the three main classifications of the comparative elements with their attributes under them.

Account and Character

This comparative element seeks to identify the presentation of the accounts and the characters presented in these accounts in terms of the martyrs and the persecutors. It therefore captures three main elements; the storyline, character presentation of the martyrs, and identity of the persecutors. These comparative elements seek to bring out the similarities and differences to see if the accounts supplement, corroborate, or contradict themselves.

Storyline

The narrative accounts in their presentations capture three main facets of the persecution and martyrdom of the early Christians. They present elaborate events before the trial. Second, these narratives present a vivid account of the trial and judgments. The third aspect of the procedure of the martyrs captures the post-trial events as well as a conclusion to the account. This aspect gives information about the author or editor(s) of the texts.

The pre-trial events in the account of the martyrdom of Polycarp describe his escape from arrest.[72] He is described in the texts as seeing a vision of his martyrdom while in exile.[73] He was later picked up by the police-like state forces to the amphitheater for trial.[74] The *Martyrdom of Perpetua* accounts for the time of the martyrs in prison while awaiting their trial.[75] Perpetua describes how she was visited by her father, who tried to persuade her to recant so that she might escape martyrdom.[76] These sections present the character of the martyrs to influence the thoughts and actions of the Christians so that they hold strong to the faith.

---

72. Martyrdom of Polycarp, 5:1.
73. Martyrdom of Polycarp, 5:2.
74. Martyrdom of Polycarp, 6–8.
75. *Martyrdom of Perpetua*, 1–3.
76. *Martyrdom of Perpetua*, 3.

The trial and judgment sections of the narrative martyrs show the passion of the martyrs. In the account of the martyrdom of Polycarp, the account presents the interaction with the governor as well as the general public. This section also captures how he was judged to execution by fire[77] and explains why he was not thrown to the beasts.[78] It is interesting that this account also captures the role of the public as major actors in the execution of Polycarp by inciting the governor[79] and gathering sticks for the burning.[80] The account of the *Martyrdom of Perpetua* expresses the interactions between the martyrs and the governor as well as the judgment given based on the interactions. What is more interesting in this account is that the governor did not execute the martyrs immediately after the judgment but allowed days to pass so as to celebrate the emperor's birthday with their martyrdom.[81] The account does not lose track of the activities of the martyrs between their judgment and execution of the judgment and the celebration of a love feast.[82] This section on the trial and judgment helps one to clearly appreciate the pains, conditions, and legal process used in the persecution and martyrdom portrayed by the narrative accounts.

The post-execution section of the texts accounts for what happened after the death of these martyrs and contains concluding remarks by the authors or editors of these accounts. In the account of the martyrdom of Polycarp, this section provides an apology for the Christian veneration of Polycarp's remains.[83] The alternative section of the *Martyrdom of Polycarp* captures in its conclusion, prayer, and the memory of Polycarp as attested by a later church father Irenaeus.[84] The *Martyrdom of Perpetua* concludes with a prayer for the martyrs and an encouragement for the church to look up to the examples of these Christians.[85]

---

77. Martyrdom of Polycarp, 8:3; 11:2; 16.
78. Martyrdom of Polycarp, 12:2.
79. Martyrdom of Polycarp, 3:2.
80. Martyrdom of Polycarp, 13:1.
81. *Martyrdom of Perpetua*, 6:7–8; 16:3.
82. *Martyrdom of Perpetua*, 7–17.
83. Martyrdom of Polycarp, 17.
84. Martyrdom of Polycarp (Alternative ending).
85. *Martyrdom of Perpetua*, 21:11.

To this end, the three facets of the accounts tell the story of the events of these martyrdoms before the trial, during the trial, and after the trial. This is quite normal in literature or a narrative plot where there is a rising (just like the pre-trial events), climax (the trial), and anti-climax (post-execution) phases in the texts.

Character of the Martyrs

This section tries to picture the personality and attitude of the martyrs as portrayed by the texts. It presents how the martyrs are described in the texts as also their dispositions and attitude to hostilities.

In the account of the martyrdom of Polycarp, he is described as being tried and executed on his own (although the account mentions that he is the twelfth to be martyred in Smyrna),[86] while the account of Perpetua and Felicity presents a group of catechumens and their teacher.[87] Apart from Polycarp, Perpetua, and Sataurus, the other characters in these texts were people of low social status, either slaves or freedmen. We can argue that the text presents the persecution and martyrdom as affecting people who were new to the faith since most of them were catechumens, as well as the mature members of the faith, the teacher Sataurus. The hostilities are thus presented as comprehensive; irrespective of sex and social status.

Furthermore, the narrative martyr Texts presents the martyrs as examples for the succeeding Christians.[88] Polycarp is presented as the schoolmaster and father of the Christians by the crowd although the public saw him as the destroyer of the Roman gods.[89] The Christians also described him as a godlike old man, a blessed person,[90] a prayerful person, and hospitable even to his enemies.[91] Above all, he is presented in the text as steadfast even in the face of adversity.[92] The governor attempted to persuade Polycarp to recant by saying:

---

86. Martyrdom of Polycarp, 19:1.
87. *Martyrdom of Perpetua*, 2:1.
88. *Martyrdom of Perpetua*, 21:11; Martyrdom of Polycarp, 1:2.
89. Martyrdom of Polycarp, 12:2. By describing Polycarp as the destroyer of the gods, the Christians felt very good and victorious.
90. Martyrdom of Polycarp, 7:3; 12:2.
91. Martyrdom of Polycarp, 7.
92. Martyrdom of Polycarp, 9:2–3.

Have respect for your age … swear by the Genius of the emperor. Recant. Say, 'Away with the atheist …swear and I will let you go. Curse Christ.[93]

Polycarp responded with the famous statement: "For eighty-six years I have been his servant and he has done me no wrong. How can I blaspheme against my king and savior?"[94] Polycarp is thus presented as courageous and his courage is depicted as exemplary for succeeding Christians.[95] The account of Polycarp's martyrdom depicts that he was ready to die, to the extent that he took off his clothes by himself, something his fellow Christians would have felt privileged to do for him.[96]

Martyrdom is seen as the will of God for their lives,[97] and an exhibition of their courage and love for God. Polycarp is seen as a "noble ram":[98] he did not even feel the pain because he was like bread and precious minerals being purified.[99] Such positive remarks about the martyrs are similarly present in the case of Perpetua and Felicity where martyrdom is used to depict God's favor and spiritual strength,[100] his will,[101] and the day of victory.[102] The martyrs are presented as joyous and happy when they were condemned to the beast because it was their day of victory and baptism.[103] The extent of Perpetua's steadfastness from a Christian perspective is shown in the text when she refused all the efforts of her father to make her recant, while he was being beaten with rods and his beard was pulled.[104] Yet Perpetua would not recant although she was aware that her father was doing all that out of love.[105] Due to her resolve to remain a Christian, she asked her father to "vanquish along

---

93. Martyrdom of Polycarp, 9:2.
94. Martyrdom of Polycarp, 9:3.
95. Martyrdom of Polycarp, 1:2.
96. Martyrdom of Polycarp, 13:2.
97. Martyrdom of Polycarp, 2:1; 5:2.
98. Martyrdom of Polycarp, 14:1.
99. Martyrdom of Polycarp, 2:2–3; 15:2.
100. Martyrdom of Perpetua, 1:1; 15:1–3.
101. Martyrdom of Perpetua, 5:6.
102. Martyrdom of Perpetua, 18:1.
103. Martyrdom of Perpetua, 18:1; 20:11; 21:2.
104. Martyrdom of Perpetua, 6:5; 9:2–3.
105. Martyrdom of Perpetua, 5:2.

with his diabolical arguments."[106] These positive remarks in the texts to a large extent portray the Christian martyr ideology of encouraging the Christians and presenting an attraction to the non-Christians.

Identity of the Persecutors

The question here is to identify those who were presented in the texts and involved in the persecution and martyrdom of the early Christians. Based on the narrative martyr texts, the public and the authorities played significant roles. The public in the martyrdom of Polycarp includes Jews and other non-Christians. It is very significant in this account that it is the public who requested that Polycarp be martyred[107] and they further "swiftly collected logs and brushwood from workshops and baths and the Jews as is their custom zealously helped them with this."[108] The role of the crowd in the *Martyrdom of Perpetua* cannot be overemphasized. Their interest is seen in their rush to the forum for the trial and to the amphitheater where the martyrs were executed.[109]

The other category of persecutors included the authorities. Their role is seen in the use of the institutions and facilities of the empire as well as in the personal involvement of the governor. In the martyrdom of Polycarp, the municipal authority and law enforcers who were likely to be armed were involved in the persecution, and the arena was used both for the trial and the execution which were conducted by the governor.[110] The argument is that these institutions and facilities of the city and the empire could not have been used without the authorization of the governor or without the governor assuming that the emperor would approve. In the *Martyrdom of Perpetua*, the account mentions soldiers, the forum, prisons (both city prison and military prison), and where the city's prison was under the control of the municipal authorities the military prison would have been under the control of the governor of the province.[111]

Furthermore, it is significant to note that these accounts identify the governor as the interrogator and judge in the trial of the Christians. In the account

---

106. Martyrdom of Perpetua, 3:3.
107. Martyrdom of Polycarp, 3:2.
108. Martyrdom of Polycarp, 13:1.
109. Martyrdom of Perpetua, 6:1, 18.
110. Martyrdom of Polycarp, 4, 5:1, 6:2, 8:2, 9.
111. Martyrdom of Perpetua, 2, 3:7–9, 5–6, 15–16, 18–21.

of the *Martyrdom of Perpetua*, the martyrs are described as being executed in honor of the emperor:[112] the governor said he was going to kill them during the celebration of the emperor's birthday.[113] This is interesting because though the emperor was not going to be present in this Roman African region on that day, the governor was sure the emperor was going to be pleased with this celebration. Given this, it is logical to say that indeed the governor and even the emperors were presented as being involved in the persecution and martyrdom of the Christians.

Therefore, the narrative martyr texts present a spectrum of persecution where different roles are assigned to the emperor, governors, their institutions and facilities, municipal authorities, and the general public that may include the Jews.

Accusation

The harmonization of the narrative martyr texts includes similarities and differences in terms of the accusations that were leveled against the Christians. This section, therefore, helps to understand the legal framework which the Christians faced and encompasses four elements; the legal process, the charges and allegations, motives of the persecutor, and the demand of the authorities to the Christians to recant.

Legal Process

The legal prosecution of the early Christians has been a subject of discussion among scholars for years. Sherwin-White has been one of the leading voices in this area and he strongly argues that the Christians faced a legal process called *cognitio extra ordinem*.[114] This is a judicial process where the governor plays the dual roles of the questioner and judge.[115] The narrative martyr texts underpin Sherwin-White's view. In both texts used in this book, the governor is presented as both the interrogator as well as the judge who passed the sentence,[116] even if we see the police administration and the military tribune

---

112. Martyrdom of Perpetua, 16:3.
113. Martyrdom of Perpetua, 16:3.
114. Sherwin-White, "Early Persecutions and Roman," 203–4.
115. Sherwin-White, 203-204.
116. Martyrdom of Polycarp, 3:1, 9–12; Martyrdom of Perpetua, 6.

playing major roles in both accounts.[117] Unlike the classic (republican) Roman judicial system, there were no long and formal speeches by the accuser or the defendant (or on their behalf) where the evidence was presented.

The process adopted in the persecution and martyrdom of the early Christians as presented in the texts suggests that the crime must be seen as crucial since it demanded the attention of the governor himself. This is also more important because the governors in the provinces did not have much time to spare, hence, for them to devote so much time to the hostilities against the Christians shows that it was important to them.[118] It can also be argued that it was part of the narrative strategy to focus on the process rather than the form. These indicate that the charges against the Christians must have been very serious and were therefore handled by a higher authority in the provinces herein the governor, who enquired and passed judgment.

Charges and Allegations

The main legal charge against the Christians in the narrative martyr texts is the charge of the name: Christian. The martyrdom of Polycarp captures the judgment of the governor who said, "Polycarp has confessed that he is a Christian."[119] Again in the martyrdom of Perpetua and her companions, the governor asked Felicity, "Are you a Christian?"[120] and after her answer, the judgment followed. The charge of the name in essence encompassed a whole range of negative characterizations such as atheism, incest, and cannibalism among others.[121]

In terms of allegations based on the narrative martyr texts, the public in most cases initiated the persecution and martyrdom of the early Christians. These allegations were often influenced by non Christians observation of the Christians, who they often misunderstood.[122] In the account of the martyrdom of Polycarp, the public requested for his arrest based on the allegation that he was an atheist.[123] Again, after the judgment was announced, the mob ex-

---

117. Martyrdom of Polycarp, 5:1, 8:2; Martyrdom of Perpetua, 16:2, 18–21.
118. Urch, "Procedure in the Courts," 95.
119. Martyrdom of Polycarp, 12:1.
120. Martyrdom of Perpetua, 8:4.
121. Benko, *Pagan Rome*, 1–24.
122. Boamah, *Magic and Obstinacy*, 77–102.
123. Martyrdom of Polycarp, 3:2.

claimed, "Here is the schoolmaster of Asia – the father of the Christians – the destroyer of our gods – the one that teaches the multitude not to sacrifice or do reverence!"[124] The demand for Perpetua and her companions to perform the sacrifice equally feeds into this theme of atheism, since they allegedly offended the gods by not offering them sacrifices.[125] Governor Hilarianus attempted to persuade Perpetua to sacrifice because of her father's "grey head."[126] When Perpetua refused, he quickly asked: "Are you a Christian?"[127] This shows that Christians were accused of dishonoring the Roman gods by not offering sacrifices.

The public deemed it offensive for anybody to do things against the *pax Romana*. What made this charge of ungodliness even more serious was the relationship between ungodliness and *superstitio*. Beard, North, and Price as well as Janssen describe *superstitio* as an endemic disease that was not to be tolerated but must be quickly cut off.[128] In the account of the *Martyrdom of Perpetua*, the mob raised the allegations that the Christians were criminals and magicians.[129] The charge of criminality could be due to the idea that Christians met at night in secret places. The non-Christians were not privy to what the Christians did at their meetings; therefore, they labeled them as criminals.[130] They were considered magicians because they seemed to have certain powers that only magicians seemed to possess.[131]

Motive of the Persecutors

Having identified those who were presented as involved in the persecution and martyrdom, it is significant to discuss whether their motives are presented in the texts. The question is: Did the authors of these narrative texts care to even present (or misrepresent) the motives of the persecution? These motives are possibly based on the character of the opponents or the persecutors. The Jews who were part of the public were most likely motivated by the desire to

---

124. Martyrdom of Polycarp, 12:2.
125. Martyrdom of Perpetua, 6.
126. Martyrdom of Perpetua, 6.
127. Martyrdom of Perpetua, 6.
128. Beard, North, and Price, *Religions of Rome*, 217; Janssen, "'Superstitio' and the Persecution," 134–39.
129. Martyrdom of Perpetua, 15:3; 16:2.
130. Benko, *Pagan Rome*, 1–24.
131. Ste. Croix, "Why Were the Early Christians?" 8; Boamah, *Christian Magic*, 62–79.

establish their distinction from Christianity (Acts 4:1–22) since much of the Roman public could not tell the difference between the Jews and Christians in the Roman Empire.[132]

For the general public, it can be argued that they were moved by the desire to keep the peace of the empire known as the *pax Romana*. To the Romans, the peace of the empire was guaranteed by the gods, and if the gods were angered, this peace would be destroyed.[133] This peace with the gods, *pax deorum*, was very important such that anybody who did not worship or sacrifice to the gods must be made to appease them to avoid calamities and plagues. Millar suggests that "there is ever-increasing evidence that the emperor-cult had an important place in public, religious and private life."[134] In this regard, the public's major allegation against the Christians was their unwillingness to worship any god except their own; this for the Romans equaled atheism. In the account of the martyrdom of Polycarp, it is said when the public asked for Polycarp's arrest, their statements included the allegation of atheism: "Away with these atheists! Go and get Polycarp!"[135] Similarly, in the martyrdom of Perpetua, her father is described as encouraging Perpetua to sacrifice to avoid execution; he said "Perform the sacrifice."[136]

The narrative martyr texts indicate that the motives of the governors and emperors were not only religious but also political in nature to ensure allegiance to the emperor. The governors wanted to ascertain the Christians' respect and allegiance not just to the emperor but the entire empire. Urch argues that "the primary function of the governor was to maintain order in his province."[137] The maintenance of law and order in early Roman society, according to the worldview of the Romans, was a religious function underpinning a political agenda.[138]

---

132. Boamah, *Christian Magic*, 48–49.
133. Ste. Croix, "Why Were the Early Christians?" 24–25.
134. Millar, "Imperial Cult," 147.
135. Martyrdom of Polycarp, 3:2.
136. Martyrdom of Perpetua, 6:2.
137. Urch, "Procedure in the Courts," 95.
138. Beard, North, and Price, *Religions of Rome*, 313–63; Turcan, *Gods of Ancient Rome*, 105–6, 134–45.

Demand

During the trials, the authorities ordered the Christians to appease the Roman gods by offering sacrifices to restore the *pax deorum*.[139] This demand was based on the fact that in a court of law, the victim must be appeased. In the legal framework against the early Christians, Ste. Croix maintains that charges against the Christians bordered on what they refused to do (their failure to sacrifice) and not on what they did.[140] The account of the martyrdom of Polycarp reveals the governor asking Polycarp to "swear by the Genius of the Emperor. Recant. Say, 'Away with the atheist'";[141] earlier on, he had asked Polycarp to say "'Caesar is Lord' to perform the sacrifice and so forth, and thus save your life."[142] Further the governor, possibly hopeful, asked Polycarp to "Curse Christ!"[143] On the other hand, the *Martyrdom of Perpetua* captures the governor requiring Perpetua and her companions to "offer the sacrifice for the welfare of the emperors."[144]

This demand to sacrifice and to curse Christ is contrary to the teachings of Exodus 20 and Deuteronomy 5. The Christians considered a sacrifice to other gods as a sin and would, therefore, not entertain it in any way. It is argued that the originator of this test was Pliny who required confessing Christians to perform the sacrifice and curse Christ, a demand which Emperor Trajan also endorsed.[145]

Action

After understanding the legal framework of the persecution and martyrdom of the early Christians in the second century Roman Empire as presented in the narrative martyr texts, it is crucial to examine the nature of the persecution as presented in these texts. What did the Christians suffer, did they attack their persecutors, and did they have the opportunity to defend themselves from the accusations? The comparative elements considered here are the form of suffering and polemics including defense and apology.

---

139. Fowler, *Religious Experience*, 169–74.
140. Ste. Croix, "Why Were the Early Christians?" 24–26.
141. Martyrdom of Polycarp, 9:2.
142. Martyrdom of Polycarp, 8:2.
143. Martyrdom of Polycarp, 9:3.
144. Martyrdom of Perpetua, 6:2.
145. Pliny, 10.96:1–4.

Form of Suffering

How did the narrative martyr texts describe the form of persecution? What were the martyrs subjected to, in terms of sufferings, punishment, and execution? The torments and forms of punishment described were varied. In the narratives, the form of punishment interacts with the other events described such as time, place, and context. In the martyrdom of Polycarp, for example, the crowd requested that he be given to the beast but the one in charge of the beast, Philip the Asiarch, prompted that " the days of the animal games were past,"[146] which implies that beasts could have been used if only the time had been right. Since the time had passed, Polycarp was instead burnt to death.[147] Before this, other martyrs and slaves from Polycarp's household were tortured, whipped, and made to lie on broken shells.[148] While the slaves were tortured to make them reveal the whereabouts of Polycarp, the martyrs, however, were tortured to force "them to deny the faith."[149] Polycarp was also threatened many times by the governor who tried to persuade him to recant, but in his case, no torture was applied.[150]

Perpetua and her companions also faced many forms of suffering. In their case, they faced house arrest,[151] imprisonment both in the city and military dungeon which Perpetua described as dark and uncomfortable.[152] She confesses that, "a few days later we were lodged in the prison; and I was terrified, as I had never before been in such a dark hole."[153] Her father was beaten in her sight with a rod just to get her to recant, hence she remarks: "I felt sorry for his pathetic old age."[154] Just before their martyrdom, her father visited them in the dungeon in all sorrow and " started tearing the hairs from his beard and threw them on the ground."[155] Again, Perpetua remarks: "I felt sorry for his

---

146. Martyrdom of Polycarp, 12:2.
147. Martyrdom of Polycarp, 11.
148. Martyrdom of Polycarp, 2 and 6.
149. Martyrdom of Polycarp, 2:2.
150. Martyrdom of Polycarp, 11.
151. Martyrdom of Perpetua, 3.
152. Martyrdom of Perpetua, 3:5–8.
153. Martyrdom of Perpetua, 3:5.
154. Martyrdom of Perpetua, 6:6.
155. Martyrdom of Polycarp, 9:2.

unhappy old age."[156] Perpetua thus also describes how family ties between pagan and Christian members of the same family could add an extra emotional dimension to the physical torments and the anxiety associated more directly with the persecution. Perpetua and her companions were made to fight the beasts where a leopard, a bear, a boar, and a heifer were used in the game to entertain the mob in celebration of the emperor's birthday.[157] They also faced the gladiators[158] and were ultimately killed with the sword.[159]

It is suggested that there are three progressive stages of persecution and martyrdom employed in the narrative martyr texts. In the first place, the governor tried to persuade or threaten them to recant. Second, there was some form of physical torture of some of the martyrs to make them recant. Third, they were subjected to degrading, painful and spectacular deaths by fire, animals, and stabbing. These three stages of torture and forms of martyrdom are present in both the narrative martyr texts where the sufferings were horrific. The martyrs are presented as heroes and victors based on their endurance to encourage other Christians to stand firm. This is seen in the final words of Saturus, who is described as having converted to Christianity under the influence of the martyrs, to a soldier, Pudens. He said to him, "Good-bye. Remember me, and remember the faith. These things should not disturb you but rather strengthen you,"[160] after which he dipped a ring into his wounds and handed it to Pudens "as a record of his bloodshed."[161]

Polemic

It is important in an analysis of this nature to compare the level of polemic attacks on the persecutors by the authors of these texts. All the narrative accounts contain polemic elements, where the persecutors are derided. In Polycarp's account, the authorities are branded as inhuman, tyrannical, impious, evil, vicious, and even jealous.[162] The account also describes the public as

---

156. Martyrdom of Polycarp, 9:2.
157. Martyrdom of Perpetua, 19.
158. Martyrdom of Perpetua, 19:5.
159. Martyrdom of Perpetua, 21:9–10.
160. Martyrdom of Perpetua, 21:4–6.
161. Martyrdom of Perpetua, 21:4–6.
162. Martyrdom of Polycarp, 2:3, 3:1, 11:2, 16:1, 17:1.

devils, predatorial, atheists, and lawless.[163] On the other hand, in the account of the martyrdom of Perpetua and her companions, the authorities are called devils[164] while the public is described as foolish and cruel; Perpetua's father's arguments are described as diabolical.[165] In terms of number and intensity, therefore, the authorities lie in the first line of attack and then the public is equally attacked polemically.

Defense and Apology

It is already established that the martyrs were not allowed to give long formal speeches for the defense. This section attempts to find out if the martyrs were described as being allowed to offer a brief defense of their convictions or address some of the charges against them based on the Christian doctrines and practices. Further, this section examines whether the martyrs are described as offering an apologetic defense in situations where they are not faced with the governor, but with other persecutors or other outsiders.

The two narrative martyr texts describe only a few such instances of defense and all of them are described as brief. In the *Martyrdom of Perpetua*, neither Perpetua nor her companions are described as giving any apology or offering any defense when interrogated by the governor – they simply confessed that they were Christians and Perpetua refused to recant.[166] In other settings, Perpetua is, however, described as offering brief apologetic defenses for herself and/or her companions. When her father asked her to denounce Christianity, she pointed to a water pot and asked her father if that could be called by another name and since the answer was obviously "no," Perpetua retorted that she too was a Christian and could not be referred to with any other name.[167] Here, she defended herself against her father and not the governor. At another time when she felt they were not well treated in the military prison, she complained to the officer of the prison and claimed that they should be treated better since they were the "most distinguished condemned prisoners," and condemned to die at the celebration of the emperor's birthday.[168]

---

163. Martyrdom of Polycarp, 3:1; 6:1, 9:2.
164. Martyrdom of Perpetua, 20:1.
165. Martyrdom of Perpetua, 3:3, 20:2, 8.
166. Martyrdom of Perpetua, 6.
167. Martyrdom of Perpetua, 3:1–3.
168. Martyrdom of Perpetua, 16:3.

Again and even more significantly, when in these celebratory games, "men were forced to put on the robes of the priest of Saturn, the women the dress of the priestess of Ceres,"[169] it is noteworthy that the account says "Perpetua strenuously resisted this to the end."[170]

In both cases, Perpetua is described as prevailing. In the account of Polycarp, it is interesting that he requested a day to teach the governor on the Christian doctrines, possibly to offer an apology, but that was turned down.[171] Furthermore, the author of the text offers a strong apology directed to the Christian readers of the text about who the Christians worshiped.[172] This apology was occasioned by a petition to the governor by Nicetes (the father of the police-captain Herod and brother of Alce, who was a Christian), who, according to the author, persuaded the governor not to hand over Polycarp's body. Nicetes, according to the author, was under the influence of the Jews, and he argued, that the Christians might otherwise worship Polycarp instead of Christ. The author argues apologetically, that they would never worship anyone except Christ because he died to save sinners although he was innocent.

It can, therefore, be suggested that apology and defense are not very prominent in the narrative martyr texts although they are not absent. The little apologetic content in these texts is both formal and informal. These apologies also defend the Christian religious foundation in terms of what they worship and their unpreparedness to worship the pagan gods.

Other Peculiar Features

This section identifies other peculiar features of the persecution and martyrdom addressed by the texts that are very prominent in the texts. Two issues are unique to Polycarp's martyrdom. In the first place, the account deals with voluntary martyrs. These are people who desired to possibly show off and hence report themselves to be martyred because of being Christians. However, this account links these voluntary martyrs to apostates who become cowards by later renouncing their faith.[173] The text, therefore, discourages

---

169. Martyrdom of Perpetua, 19:4.
170. Martyrdom of Perpetua, 19:4.
171. Martyrdom of Polycarp, 10:1.
172. Martyrdom of Polycarp, 17.
173. Martyrdom of Polycarp, 4.

such acts as voluntary martyrdom. The second unique issue in this account is the question of burial; in this account, it is clear that after Polycarp was cremated, the disciples picked what they could of his remains and provided a befitting burial of his ashes.[174] The *Martyrdom of Perpetua* does not tell the readers where and how they were buried.

When the two accounts are compared, the narrative martyr texts bring to the fore the role of persuasion. The texts capture frantic efforts, especially by the governors, to get these martyrs to recant and escape death, a procedure that may be reminiscent of the correspondence between Emperor Trajan and Governor Pliny. According to the texts, the persecutors' ultimate desire was for the Christians to "repent" to uphold the Roman order. Furthermore, these narrative martyr texts are heavily influenced by the Scriptures. A cursory reading of the scriptural references as indicated in the footnote of Musurillo's collections shows remarkably that both accounts have thirteen scriptural references with nine New Testament and four Old Testament verses in each text. Heffernan also identifies a wide range of scriptural influences in the account of the martyrdom of Perpetua and her companions.[175] This may already show how Scriptures were used at the time. Hartog affirms the heavy dependence on Scriptures in the account of the martyrdom of Polycarp, which according to him resembles the Greek Bible, especially the Septuagint and the New Testament.[176]

A final, major feature of these narrative martyr texts is the role of visions. In the account of the *Martyrdom of Perpetua*, five visions are narrated; the first vision was narrated by Perpetua following her brother Saturus's request to her about discerning what would happen to them. Polycarp also saw a vision before his arrest and he was shown how he was going to die by burning. It is strongly argued that since these visions were to a large extent eschatological, they seemed to have encouraged the martyrs to hold on to their faith while invariably making them obstinate against the non-Christians, especially the governors.[177]

---

174. Martyrdom of Polycarp, 18:2.
175. Heffernan, *Passion of Perpetua and Felicity*, 527–29.
176. Hartog, *Polycarp's* Epistle, 209–11.
177. Boamah, *Christian Magic*, 103–28.

These particular aspects of the narrative martyr texts show important features of the hostilities against the Christians which may need further investigation. Although some parts of these are addressed in academia, more questions could be asked to help understand them better.

Protocol Martyr Texts

The protocol martyr texts in this book refer to accounts of the martyrs that resemble court interactions. This class of texts is sometimes referred to as acta martyr texts, but for the purpose of this book, it shall be designated as protocol martyr texts, based on the style of the texts compared to the narrative martyr texts. This book uses the account of the *Scillitan Martyrs* and the *Martyrdom of Justin and His Companions*.

These texts are compared in what is labeled as harmony to establish similarities and differences in the image they paint of the persecution. This harmonized picture of the protocol texts is later compared to the harmonized picture from the narrative martyr texts. The comparative elements employed in the narrative martyr texts analysis are similarly used here.

Account

This section examines how the accounts are presented as well as the presentation of the characters in the texts. It encompasses the storyline of the account, identity of the martyrs, and the persecutors.

Storyline

The protocol martyr texts capture the courtroom interaction and their judgment. The trial activities are thus in focus. The account of the Scillitan martyrs consists mainly of the dialogue between the martyrs and the governor during the interrogation followed by the sentencing of the martyrs and then a passage describing how the martyrs praised God.[178] This is similar to the case of Justin and his companions. For example, in recension A, the culprits were presented before the governor, interrogated, and then sentenced to death.[179] An interesting feature in the protocol martyr texts is the fact that although they were presented in a group, the governor then interrogated them on the

---

178. Scillitan Martyrs, 2–17.
179. Martyrdom of Justin, 2–6 (recension A), 2–5 (recension B), 2–5 (recension C).

charges individually. Finally, they were judged with mention of their names, but with a common verdict.[180]

It is concluded that the procedure or storyline of the protocol martyr texts is straightforward. It captures the trial and only very little of the post-trial events. There is no mention of the arrest of the martyrs.

Identity of the Martyrs
In this group of texts, there is not much information concerning the martyrs. Their names are provided and they are, through their confessions and words, presented as very courageous persons. In the account of Justin and his companions, it is stated in recension B that one of them, Evelpidtus, was a slave of the emperor.[181] They are presented as very resolute persons who would not give up their faith.[182] Furthermore, they are presented as very happy when their death sentence was published after the interrogations.[183] Recension C of the martyrdom of Justin and his companions suggests that these young Christians were from various cities in the empire.[184] Similarly for the Scillitan martyrs, their names are provided and they showed joy when they were sentenced to death for being Christians.[185]

It is mostly accepted that apart from their leaders, the other martyrs were likely to be catechumens, students, slaves, or generally people of low social status. The characterization of these martyrs as presented in the texts is rather very scanty but they are projected as exemplary members of the Christian community.

Identity of the Persecutors
Since the protocol texts capture the trial session of the persecution and martyrdom of the Christians, the identifiable persecutor in these texts is the governor. The governor himself interrogated the martyrs and passed judgment.[186] As highly placed authorities of the Roman Empire, governors are thus

---

180. Martyrdom of Justin, 5:6 (recension A), 5:8 (recension B), 5:2 (recension C); Scillitan Martyrs, 14.
181. Martyrdom of Justin, 4:3 (recension B).
182. Martyrdom of Justin, 3–5 (recension A), 2–5:6 (recension B), 3–5 (recension C).
183. Martyrdom of Justin, 6 (recension A), 6 (recension B).
184. Martyrdom of Justin, 2–4 (recension C).
185. Scillitan Martyrs, 1, 15.
186. Martyrdom of Justin, 2–5 (recension A), 2–5 (recension B), 3–5 (recension C).

presented as intimately and actively involved in the persecution and martyrdom of the early Christians. The account of the Scillitan martyrs similarly shows the active roles of the proconsul Saturninus who interrogated and passed judgment for the execution of the early Christians.[187]

Accusation

This section considers the legal framework adopted in prosecuting Christians. This category of the comparative elements harmonizes the legal processes adopted, the charges and allegations, motives, and the demand of the authorities as presented in the protocol martyr texts.

Legal Process

The protocol martyr texts present a legal process that follows the *cognitio extra ordinem* where the authority is seen as the interrogator and the judge. In the accounts, the martyrs were presented before the magistrate who asked questions with regard to their meeting places, activities after conversion, and eventually determined their fate.[188]

The authorities are described in the protocol martyr texts as active in the persecution and as considering it important to persecute Christians. There is no mention of any *delator (denouncer)* to charge the martyrs. *Cognitio extra ordinem*, according to Sherwin-White, was not the most commonly used procedure in Roman imperial times.[189]

Charges and Allegations

The legal charge against the Christians was concerning the name "Christian". In these texts, the authorities were very emphatic in asking the martyrs individual questions such as "Are you a Christian too? You are not also a Christian, are you?"[190] In most cases right after these questions, the judgment for their execution followed. In the account of the Scillitan martyrs, when the proconsul encouraged the martyrs to offer sacrifice, Vestia responded, "I am a Christian;" Secunda said, "I wish to be what I am." Then the proconsul

---

187. Scillitan Martyrs, 2–14.

188. Martyrdom of Justin, 2–5 (recension A), 2–5 (recension B), 2–5 (recension C); Scillitan Martyrs, 2–14.

189. Sherwin-White, "Early Persecutions and Roman," 203–4.

190. Martyrdom of Justin, 4:1, 8 (recension A).

Saturninus said to Speratus, "Do you persist in remaining a Christian?", to which Speratus responded, "I am a Christian."[191] Additionally, the judgment that followed the sentencing began by naming the martyrs and after which it read "have confessed that they have been living in accordance with the rites of the Christians."[192] Therefore, it is without a doubt that the confession of being a Christian is presented as the foundation for the verdicts. Analyzed carefully, however, it is clear that the texts present underlying allegations that explain why the confession of being a Christian was seen as a confession that entailed the death penalty. Sometimes, it was the magistrate who brought up such allegations and at other times, the martyrs defended themselves without the magistrates bringing them up. Such underlying allegations included ungodliness, cannibalism, incest, magic, etc.[193]

The account of the Scillitan martyrs presents allegations against the Christians based on the interrogations of the proconsul. Allegations such as Christianity being madness, atheism, folly, and the Christians as being obstinate were identified.[194] Further, when encouraged by the proconsul to return to his "senses," one of the martyrs, Speratus, answered in a way that seemed to anticipate allegations of wickedness ("We have never done wrong; we have never lent ourselves to wickedness").[195] The interrogations in the martyrdom of Justin and his companions similarly stress these allegations. The magistrate asked questions like, "what sort of life do you lead?",[196] which may be premised on the allegation of social vices such as magic, sorcery, cannibalism, incest, and debauchery, among others. The governor also inquired about where they met.[197] This question resonates with the rumors that the non-Christians believed the Christians met in secret places to do their nefarious activities.[198]

---

191. Scillitan Martyrs, 9-12.
192. Scillitan Martyrs, 14.
193. Engberg, *Impulsore Chresto*, 194; Benko, *Pagan Rome*, 1-24.
194. Scillitan Martyrs, 2, 4, 8.
195. Scillitan Martyrs, 2.
196. Martyrdom of Justin, 2 (recension A).
197. Martyrdom of Justin, 3 (recension A), 3 (recension B), 2:4 (recension C).
198. Engberg, *Impulsore Chresto*, 188; Sherwin-White, "Early Persecutions and Roman Law Again," 783-84; Walsh, "On Christian Atheism," 258.

Therefore, the questions asked by the authorities and the answers provided by the martyrs present the image that strong prejudices against the Christians influenced the hostilities against them in the empire.

Motives of Persecutors

It is without a doubt that the motives of the authorities in this category of texts are presented as both political and religious. This is seen as interrogation in the text. The account of the Scillitan martyrs presents that just after the names of the martyrs were presented, "The proconsul Saturnius said, 'If you return to your senses, you can obtain the pardon of our lord the emperor.'"[199] This statement points, to a large extent, to the proconsul's prejudice that they could be practicing something close to *superstitio* which offended the gods. In response to this suggestion, the leader "Speratus said, 'we have never done wrong; we have never lent ourselves to wickedness. Never, have we uttered a curse.'"[200] This response shows he was also addressing some of the social vices believed to be characteristic of the Christians.

Furthermore, the proconsul reacted to this statement by saying, "we too are religious people, and our religion is a simple one: we swear by the genius of our lord the emperor and we offer prayers for his health – as you also ought to do."[201] The political aspect is seen in his last words in the obligatory duty of the citizens to the emperor – the prayer. Again, this reaction points to the fact that among the Romans, the emperor was seen as both a religious and a political leader. The accounts of the martyrdom of Justin and his companions are even more interesting. The governor asked the martyrs questions about the kind of lives they lived, where they met, and other inquiries that point to some of the allegations of *superstitio* to stress his religious motives. He also demanded them to offer sacrifice, which is more political. In recension B, the author quotes the words of the governor as saying to Justin unequivocally: "'First of all, you must obey the gods and submit to the order of the emperors.'"[202]

The authorities in these accounts are described as presenting, in their interrogation and verdicts, the Christians as jeopardizing the *pax deorum* and

---

199. Scillitan Martyrs, 2.
200. Scillitan Martyrs, 3.
201. Scillitan Martyrs, 4.
202. Martyrdom of Justin, 2 (recension B).

the *pax Romana*, and thus the governors are described as being motivated by their desire to restore such peace either by forcing Christians to recant and sacrifice or by punishing them. Apart from this religious motivation, the emperor needed to be assured of the allegiance of the Christians.

Demand

In most cases during the trial of the early Christians, it is interesting that when the martyrs confessed to being Christians, the governor demanded from them the offering of sacrifice to the Roman gods and/or swearing by the *genius* of the emperor.

All the accounts in the protocol martyr texts request the martyrs to swear by the *genius* of the emperor and offer sacrifice. The proconsul in the account of the Scillitan martyrs suggested to the martyrs to swear and when they refused, his judgment in part reads: "and whereas those allowed to return to the usage of the Romans they have persevered in their obstinacy."[203] Being Roman means praying to the *genius* of the emperor.[204] The same requirement is demanded in the martyrdom of Justin and his companions. The judgment reads: "Those who have refused to sacrifice to the gods are to be scourged and executed under the law (recension A); those who have refused to sacrifice to the gods and yield to the emperors' edict are to be led away to be scourged and beheaded under the law (recension B)."[205]

The authorities would want the Christians to sacrifice as the general Roman populace would do. However, the Christians saw it as idolatry and hence could not bring themselves to do that, since it was against their faith.

Action

These comparative elements have considered the nature of the persecution and martyrdom of the early Christians in the Roman Empire. This section aims to understand what the oppressors did to the Christians after the charges were proved. It, therefore, comprises the form of suffering, polemic attacks, and their defense and apology.

---

203. Scillitan Martyrs, 14.
204. Turcan, *Gods of Ancient Rome*, 134–39.
205. Martyrdom of Justin, 5:6 (recension A), 5:8 (recension B), 5:2 (recension C).

Form of Suffering

According to the texts, the Scillitan martyrs were condemned to be executed by the sword, and eventually, they were beheaded.[206] In the account of the martyrdom of Justin and his companions, recension A talks about the martyrs being scourged and executed;[207] recension B similarly talks about scourging and beheading of the Christians,[208] while recension C points to cruel torment, death by the sword, and chastisement by whips.[209]

These forms of persecution and martyrdom can be classified into two; physical torture and the ultimate punishment, death. The physical torture including scourging, whipping, and various chastisements are only found in Justin's martyrdom. The ultimate form used to claim the lives of these Christians was the cutting off of their heads.

Polemic

The protocol martyr texts also made some counterattacks on the persecutors of the early Christians in the Roman Empire. Although the account of the Scillitan martyrs does not present any direct attacks on the persecutors, the account of the martyrdom of Justin and his companions has a strong polemic content. All three recensions of the martyrdom of Justin and his companions begin with charges by the authorities as being "wicked," "idolaters," and "impious."[210] The recension C includes other direct charges of the authorities as being a "plague" and "terrible." All the direct attacks are made against the authorities and not the public.

Defense and Apology

It must be stressed that the accounts of the persecution and martyrdom of the Christians as portrayed by the protocol martyr texts emphasize how the martyrs defend the Christian faith. The account of the martyrdom of the Scillitans tries to cleanse Christianity of the social vices they were allegedly engaging in by suggesting that they had done nothing wrong; they did not

---

206. Scillitan Martyrs, 14, 17.
207. Martyrdom of Justin, 5:6 (recension A).
208. Martyrdom of Justin, 5:8 (recension B).
209. Martyrdom of Justin, 4:1; 5:1; 6:1 (recension C).
210. Martyrdom of Justin1 (recension A), 1 (recension B), 1 (recension C).

support wickedness or curse people.[211] The martyrs in this account further argued that they were responsible members of the society since they paid their taxes, did not steal, and explained that the God they serve is invisible.[212] The account of the martyrdom of Justin and his companions also explained that the Christians were blameless and their doctrines of God's omnipresence, Jesus as the creator, Christian apocalypse, and many other Christian beliefs and practices were relevant to their worship.[213] These defenses offered by the Christians during the interrogations in this class of martyr texts try to explain the Christian beliefs and practices as well as make the Christian faith appealing to the non-Christians. Therefore, to a large extent, they have a strong evangelistic appeal.

Other Peculiar Features

It is important to stress that these accounts of martyrdom in the protocol martyr texts bring to the fore some other peculiarities that are very interesting. In the first place, there is little presence of scriptural influences in the texts. However, some imageries and ideas used in the texts have scriptural backing. Justin, for instance, cites from Jeremiah 23:24, stating that "God is not circumscribed by place; invisible, he fills the heavens and the earth."[214]

The accounts touched on burial as a practice of the early church. In recension B of the martyrdom of Justin and his companions, the Christians had to even "secretly" steal the bodies of the martyrs for burial.[215]

A major peculiarity of the protocol martyr texts is the element of conversion. The accounts show that some of the martyrs, especially in the martyrdom of Justin and his companions, are second-generation Christians.

Similarities and Differences

This section brings together the two classes of the martyr texts to identify possible similarities and differences in the way they portray the persecution and martyrdom of the Christians in the Roman Empire during the second

---

211. Scillitan Martyrs, 3.
212. Scillitan Martyrs, 5–6.
213. Martyrdom of Justin, 2:5; 5:1–6 (recension A), 2:3–7; 3:1–3; 4:7–8; 5:1–8 (recension B), 2:1–3; 4:1–6 (recension C).
214. Martyrdom of Justin, 3:1 (recension B).
215. Martyrdom of Justin, 6 (recension B).

to early third centuries. This comparison helps to see if the texts corroborate, supplement, or even contradict each other. The narrative martyr texts have one way of describing these hostilities while the protocol martyr texts also seem to strengthen other aspects. The attempt, therefore, is to synchronize the issues these texts raise in the persecution and martyrdom. The synchronization here is presented through the comparative elements used in discussing the narrative and protocol martyr texts.

Account

This category compares the storyline or the flow of events in the texts and the identity of both the oppressors and the oppressed. Such a comparison helps to understand the two categories of the martyr texts, the presentation of the accounts, and who was involved in these hostilities. The following section looks into the nature of the accounts of the persecution and martyrdom as captured by the martyr texts while stressing their convergent and divergent viewpoints.

Storyline

The two kinds of martyr texts differ in their focus; while the narrative accounts are detailed, the protocols are short and straightforward. The narrative accounts take into consideration the issues before, during, and after the trial, but the protocol accounts focus on the trial issues.

Since the protocol accounts often present in-depth accounts of the trial session, they are focused on the dialogue between the magistrate and martyrs, whereas the narrative accounts, in comparison, seem to rush through. The pictures presented by the two kinds of texts, therefore, complement each other.

Identity of Martyrs

The narrative and protocol martyr texts agree in their presentation of the characters of the martyrs. They are described with positive remarks especially as highly courageous and worthy of emulation by the later Christians. This glorification of the martyrs in the texts makes it clear that, to a large extent, these texts were written by Christians with a large Christian congregation in mind.

Identity of the Persecutors

Again, the two classes of texts agree with regard to who was involved in the persecution and martyrdom of the Christians. The texts suggest that the persecutors included both the non-Christian public and those in authority. While the narrative texts emphasize the role of the public and in the account of the martyrdom of Polycarp, there is special mention of the Jews, the protocol texts are silent about the public. The authorities are also active in the narrative texts, but here we see a spectrum of authorities from municipal authorities and local police to Roman soldiers and governors and we see the use of public facilities and spaces like prisons, forums, and amphitheaters. Therefore, the narrative accounts capture the authorities and the public while the protocol accounts exclude the public.

Accusation

This subsection captures the legal procedure adopted, charges and allegations, motive, and the demand of the authorities and therefore, gets into the legal framework of the hostilities.

Legal Procedure

All the processes presented in the texts followed the *cognitio extra ordinem* procedure. Both the narrative and protocol martyr texts agree that the legal method adopted is what Sherwin-White suggests in his writings.[216] The involvement of magistrates and Rome's urban prefects in the prosecution of Christians shows how seriously the authorities took the threat of the Christians.

Charges and Allegations

As stated earlier, the primary charge with which the Christians were saddled was the charge associated with the name Christian. The charge of the name entailed, however, that there were negative traits or crimes associated with the name: these included the allegations of *superstitio*, magic, social vices, and many others.[217] These allegations are generally social but may have some religious and political implications.

---

216. Sherwin-White, "Early Persecutions and Roman," 203–4.
217. Engberg, *Impulsore Chresto*, 187–91.

Motives

The motivation was predominantly religious and political. The persecutors sought to maintain a peaceful relationship between the gods and the people – *pax deorum*. Further, the Christians' unpreparedness to offer sacrifices to the *genius* of the emperor created doubt concerning the allegiance of the Christian.

Demand

After the Christians admitted that they were Christians, the authorities demanded that they appease the gods by offering sacrifice. This demand was an attempt to restore the broken relationship that existed between the gods and the Romans. The Christians could not do this since it was against the first two requirements of the Decalogue.

Action

This section of the comparative analysis seeks to reveal how the judgments were implemented in both the narrative and protocol accounts. The form of suffering, polemics, and their defense and apology are analyzed from the texts.

Form of Suffering

The narrative accounts suggest that there was psychological and physical abuse inflicted on Christians and even death. In the protocol accounts, the emphasis is placed on physical abuse which included whipping and scourging, and execution as the ultimate punishment. To this end, the narratives expose the reader to the pain the Christians suffered psychologically and physically while the protocol texts focus on their decapitation and physical torture.

Polemic

The two classes of texts attack the authorities and the general public with some countercharges. The protocol texts directly attack authorities alone while the narrative texts, also attack the public, besides the authorities, directly. This difference between the texts could be attributed to the nature of the texts.

Defense and Apology

The protocol accounts, compared to the narrative accounts, present a more detailed perspective on the defense and apologies by the Christians. It was only in the martyrdom of Polycarp that there is some formal apology of who the Christians worship.²¹⁸ It was not even offered by the martyr (Polycarp) but by the narrator when it is suggested that the Christians might steal the body of the martyr to worship it. Also, Polycarp himself requested such a debate but he was refused.²¹⁹ The account of Perpetua and her companions also has some defense but these cannot be described as formal.²²⁰ The protocol accounts have a lot of apologetics and defense content as seen in the way the martyrs tried to address some of the prejudices against the Christians. In effect, the protocols offer some defense and apology while the narratives are almost silent on defense and apology.

The nature of the hostilities based on the synthesis of the two classes of texts shows some agreements and disagreements. The differences do not reveal a contradiction but complementary elaboration; what is not covered in the protocol texts (pre- and post-trial events) are covered in the narrative texts; what is in absolute focus in the protocol texts (dialogue between judge and martyr) is also not elaborated in the narrative accounts.

Other Peculiar Features

Apart from the comparison of these two sources, some peculiarities can be also compared. In the first place, they both make use of scriptural texts and references. They cite from the Old and New Testaments to support and progress their arguments. Second, they both agree that, although some martyrs were in a group, they faced the charges individually. Furthermore, the accounts present from a non-Christian perspective the obstinacy of the martyrs.

The accounts however differ in terms of the fact that the narratives touch on the role of visions in these hostilities while the protocols do not record anything about visions. Also, the protocols touch on the issue of conversion which shows that many of the Christians were converted by their parents.

In general, it can be seen that the narrative and protocol accounts have some important convergences with very few differences but no contradictions. The few nuances in the texts complement each other strongly about the general picture of the persecution and martyrdom of the early Christians in the Roman Empire from the second century.

---

218. Martyrdom of Polycarp, 17.
219. Martyrdom of Polycarp, 10.
220. Martyrdom of Perpetua, 3:1–3, 16:3, 18:4.

Conclusion

This chapter has shown the three main factors which influenced the writing of martyr texts. First, there was the need to relate with other Christians abroad. Second, it was necessary to record the history of Christian developments and third, to build a Christian identity. These factors and purposes largely connect to bring to the fore the corroborative and supplementary roles of the two classes of texts.

Regarding the central question of this chapter, it is clear that there are striking similarities in the narrative and protocol forms of the martyr texts. The legal process, charges, allegations, and motives, as well as forms of suffering have the same representations in both texts. It is argued that the levels of overlap and similarity in the images painted by all four texts demonstrate there was a historical reality behind the images provided by the texts.

Besides these similarities, there are a few nuances but not contradictions between these forms of texts. Some of the nuances are seen in terms of the storyline, the character of the persecutors, and the apologetic contents of the texts. To a large extent, these nuances do not contradict but rather supplement each other. The various nuances identified stress the influence of the form of the text on the content since an author who intends to write in a protocol form does not have the time to include what happened before the arrest of the martyrs or the events after the martyrs were killed. Conversely, such authors have an increased focus on the dialogue between martyr and governor, thereby focusing more on apologetics and defense when compared to the narrative style of writing.

Based on this result, it is suggested that scholars should make use of both the protocol and martyr texts to clearly understand the persecution and martyrdom of the early Christians. Using one form without the other may cause one to lose sight of some crucial aspects of the entire phenomena where the hostilities are concerned, but a corroborated and supplementary use of the two will contribute to a better understanding of the situation at the time.

CHAPTER FOUR

"You Killed Us" – Apologetic Texts

The persecution and martyrdom of the early Christians in the Roman Empire was prevalent both in Rome and in the other parts of the empire. John Granger Cook suggests that the Romans perceived the Christians as "others" because they did not seem to fit into the Roman identity construction.[1] The non-Christians felt that the doctrine and practices of the Christians to a large extent were against the Roman social order. To correct such notions, Christian authors wrote this genre of texts called the apologetics to equip Christians with a prepared defense as well as provide them with the ability to convert some high-profile personalities of the empire. It is in this light that the title "You Killed Us" is employed to express the Christian idea that by addressing a mostly non-Christian audience, the texts were written to complain about the way they were wrongly accused and treated.

The apologetic texts further include Christian descriptions of the persecutions, the persecutors, and the presentation of their allegations, to which the apologists, in turn, offer a defense. This chapter, therefore, explores the image of the persecution and martyrdom of the early Christians projected by the apologetic texts to identify if their picture of the hostilities against the Christians supplement, corroborate, or contradict each other.

Most scholars, including Ulrich[2] and Engberg,[3] agree that the division of the apologetic texts is based on their explicit addressees. This is important because although most of the apologies are addressed to outsiders

---

1. Cook, *Roman Attitude*, 2.
2. Ulrich, "Apologetics and Apologies," 11–12.
3. Engberg, "Truth Begs No Favours," 182–83.

(non-Christians), some of them are addressed to the authorities such as the emperors or magistrates, while the others are addressed to the general public. Engberg designates the apologetic texts addressed to the authorities as apologies and those addressed to the general public as part of the bigger corpus of apologetic texts.[4]

The main objectives of this chapter are twofold; first, to develop a comprehensive picture of the persecution and martyrdom as portrayed by the apologetic texts. The comparison is to find out to what extent the two categories of texts supplement, corroborate, or contradict each other with regard to the hostilities against the Christians, as was done in chapter three. The essence of the similarity (which may imply a corroborative or supplementary) or a possible difference (which may imply contradictory accounts) helps to address the second objective, which is a discussion of the submission status of the apologies. This second objective is crucial because some scholars maintain that the apologetic texts addressed to the authorities were not intended for submission. This book, therefore, contributes to the age-long debate on the premise that a very close similarity between the two classes of apologetic texts based on the comparative elements would suggest that the apologies were not intended for submission while a level of difference would suggest an intention for submission. This implies that if the apologetic texts addressed to the authorities are the same as those addressed to the public, then the apologies were not intended for submission and the reverse may, therefore, be true. Given this book's adoption of Kennedy's rhetorical critical model which focuses on the speaker or author, audience, discourse, and context or occasion of a text, a preliminary discussion on the nature, factors, and purposes of the apologetic texts will be done.

Submission Status of Apologies

A major feature of the apologetic texts is the explicit nature of its addressees, although this is not a peculiar feature because letters equally have explicit addressee(s).[5] However, there is a strong debate among scholars on whether these apologies were intended to be submitted to those they explicitly address.

---

4. Engberg, 183; Engberg, "From among You," 51.
5. Jacobsen, "Apologetics and Apologies", 20–21.

Even though almost all scholars agree that the addressees were not the only people intended to read the text, scholars disagree on the intent of the authors regarding the reading of the texts by their addressees. The texts certainly had internal audiences[6] in mind apart from the external group they possibly address. However, the debate centers around the intent of the authors with regard to ensuring that the addressees who were usually non-Christians (the public and the authorities) received and read the texts.

Alexander suggests that "apologetics, as we have seen, often fail to reach the dramatic audience to whom it is ostensibly addressed."[7] Some scholars argue that the address to the authorities was only a literary device, intended to heighten interest in the text through the application of such prominent addressees.[8] Lesley Bernard seems to be in this category when he remarks on Justin's apologies by stating that "Humanistic Jewish writers before Justin had used similar modes of addressing to ensure that their works were well received by the public for whom they were designed."[9] To this class of scholars, the apologists only applied the names of the authorities to attract readers for these texts.

On the other hand, some scholars also maintain that it was standard practice in the Roman Empire where small books on different issues were sometimes written to communicate to emperors and magistrates.[10] Such small books, *libellus* in Latin and *biblidion* in Greek which can be translated as "small scroll," were submitted to a magistrate or an emperor with a petition.[11] This group of scholars, therefore, suggests that it is likely that these texts could have been intended for submission to the authorities. Jacobsen is one of those who strongly maintain that the apologies were at least intended for submission.[12] The basis of his strong suggestion is that the apologetic texts touch strongly on political issues especially with regard to the legal status of the Christians in the empire.

---

6. Jacobsen, "Apologetics and Apologies", 16.
7. Alexander, "Acts of the Apostles," 44.
8. Jacobsen, "Apologetics and Apologies," 13–17.
9. Bernard, *St. Justin Martyr,* 6.
10. Engberg, "Condemnation, Criticism and Consternation,"201–3.
11. Skarsaune, "Justin and The Apologists," 123.
12. Jacobsen, "Main Topics," 107.

In the light of this seeming confusion, I provide a few scientific solutions by adopting a systematic comparison between the subcategories of the apologetic texts in this chapter and the martyr texts in chapter three to address the issues. This comparison is based on the argumentative strategy of the texts. In the first place, among the apologetic texts, it is assumed that those written to the general public may have a strong polemic approach as compared to those addressed to the authorities and less inclined toward discussing the legal procedure in detail. Geoffrey Dunn agrees with the premise that the polemic content of a text that is intended to be read by a particular group is less polemical toward that audience.[13] Kahlos defines polemic as a strong verbal or written attack on a people, beliefs, and practices to destabilize an opponent's position in order to highlight that of the polemist.[14] Again, in this light, the sources of the argument as presented to the general public may use both Christian and non-Christian sources while those addressed to the authorities may depend on philosophy, logic, and legal arguments in addition to the Christian and non-Christian sources.

On the other hand, where the apologetic texts are compared to the martyr texts, it is anticipated that if the apologies were intended for submission, the martyr texts will focus on religious charges while the apologetic texts will deal with political issues. Furthermore, the apologies will present a more aggressive defense as compared to the martyr texts (if there are any apologetic aspects of the texts). Additionally, the martyr texts are most likely to use Christian sources in their works as compared to the apologetic texts which may employ both Christian and non-Christian sources as well as philosophical, logical, and legal arguments. The reverse of these issues would therefore mean that the apologies were never meant to be submitted when compared to the martyr texts. In essence, if the results of the external comparisons are different, then it is logical to argue that the apologies were meant to be submitted but if the comparisons show that the martyr texts and the apologetic texts are similar in these same respects, then the conclusion suggests that the apologies were not intended for submission.

---

13. Dunn, "Rhetorical Structure in Tertullian's," 50.
14. Kahlos, *Debate and Dialogue*, 62–63.

Purpose And Audience

Reading between the lines of the apologetic texts show four key purposes for writing these texts. It is easy to identify the purposes of the texts by identifying the audience or addressees of the texts. Apologies largely address out-group members since the texts complain and defend a cause of action. Nonetheless, a great majority of scholars agree that apologetic texts are not only limited to out-group members but have attention for in-group members also.[15] Young suggests that "their objective (apologetic texts) was not simply defending themselves against charges. Their common intent is the justification of an anomalous social position in the eyes of others or themselves."[16]

In this section, the purposes of the apologetic texts become clear when the audience is identified, as was done in chapter three. First, the Christian apologetic texts are written to the authorities of the Roman Empire which includes the emperors or the provincial authorities. The authors sought by writing to the authorities to stop the action of the persecution and martyrdom. Therefore, the apologists explain the Christian identity and complain about the processes they face by appealing to natural justice.[17]

Second, the authors of the apologetic texts explicitly addressed their texts to the general public. The apologists targeted the general public because they usually acted as the plaintiffs who bring the accusation against the Christians in the trials. They are not just addressed to stop the persecution and martyrdom but, even more importantly, to convert them to Christianity.[18] Molly Whittaker's commentary on *Ad Graecos* suggests that "essentially hortatory rather than didactic. His (Tatian's) main concern is to urge pagan readers to leave the error of their ways in order that they may turn to the truth."[19]

Third, the Christian apologists sought to construct the Christian identity by generally addressing the authorities and the general public.[20] Kahlos affirms that apologetics and polemics are often used to reinforce a group's

---

15. Jacobsen, "Main Topics in Early Christian," 106; Ulrich, "Apologists and Apologetics," 2–6.

16. Young, "Greek Apologists," 104.

17. Alexander, "Acts of the Apostles," 106; Frosini, "Theory on Natural Justice," 102; Lloyd, "Natural Justice," 218; de Smith, *Judicial Review*, 136.

18. Justin, *First Apology*, 68.

19. Tatian, *Oratio Ad Graecos*, xv.

20. Young, "Greek Apologists," 102.

identity.[21] By writing these texts, the apologists complain that the perpetrators of these hostilities did not understand Christian beliefs and practices and therefore they intend to correct such misconceptions of Christianity. The question of identity is a demarcation of "otherliness," so the apologist defines how Christians are unique from the other religious, social, and even political organizations.

Fourth, though not explicit, the apologetic texts were intended to be read by the Christians too.[22] The apologists wrote to encourage the Christians to stand firm in arguments against the non-Christians.[23] They sought to equip and educate other Christians to be able to argue out their faith with the non-Christians. This was important because the Roman Empire, owing to the influence of Hellenization, loved philosophy and debate. Therefore, the Christians needed to be able to argue what they believe and why they do the things they do. This is why an explanation is an important component of apologetic texts.

All in all, Christian apologists wrote to the authorities of the empire to halt the Christian opposition, win the public to Christianity alongside the construction of the identity of the Christians, and equip the Christians in the debate regarding the Christian faith.

Background of the Apologetic Texts

It is very important at this point to explore the texts that are to be used for the internal comparison of the apologetic texts. This is crucial because this chapter seeks to compare the texts written to the authorities with those written to the general public. It is essential to understand the features of the individual texts and their authors. In all, six different texts and three authors are discussed in this chapter. Four of the texts are addressed to the authorities and two addressed to the general public. It is interesting that in terms of authorship, one person (Justin Martyr) wrote two apologies to the authorities (*First Apology* and *Second Apology*) while his student (Tatian) wrote to the public (*Oratio Ad Graecos*). Another author (Tertullian) wrote two apologies

---

21. Kahlos, *Debate and Dialogue*, 56–57.
22. Engberg, "Truth Begs No Favours," 178.
23. Price, "Latin Christian Apologetics," 105–6.

(*Apologeticum* and *Ad Scapulam*) to the authorities and one (*Ad Nationes*) to the public. The texts are compared to identify if the authors changed their styles based on implicit addressees.

Justin Martyr

Ulrich from a modern perspective describes Justin as the "most important second-century apologist."[24] Justin gives a lot of information about his background and conversion in one of his texts, *Dialogue avec Trypho*.

Justin's date of birth is not certain but most scholars agree that it must have been in the early second century and that he was of pagan parents in Flavia Neapolis in Syria Palestine, modern-day Nablus.[25] Lesley Bernard suggests that Justin's ancestors must have settled in Flavia Neapolis as colonists after its establishment.[26] Justin refers to himself as a Samaritan[27] but Ulrich and Bernard suggest that his labeling refers to his hometown rather than to his religion because his life does not suggest he was ever a religious Samaritan.[28] His grandfather's name, Bacchius, is Greek while his father's name, Priscus, is Latin.[29]

He had a gentile upbringing while his education was Greek at various philosophical schools.[30] He started as a Stoic, but opining that he was not learning anything new about God he left for the Peripatetic school; but when he was asked to pay tuition, he felt good philosophers should not take money before teaching, so he then approached a famous Pythagorean and asked to be trained at the Pythagoras school. However, to be trained in the school of Pythagoras the student needed to know music, astronomy, and geometry. Unfortunately, Justin did not have these qualifications so he was dismissed. In his troubled moments, the thought of the Platonists came to mind, and he was submitted to the Platonist school where he received training and was able to thrive. Justin can, therefore, be said to have trained in four philosophical schools, from Stoic to Peripatetic through Pythagorean to Platonism. It was

---

24. Ulrich, "Justin Martyr," 15: 51; Bediako, *Theology and Identity*, 136.
25. Justin, *First Apology*, 1:1.
26. Bernard, *Justin Martyr*, 5.
27. Bobichon, *Justin Martyr*; Falls, *First Apology*, 29:1; 120:6.
28. Ulrich, "Justin Martyr," 51; Bernard, *Justin Martyr*, 5.
29. Bernard, 5.
30. Justin, *Dialogue avec Trypho*, 2; Ulrich, "Justin Martyr," 51, Bernard, *Justin Martyr*, 6.

while he was training as a Platonist that he met an old man who spoke to him about Christianity.[31]

Justin received a Christian education and saw himself as a Christian philosopher.[32] He, therefore, established a school to train Christians. Bernard suggests that his school was probably a mobile school where he taught different kinds of people at various places. It is believed that some of his students came to him in Rome.[33] Some of his students were Evelpistus (one of his companions who died with him), Tatian (the Assyrian), Irenaeus (from Smyrna), and many others.[34] He also gave himself up for the writing of texts, especially apologies. Three of his texts have survived; *First* and *Second Apologies* as well as the *Dialogue avec Trypho*.[35] Young summarizes the central theme of Justin's apologetic thoughts as: "Justin tries to challenge the justices of condemning Christians just for being Christians by confronting misconceptions and rumours on one hand while setting out their doctrines and ethics as philosophical and true on the other."[36] He was vehement in defending the Christian faith from the Romans, Jews, and dissents. Justin died as a martyr at the time of Emperor Marcus Aurelius and Bernard suggests that he may have been young when he died.[37] His martyr account has been analyzed in the previous chapter. Justin himself, together with his student Tatian, suggested that he might have been reported as a Christian by his Stoic competitor Crescens.[38]

For this work, Justin's two main apologies are discussed and compared with Tertullian's *Apologeticum* and *Ad Scapulam*. These four texts are all addressed to authorities. Subsequently, the four texts are compared to selected apologetic texts addressed to the general public. The features and characteristics of the two apologies are therefore discussed below.

---

31. Justin, 3; Bernard, 6–7.
32. Bediako, *Theology and Identity*, 139–46.
33. Bernard, *Justin Martyr*, 12.
34. Bernard, 13.
35. Ulrich, "Justin Martyr," 53; Bernard, 5.
36. Young, "Greek Apologists," 83.
37. Ulrich, "Justin Martyr," 52.
38. Justin, *Second Apology* 3:1; Tatian, *Oratio Ad Graecos* 19:1.

First and Second Apologies

Most scholars seem to agree that Justin's two apologies are related and that they are supposed to be one text. The *First Apology* is addressed to the Emperor Antoininus Pius and his son Marcus Aurelius and his later co-emperor Lucius Verus.[39] However, Oskar Skarsaune suggests that it had the emperor, senate, and the Roman people in mind to appeal to them to stop the persecution and martyrdom of the early Christians in the Roman Empire.[40] Ulrich divides the *First Apology* which has sixty-eight chapters and a rescript from the Emperor Hadrine to Manucius Fundanus into five main parts.[41]

1. Chapters 1–12   Defense against the charge of atheism
2. Chapters 13–29   The teachings of Jesus
3. Chapters 30–60   Jesus as the son of God
4. Chapters 61–67   Christian sacraments (Eucharist, baptism) and Sunday meetings
5. Chapter 68–end   Legal and political basis of his apology

For the *Second Apology*, Ulrich divides the fifteen chapters into four main subsections.[42] These are:

1. Chapters 1–4   Hostilities of demons to God
2. Chapters 5–7:8   Apocalyptic themes with emphasis on the eternal fire
3. Chapter 7:9–end   Justin's logos doctrine
4. Chapter 8   Failure of philosophy

On the other hand, Bernard offers another in-depth categorization of the texts.[43]

1. Chapters 1–2   Appeal for justice
2. Chapters 3–5   Defend Christianity against some scandals
3. Chapters 6–12   The charge of atheism
4. Chapter 13   Christianity as monotheism

---

39. Bernard, *St. Justin Martyr*, 6.
40. Skarsaune, "Justin and The Apologists," 123.
41. Ulrich, "Justin Martyr," 53–54.
42. Ulrich, "Justin Martyr," 54.
43. Bernard, *St. Justin Martyr*, 6– 8; 15–17.

5.	Chapters 14–20	Christianity as a moral religion
6.	Chapters 21–22	Pagan stories which model and corrupt Christian stories
7.	Chapter 23	Christ as the Messiah
8.	Chapters 24–29	Against magicians
9.	Chapters 30–53	Christianity is the fulfillment of prophecy
10.	Chapters 54–58	Roman myths are imitations of Christ
11.	Chapters 59–60	Plato depended on Moses
12.	Chapters 61–67	Christian baptism and Eucharist

Bernard's thoughts on the *Second Apology* only provide topics for the chapters without categorizations.

In sum, Young suggests that Justin sees his works in three ways: first, as a *prosphonesis* (philosopher-king) that addresses emperors who are philosophically inclined; second, as *enteuxis* (a plea or petition) – the *Second Apology*, in particular, was inspired by the recent killings of Christians; third, as *exegesis* (explanatory), projecting Christianity as the true religion.[44]

Tatian the Assyrian

Falkenberg presents the confusion surrounding a man described as a heretic by the Western church but as a theologian by the Eastern church.[45] Tatian may have been born around AD 120 in Assyria,[46] east of the Euphrates, to wealthy pagan parents[47] and possibly died between AD 180 and 190.[48] He travelled extensively and his parents gave him the best of conventional, Hellenistic education particularly in rhetoric and, at one point of time, he was initiated into a mystery cult.[49] Tatian visited Rome and became a student of Justin who he respected very much.[50] He may have been converted based on his desire for intellectual activities such as the reading of Scriptures but it is also possible that Justin played a role in his conversion. Tatian referred to himself

---

44. Young, "Greek Apologists of the Second Century," 83–84.
45. Falkenberg, "Tatian," 67.
46. Tatian, *Oratio Ad Graecos*, 42:1; Hunt, *Christianity in the Second Century*, 1.
47. Tatian, *Oratio Ad Graecos*, 11:1; Whittaker, *Oratio Ad Graecos*, ix.
48. Falkenberg, "Tatian," 67.
49. Tatian, *Oratio Ad Graecos*; 35:1–2; Falkenberg, "Tatian," 67.
50. Tatian, 18:2, 29:1; Whittaker, *Oratio Ad Graecos*, ix.

as the "herald of the truth."[51] Justin's influence on Tatian was great and there are some similarities in their life history since they were both converted by scriptural reading, belonged to pagan families, and both attacked the Roman culture.[52] Tatian also became a teacher after Justin, and Clement of Alexandria and Rhodo, who opposed Marcion, were his students.[53] To him, Christianity is an educational discipline (παιδεία – paideia), superior philosophy, and an all-embracing religion irrespective of age or sex.[54]

Later in his life, Tatian broke away from the church because of his teachings and moved to the east of Mesopotamia to form his school and sect, although Eusebius suggests that he was excommunicated in AD 172.[55] Irenaeus suggests that his breakaway was a result of pride and the sect he formed denied Adam's salvation, banned marriage, and promoted vegetarianism.[56] Tertullian similarly affirms the sect's ascetic practices and their celebration of the Eucharist with water instead of wine.[57] However, Whittaker suggests that by the fourth century, Tatian's influence on the sect had diminished.[58] Jerome and Irenaeus suggest that his sect was called Encretites.[59] He is therefore sometimes described as a heretic and/or gnostic by many scholars although Falkenberg suggests that he may not have been a major heretic after all.[60] Emily Hunt, Hawthorne, Foster, and others strongly argue against Irenaeus and Grant on their assertion that Tatian became a heretic.[61]

---

51. Falkenberg, "Tatian," 68; Whittaker, *Oratio Ad Graecos*, ix, xv; Tatian, *Oratio Ad Graecos*, 18, 20.

52. Hawthorne, "Tatian and His Discourse," 187; Foster, "Tatian,"106.

53. Whittaker, *Oratio Ad Graecos*, ix; Hunt, *Christianity in the Second Century*, 2.

54. Whittaker, xv.

55. Falkenberg, "Tatian," 67.

56. Falkenberg, 76; Whittaker, *Oratio Ad Graecos*, x.

57. Whittaker, x.

58. Whittaker, x.

59. Whittaker, x.

60. Falkenberg, "Tatian," 79; Whittaker, xvi.

61. Hawthorne, "Tatian and His Discourse," 165–67; Hunt, *Christianity in the Second Century*, 1–2; Foster, "Tatian," 116–17.

Tatian's Oratio Ad Graecos

Tatian wrote quite extensively because apart from his *Oratio Ad Graecos*, he matches the Gospels in his *Diatessaron*, while his *On Animals* is lost.[62] He even had it in mind to write a text entitled *Those Who Have Propounded Ideas about God*. Falkenberg suggests that he wrote it but that it is lost.[63] There may be other extracts by him such as *On Problems, On Perfection according to the Savior,* and *On Six Days of Creation*.[64] Hawthorne argues that Tatian's writings are influenced by philosophies especially Stoicism and Platonism.[65]

Foster suggests that Tatian's text represents an important Christian apologetic trend in the second century in defense of the faith.[66] It is generally agreed that he wrote *Oratio Ad Graecos* in Greek probably between the 150s and 170.[67] Whittaker describes his apology as hortatory rather than didactic to stress the strong evangelistic appeals although it is also full of polemics.[68] Some of the major themes this apology touches on are monotheism, logos theology, Roman ideologies such as mythologies, astrology, magic, sorcery, etc. Many of the issues Tatian raises show his close connections with Justin; especially in the way he uses Jewish ideas to argue that Christianity is older than Homer, besides his use of prophecy and chronological argument.[69] The text has extensive biblical references. A cursory count from the list provided by Whittaker shows that Tatian uses about seven Old Testament verses and thirty-four New Testament verses.[70] It is argued that Tatian gives great consideration to his audience and so does not use christological titles such as Christ, Son of Man, Savior, and logos theology.[71] This text, though an apology,

---

62. Hunt, *Christianity in the Second Century*, 2; Whittaker, *Oratio Ad Graecos*, x; Falkenberg, "Tatian," 68.
63. Whittaker, *Oratio Ad Graecos*, x; Falkenberg, "Tatian," 68.
64. Falkenberg, 68.
65. Hawthorne, "Tatian and His Discourse," 178–80.
66. Foster, "Tatian," 117.
67. Falkenberg, "Tatian," 67; Foster, 108; Hunt, *Christianity in the Second Century*, 3.
68. Whittaker, *Oratio Ad Graecos*, xv.
69. Falkenberg, "Tatian," 69.
70. Whittaker, *Oratio Ad Graecos*, xvii.
71. Falkenberg, "Tatian," 71–73; Although Whittaker does not link the absence of these elements to Tatian's audience (Whittaker, *Oratio Ad Graecos*, xvi.).

is criticized for omitting words and concepts like Christ, Christianity, Jesus, Lord, church, Savior and its lack of an appeal to the readers.[72]

Whittaker classifies Tatian's forty-two chapter apology into sixteen sections.[73]

1.	Chapter 1	Introduction and attacks the Greek culture
2.	Chapter 2–3	Attack Roman philosophy
3.	Chapters 4–7	Discuss the Christian doctrine of creation
4.	Chapters 8–11	Attack astrology and mythology
5.	Chapters 12–15	The two kinds of spirits
6.	Chapters 16–18	Against sorcery and medicine
7.	Chapter 19	Addresses philosophers especially Crescens
8.	Chapter 20	Apocalypse
9.	Chapter 21	Mythologies
10.	Chapters 22–28	Attack pagan practices
11.	Chapters 29–30	Tatian's conversion
12.	Chapter 31	Chronological arguments
13.	Chapters 32–34	Christian attitudes toward sex and age
14.	Chapter 35	Tatian's education and travels
15.	Chapter 36–41	The chronological argument again
16.	Chapter 42	Conclusion

Hunt describes this text as "an apologetic work, written to justify the position of Christianity in the Graeco-Roman world, and belongs to the stream of Hellenized Christianity that emerged after Christianity diverged from Judaism."[74]

Tertullian

Quintus Septimius Florens Tertullianus,[75] often called Tertullian from Carthage, North Africa, can be described as the most significant Christian scholar in North Africa from about the first to the third century. He was noted for his thoughts and strong opinions. It is argued that the persecution

---

72. Hawthorne, "Tatian and His Discourse," 161.
73. Whittaker, *Oratio Ad Graecos*, xviii–xx.
74. Hunt, *Christianity in the Second Century*, 19.
75. Roberts and Donaldson, *Ante-Nicene Fathers*, 3:3; Willert, "Tertullian," 164.

and martyrdom of the Christians were visited on the African province of the Roman Empire as far back as the reign of Commodus around AD 180 during the time of Vigellius Saturninus as proconsul who killed the first Christians when he was a governor.[76] Soon after that incident, Saturninus again eliminated some other Christians known as the Scillitan Martyrs who are said to have been murdered on 17 July 180.

Wilbert believes Tertullian was born in AD 160.[77] Barnes, however, believes he was born between AD 155 and 170.[78] Coxe pushes for a much earlier date of AD 145.[79] Tertullian was a Stoic philosopher and this made him susceptible to Christianity. He probably became a Christian around AD 193 as a result of observing the courage of the martyrs and because of his understanding of Christianity as a moral religion.[80] As a Christian, he is believed to have been a catechumen teacher who prepared baptismal candidates.[81] Coxe suggests that he was a presbyter.[82] Glover suggests that he was not liked by the church because they saw him more like a Puritan.[83] However, Tertullian may have studied literature, language, rhetoric, and law.[84] Many scholars including Willert and Coxe suggest that he lived in Rome and practiced as a lawyer[85] although Barnes disagrees strongly with both positions based on his assertion that Tertullian may never have lived in Rome.[86] Tertullian was married but subsequently bereaved and hence he lived with his son Caracalla and died a martyr at an old age around AD 230 or 240.[87]

Most of the information about Tertullian is retrieved not only from his writings but also from the writings of three church fathers – Jerome, Eusebius,

---

76. Barnes, *Tertullian*, 60.
77. Willert, "Tertullian," 164.
78. Barnes, *Tertullian*, 1; 59.
79. Roberts and Donaldson, *Ante-Nicene Fathers*, 3:5.
80. Willert, "Tertullian," 163; Barnes, *Tertullian* 2; However, Coxe suggests that he became a Christian in AD 185 but does not explain what attracted him to this faith. Roberts and Donaldson, *Ante-Nicene Fathers*, 3:3-4.
81. Willert, "Tertullian," 164.
82. Roberts and Donaldson, *Ante-Nicene Fathers*, 3:5.
83. Tertullian, *Apology*, ix.
84. Tertullian, xvi; Willert, "Tertullian," 164.
85. Willert, "Tertullian," 164; Roberts and Donaldson, *Ante-Nicene Fathers*, 3:3-5.
86. Barnes, *Tertullian:*, 58.
87. Barnes, 2, 59–60.

and Augustine.[88] Jerome holds that Tertullian was a son of a centurion and that he was ordained. Augustine tells his readers that although Tertullian became a Montanist probably in the third century,[89] he later left Montanism to form his sect which was called Tertullianistae. Eusebius suggests he was a famous lawyer.

However, Barnes disagrees with the descriptions by the three church fathers.[90] He disagrees with the claim that Tertullian was a priest since Tertullian never suggests this in his arguments but describes himself twice as belonging to the laity. Barnes believes that he was often referred to as a priest because some of his writings are sermonic. However, he suggests that Jerome may have referred to Tertullian as a priest because he admired Tertullian and like himself (Jerome), Tertullian was not well treated by the Roman clergy. Coxe agrees with the idea that Tertullian agreed with Montanus's opinions because of "the envy and contumelious treatment of the Roman clergy."[91] Barnes is even not sure that Tertullian's father was a soldier in the first place since his father's title as "centurion proconsularis" may not have been in existence because no centurion had the title "proconsularis." Again, Tertullian is often associated with a Tertullian who wrote some important legal textbooks but Barnes disagrees because the Christian Tertullian seemed much younger than this lawyer and again there are some occasions where the Christian Tertullian displays legal accuracies and some unpardonable inaccuracies and, thus, he could not have been a lawyer.

Tertullian is believed to have written extensively. Willert suggests that he has about thirty-one manuscripts to his credit although Barnes has a record of thirty-two.[92] Glover describes him as sometimes even too clever to a fault.[93] Barnes again suggests that it took him about sixteen years to write all his texts, thus the period spanning AD 196–212.[94] Many of Tertullian's works are polemics against heresies, Gnosticism, and Marcionism. Yet many of his writings are influenced by Montanist ideas.

---

88. Barnes, 57–58.
89. Roberts and Donaldson, *Ante-Nicene Fathers*, 3:5; Willert, "Tertullian," 159.
90. Barnes, *Tertullian*, 3–29.
91. Roberts and Donaldson, *Ante-Nicene Fathers*, 3:5.
92. Willert, "Tertullian," 159; Barnes, *Tertullian*, 55.
93. Tertullian, xvi.
94. Barnes, *Tertullian*, 58.

Barnes further believes that the dating of Tertullian's works may have been influenced by his attacks on Bishop Callistus[95] since he is a lawyer and priest. Therefore, he suggests methodology as a means of dating these texts based on allusion to historical events, a reference to other texts, doctrines, style, and conclusions.[96] He suggests a strong relationship between the useful texts. He suggests that *Apologeticum* was a remolding of *Ad Nationes* since both were written around the same period: *Ad Nationes* was written in the summer of AD 197, while *Apologeticum* was written in the autumn of the same year. *Ad Scapulam* was written about fifteen years after *Apologeticum* in AD 212.[97]

Notwithstanding the impressive contributions of Tertullian to Christianity in Carthage, Coxe and other scholars are not sure how Christianity entered the African province.[98] Barnes suggests that Christianity came to this region during the apostolic age.[99] He defines two major scriptural instances from the Acts of the Apostles to back his arguments. In the first example, he depends on Acts 2:10 – the Pentecost experience where those in Jerusalem at the time included Libyans who were Africans. His second example is from Acts 8:26–40 where the apostle Philip encountered an Ethiopian eunuch who he baptized.

Lamin Sanneh and other scholars such as Bediako agree with these two instances but go even further to touch on other inferences from Scriptures, historical sources, and other sources of oral tradition to show that Christianity had been in Africa probably soon after the crucifixion of Christ.[100] Sanneh, for instance, argues that after the birth of Christ he was taken to Egypt (an African land), and in Mark 15:21 Simon of Cyrene, the one who helped Jesus carry his cross was from Africa (Cyrene was a Roman province of Libya); this same Simon was the father of Rufus and Alexander who were major contributors to Christianity in Africa. Furthermore, Sanneh refers to Eusebius who suggests that both Mark (the writer of the first Gospel account) and apostle Thomas visited African lands. Therefore, Sanneh and other scholars attribute Christianity in Africa to immediately after the time of the ministry of Jesus.

---

95. Barnes, 30.
96. Barnes, 30–56.
97. Tertullian, *Apology*, xxii; Barnes, *Tertullian*, 48.
98. Roberts and Donaldson, *Ante-Nicene Fathers*, 3:3.
99. Barnes, *Tertullian*, 63–64.
100. Sanneh, *West African Christianity*, 1–13; Bediako, *Jesus in Africa*, 20–45.

Although some scholars suggest that Christianity in Carthage was predominantly Jewish, Barnes strongly disagrees with this position because Carthage was a busy, cosmopolitan town where Christianity spread very fast and was spearheaded by the rich and educated. He refers to the example of the martyr Perpetua who was of the senatorial rank and concluded that by AD 212, Christians were in the majority.[101] Coxe suggests that by the beginning of the third century, there was a council of about seventy bishops which was presided over by the bishop of Carthage, Bishop Agripupinus.[102] If this is true, then it is without a doubt that Christianity had visibility in the African province by the third century. Carthage, being a Roman province invariably attracted hostilities for the Christians there, which Ste. Croix describes as the "baptism of blood".[103]

Tertullian's Apologeticum

Tertullian in this text addresses the Roman governor but had in mind other readers, especially the emperor.[104] *Apologeticum*, with two distinct manuscript traditions, is seen as a phenomenon rare in Latin paleography.[105] Barnes picks up the traditions that Tertullian's *Apologeticum* has two recensions, where the first version labeled the *Fuldensis* is the draft of rewriting the *Ad Nationes* with which Willert agrees,[106] while the second the *Vulgate* version is the final and polished text.[107] Barnes and Willert agree on AD 197 as the date of its authorship.[108]

In this text, Tertullian deals with some political themes of the time because of political instabilities at the time of writing.[109] Tertullian argues strongly and extensively against the worship of the emperor and the idea of child infanticide among Christians in this text.[110] Willert suggests that the struc-

---

101. Barnes, *Tertullian*, 63–69.
102. Roberts and Donaldson, *Ante-Nicene Fathers*, 3:3.
103. Roberts and Donaldson, 3:3.
104. Tertullian, *Apologeticum*, 1:1, 9:6, 30:7, 44:2, 45:7, 50:12; Willert, "Tertullian," 162.
105. Tertullian, *Apology*, xxi.
106. Willert, "Tertullian," 160.
107. Barnes, *Tertullian*, 14.
108. Willert, "Tertullian," 159; Barnes, *Tertullian*, 55.
109. Willert, 161–63.
110. Tertullian, *Apologeticum* 28–35; Barnes, *Tertullian*, 13; Willert, 163.

ture of the text consists of *exordium* (introduction), *narration* (description of case), *propositio* (topic list), *argumentatio* (argumentation), *confirmatio* (evidence), *confutatio* (counterevidence), and a *peroratio* (close).[111] The text is structured into three main sections, where the body of the text addresses three main charges:

1. Chapters 1–3   Introduction
2. Chapters 4–45   Main issues
   a. Chapters 7–9   Ethical charges
   b. Chapters 10–16   Religious charges
   c. Chapters 28–35   Political charges
   d. Chapters 36–45   Christians as model citizens
3. Chapters 46–50   Conclusion

Tertullian's Ad Scapulam

Barnes and Arbesmann suggest that *Ad Scapulam* may have been written soon after 14 August 212 due to the reference made to the eclipse of the sun.[112] Although Arbesmann earlier on suggested that the reason or basis for the writing of this text was motivated by an activity of a Roman jurist Domitus Ulpianus who collected rescripts of the emperors against the Christians; this activity took place in 215 AD, three years after the writing of the text.[113] It is without a doubt that this apology is addressed to the proconsul of the African province Scapula. Tertullian in this apology grounds the Christian liberty to worship who or what they want on the natural right of a person to choose their religion. Furthermore, to him, the charge of Christian disloyalty cannot be accurate because the Christians were very supportive of the social, economic, and political well-being of the Roman Empire.

A major aspect of this apology is the identity marker used; out of the five-chapter apology, three chapters begin with "We"[114] while one chapter begins with "Your"[115] to show that this text tries to draw lines between what the

---

111. Willert, 168–70.
112. Barnes, *Tertullian*, 38; Arbesmann, "Tertullian to Scapula," 148.
113. Arbesmann, 147.
114. Tertullian, *Ad Scapulam*, 1, 2, 4.
115. Tertullian, 5.

Christians believe as against the beliefs of the Roman society. Furthermore, another unique argument in this apology is built on the logic that anything that is not profitable is eschewed. This suggests that since the authorities were not benefiting or attaining the desired aim of the hostilities, they should stop it. To this end, Tertullian lists authorities who have suffered some consequences for the hostilities against the Christians. These included Vigellius Saturninus (who became blind), Claudius Lucius Herminianus (who became sick), and Caecilius Capella (who faced doom).[116]

On the other hand, Tertullian describes good authorities such as Cincius Serverus, Vespronius Candidus, Julius Asper, and Hadrian[117] who did not engage in the hostilities against the Christians. He refers to the hemorrhage suffered by Scapula to admonish him to be wise and stop the persecution of the Christians (lest the divine retribution is fulfilled on him).[118] Tertullian by this appeal to the conscience of Scapula suggests that it is not beneficial to persecute the Christians.

The chapters can be categorized into:

1. Chapter 1   Introduction and Christian obstinacy
2. Chapter 2   The doctrine of God, and the politico-religious charges
3. Chapter 3   Signs of the apocalypse and some governors' predicaments
4. Chapter 4   Roman political system and good emperors
5. Chapter 5   Growth of Christianity in the empire

Tertullian's Ad Nationes

It has already been suggested that there is a strong relationship between *Apologeticum* and *Ad Nationes*.[119] Barnes suggests that owing to the reference made to the battle of Laudanum, this text must have been written soon after the aforementioned battle, hence the position that it was written in AD 197.[120] Tertullian, in this apology, argues that Christians are facing many injustices.

---

116. Tertullian, 3.
117. Tertullian, 4.
118. Tertullian, 3.
119. Barnes, *Tertullian*, 49.
120. Barnes, 55.

He employs sarcasm, rhetoric, polemics, and other strategies to argue against political, social, ethical, and religious charges against the Christians. He argues that the main charge is with the Christian name. Tertullian, therefore, uses Tacitus's confusion in calling the Christians, "chrestoi" which means virtue (in Greek) to say the Christians are virtuous in their dealings.

This apology is also divided into two books where book two mainly addresses a non-Christian theory about the Roman gods. Varro had theorized that the gods are made of three elements. The first part is the *physical* which appeals to philosophers, the second part *mythic* which appeals to poets, and the final part *gentile* which is concerned with the nations. The apology is divided into sections as follows:

1. Chapter 1 — Introduction (Varro's theory of the gods)
2. Chapters 2–5 — The physical composition of the gods and philosophy
3. Chapters 6–7 — The mystic and the poets
4. Chapter 8 — The Gentiles and the nations
5. Chapter 9 — Criticism against Varro's theory
6. Chapter 10–16 — Criticism against Roman religious practices and the gods
7. Chapter 17 — Christian God as superior to the gods of the Romans.

Book one deals with various issues concerning the persecution and martyrdom of the Christians. It is divided as follows:

1. Chapters 1–3 — Introduction (Injustices against the Christians)
2. Chapter 4 — The virtue of Christianity and the goal of philosophy (Socrates)
3. Chapter 5 — Some questionable Christian behaviors
4. Chapter 6 — Injustice against the Christians
5. Chapters 7–9 — Some negative thoughts against the Christians
6. Chapter 10 — Roman gods as contemptible
7. Chapters 11–13 — Roman perception of the Christian worship

8.	Chapter 14	Christians accept all persons but Romans discriminate
9.	Chapters 15–16	Ethical accusations against the Christians
10.	Chapters 17–19	Christian obstinacy
11.	Chapter 20	Conclusion (only the Christian God is true).

Internal Comparison of the Apologetic Texts

The writing of the apologetic texts was influenced by the hostilities against the Christians in the Roman Empire. However, they are not used to the same degree as the martyr texts when scholars discuss the persecution and martyrdom of the early Christians in the Roman Empire. This chapter seeks to bring out the picture of the hostilities against the Christians as portrayed by the apologetic texts by dividing the texts according to their explicit recipients and comparing them with each other. This internal comparison of the apologetic texts is crucial to addressing the objectives of the study.

The comparison is structured into fourteen comparative elements in this internal comparison. These comparative elements are largely similar to those used in comparing the martyr texts in chapter three. The elements are almost in the same order, which will be an advantage for the external comparison of the two kinds of texts in chapter five. These elements are subcategorized into three main comparative forms. The first category looks at the "account" in the texts. This category tries to find out if the texts have some narrative elements as well as analyze the players in the texts by looking at the characters as persecutors and martyrs including the form of suffering of the Christians. The second category of the comparative elements looks at the "accusations" that give room for the persecution and martyrdom of the Christians. This category looks at the legal procedure of the hostilities according to the texts, the charges, and allegations against the Christians, the motives of the persecutors as well as the authorities' demands from the Christians. The final comparison dives into the argumentative form of the apologetic text to advance the position of the texts. In light of these elements, the polemic aspects of the texts and the argumentative strategies are analyzed.

Apologetic Texts to Authorities (Apologies)

The apologetic texts come in two forms depending on the addressees. Some were addressed to the authorities of the Roman Empire to try to influence the authorities to stop the hostilities against the Christians and possibly to even win them over to Christianity.

Account

This subheading here discusses the possible narrative aspect of the apologetic texts, the players in the account, and who plays what roles in the persecution and martyrdom of the early Christians. These characters include potentially both martyrs and persecutors. Again, the forms of the sufferings are also discussed.

Narrative

This comparative element tries to find out if the apologies tell the story of the martyrs. It can, however, be strongly argued that although there are some elements of storytelling, the apologetic texts do not function as a narrative. The presence of a narrative in these texts is quite minimal and not enough to be classified as containing such narratives. Justin's *Second Apology* begins with a story of a Christian woman who according to Justin is treated unfairly because she is a Christian.[121] The other apologetic texts tell little or no stories about the persecution and martyrdom. The apologists are more focused on defending the Christians of the charges leveled against them and explaining the Christian doctrines and beliefs with the motive of converting them to Christianity.

Identity of the Martyrs

It is important to know how the apologies characterize the Christians who face persecution and martyrdom. The identification of the character of the martyrs will help define the motives of the apologist. This implies that if the martyrs are guilty as charged, they will not solicit the pity of the audience because they would deserve the punishment due to them. However, the apologists present the martyrs in a positive light to affect the psychology of the audience to empathize with the martyrs while revealing their innocence and

---

121. Justin, *Second Apology*, 2.

projecting the maltreatment of the persecutors. The apologies to this extent show that the martyrs were virtuous, chaste, courageous, and innocent;[122] they even thanked God when they were sentenced. Both Justin and Tertullian explain that they were well aware that being a Christian may warrant death since Christ also suffered death.[123]

Additionally, the apologies show that these martyrs included both men and women and that the Christians included people of all ages. It implies that Christianity was without any barrier of age or sex. Again, the characterization of the Christians as giving thanks even when condemned makes the martyrs worthy of emulation. Many readers would expect that people sentenced unjustly to death would castigate, insult, or attack the judge, or plead for mercy, especially because they believe they were not allowed a fair trial. Nonetheless, the apologists present the martyrs as calm and thankful when sentenced and executed, which is a stark contrast to expected behavior. In essence, the positive character of the martyr's appeals to the audience of these texts thus portrays the Christians and martyrs as superior to condemned criminals.

Identity of the Persecutors

In terms of who was involved in the perpetuation of hostilities against the early Christians, Justin's *First Apology* identifies rumor mongers and accusers, apart from the authorities,[124] while the *Second Apology* mentions a husband who accuses his wife of being Christian.[125] Furthermore, Tertullian's *Apologeticum* mentions the populace and his *Ad Scapulam* talks about the citizens and populace.[126] In the light of these identifications, it is evident that the persecutors in the persecution and martyrdom of the Christians can be categorized into two, the public and authorities. While the public acted as accusers in reporting and presenting allegations against the Christians, the authorities turned the allegations into charges against the Christians to convict them legally.

---

122. Justin, *First Apology*, 12, 15; Tertullian, *Apologeticum*, 46; *Ad Scapulam*, 5.1.

123. Justin, *Second Apology*, 11, 12; Tertullian, *Apologeticum*, 1.13, 27.3, 50.1; *Ad Scapulam*, 1.

124. Justin, *First Apology*, 3, 4.

125. Justin, *Second Apology*, 2.

126. Tertullian, *Apologeticum*, 50.12; *Ad Scapulam*, 3.

The character of these persecutors makes it clear that the persecution and martyrdom of the Christians were widespread and included the entire machinery of the Roman Empire. Since the persecution is cast in some form of a legal system, it can be suggested that the category of the authorities included some institutions of the empire in the care of the Roman authorities. Given the characters involved, the persecutions are thus presented as widespread and comprehensive.

Form of Suffering

Justin does not provide a list of the forms of the persecutions against the Christians. However, Tertullian provides a list in his *Apologeticum* – hanging on the cross, stakes, hooks, torture, crushed, rack, lions, pander, sword, axed, and burnt alive – as some of the forms applied against the Christians.[127] He again in *Ad Scapulam* lists torture, beasts, burning, and decapitation as punishments meted out to the Christians.[128]

All the comparative elements of the account of the persecution show that the narrative content of the apologetic texts is almost absent. The Christians are projected in a positive light and the persecutors included both the authorities and the general public. Furthermore, the Christians suffered a great number of humiliating and inhumane treatments ranging from physical torture to execution.

Accusation

This comparative element discusses the apologists' picture of the legal procedure in the hostilities against the Christians. What were the accusations according to the apologists and what demands from the authorities did the martyrs face? The political administration of the Roman Empire and the legal regime applied against the Christians according to the apologetic texts will be analyzed in this section.

Legal Procedure

The type of legal process the martyrs faced cannot be deciphered clearly based on the selected texts. However, based on the little account given by Justin in his *Second Apology*, it is logical to conclude that the format was, as suggested

---

127. Tertullian, *Apologeticum*, 4.3–4, 12, 30.7, 40.2, 50.12.
128. Tertullian, *Ad Scapulam*, 3, 5.

by Sherwin-White, *cognitio extra ordinem*.[129] In this account, Justin suggests that in the first place a charge is brought against a woman by her husband but since he could not sustain it, the husband directed the accusation against his wife's Christian teacher, Ptolemaeus. The account, therefore, suggests that he was questioned by the governor Urbicus, who executed him. On the other hand, Tertullian's *Ad Scapulam* talks about "advocates and assessors."[130] Furthermore, since the other texts equally build on the problem of injustice, it can be suggested that the procedure was purely in agreement with Sherwin-White's suggestion of *cognitio extra ordinem*. In this procedure, the authority, thus the emperor, governor, or prefect, acts as the interrogator and judge. This discloses that the authorities played a significant role in the legal process used against the Christians in these hostilities.

Charges and Allegations

The public, especially those who accused the Christians before the authorities, held negative prejudices against the Christians. These prejudices gave them the energy to act as accusers against Christians. Justin's *First Apology* identifies wickedness, covetousness, conspiracy, infanticide, and incest at their meetings, as some of the allegations against them.[131] Along with ethical charges, Christians faced the charge of atheism and formally the charge of the name Christian, that is, they were simply denounced to the authorities as Christians.[132] In his *Second Apology*, Justin argues that the Christians were seen by outsiders as godless and impious,[133] therefore the charges of the name Christian and atheism were very prominent against the Christians.[134] Furthermore, Tertullian in *Apologeticum*[135] identifies allegations against Christians as being worshipers of the cross and an ass, mad, criminals, committing infanticides, incestuous, murderers, adulterous, dishonest, and treacherous people. Tertullian on his part talks about charges such as the

---

129. Sherwin-White, "Early Persecutions and Roman," 203–4; Justin, *Second Apology*, 2.
130. Tertullian, *Ad Scapulam*, 4.
131. Justin, *First Apology*, 12.
132. Justin, 6, 7, 20.
133. Justin, *Second Apology*, 3.
134. Justin, 2.
135. Tertullian, *Apologeticum*, 1.13, 2:1–6, 16.

name, atheism, treason, failures in businesses, obstinacy, and many others.[136] Additionally, in *Ad Scapulam,* the Christians were portrayed by the non-Christians as sacrilegious, thieves, and practicing magic.[137] He, therefore, touches on charges of political disloyalty, atheism, the name Christian, and other ethical issues.[138]

These allegations when classified can be seen as religious, political, social, and ethical crimes against the Roman consciousness. The most important charges against the Christians as identified by these apologies were charges of the name Christian and atheism. Additionally, political charges and ethical charges are leveled against Christians. These religious, political, and ethical charges against the Christians to a large extent were derived from the allegations by the public. It is also significant to stress that these charges were not mutually exclusive but significantly and jointly interdependent. Tertullian shows a relationship between the various charges when he says, "But the Christian, a man guilty of every crime, the enemy of gods, emperors, laws, morals of all Nature together."[139]

Motives

The apologetic texts do not state categorically what motivated the Romans against the Christians. However, based on the charges and the involvement of the authorities, it can be suggested that they were motivated by the need to keep the peace of the Roman society and the *pax deorum*. The charges and allegations were often religious and in order not to offend the gods of the Romans and to preserve the society, the Christians had to be persecuted. The persecutors were, therefore, seeking to maintain the peace with the gods known to the Romans as *pax deorum*. This idea of working to bring peace between the gods and the people was every Roman's responsibility. It implied that the Christians by not offering sacrifices and refusing to worship the Roman gods had gone against the norms of the society; the relationship between the gods and the people could be destroyed. This could bring natural disasters and many other troubles to society. Therefore, such persons needed to be dealt with to restore the *pax deorum* between the gods and the

---

136. Tertullian, 9, 10, 28.2, 42, 50.2.
137. Tertullian, *Ad Scapulam,* 2, 4.
138. Tertullian, 1, 2.3, 4.
139. Tertullian, *Apologeticum,* 2.16.

people. The idea of maintaining the peace between the gods and the people to a large extent influenced the persecutors to act against the Christians. This is important because it was believed that when there is peace between the gods and the people, there will be economic, social, and political peace and progress. Peace between the gods and the people guaranteed the safety of the Roman social setup.

Demand

According to the apologists, the accused Christians were required by the authorities to sacrifice to the gods of the Roman Empire and to swear by "the genius" of the emperor. All the apologetic texts recount the demand by the authorities that the Christians should sacrifice to the *genius* of the emperor.[140] As mentioned earlier, the martyrs refused to perform the sacrifice because it was against their faith – Justin uses this in his arguments against the ethical accusations.[141] The refusal of the Christians to perform the sacrifice proved that the Christians were a disloyal group who were against the Roman religious, political, and social order. This is why they were blamed for all the natural disasters in the Roman Empire.[142]

In the light of this analysis, it is realized that the legal procedure employed against the Christians according to the apologists was, as Sherwin-White suggested, *cognitio extra ordinem*. The allegations and charges against them covered religious, political, and ethical accusations. The persecutors were motivated by the need to keep the peace between the gods and the people. The martyrs' refusal to sacrifice proved their obstinacy and readiness to die for their faith.

Argumentation

This section compares four main issues concerning how the apologists defended the Christians against the accusations. These comparative elements analyze how Christian apologies adopted various methods to defend and explain the Christian ways of doing things. The comparative elements consider

---

140. Justin, *First Apology*, 55; Tertullian, *Apologeticum*, 28; *Ad Scapulam*, 2.
141. Justin, 5, 11.
142. Croix, "Why Were the Early Christians?" 24–25; Millar, "Imperial Cult," 147.

the presence of polemics, argumentative strategies, sources of the arguments, and the themes that are addressed by the apologies.

Polemics

The main issue is to identify if the apologists launched some form of attacks against their opponents in these texts. It is often very normal that in defenses like these, the authors will try to attack their opponents in the course of the defense. It is often assumed that apologetics may incorporate polemics. Justin in *First Apology* describes the hostilities against the Christians as "stupid," "irrational," and the accusers as "dissolute." He also attacks Jewish methods of scriptural interpretation.[143] Sometimes, Justin even sounds insulting, for example where he says: "you do not investigate the charges made against us, but, give in to unreasonable passion, and the instigation of evil demons."[144]

In *Second Apology*, Justin states that since what is being done to the Christians is "unreasonable," he is "compelled" to write this apology[145] and then attacks his so-called accuser, Crescens.[146] Tertullian is even comprehensive when it comes to the application of polemics in his apologies. In *Apologeticum*, he charges the Roman gods and the Jews while describing his prosecutor as unjust, impious, cruel, foul, and like a dog.[147] He wages strong attacks on the addressee of the text when he says, "it is you then, who are the danger to mankind, it is you who bring upon the public misfortune – you, by your contempt for God and your worship of statues.."[148] He describes the authorities as cunning, rude, cruel, enraged, and haters of the truth.[149] Similarly, in his address to Scapula, he describes the persecutors as evil, enemies of God, fighters against God, "ignorant men" and describes their gods as "demons."[150]

Such attacks on the Jews, gods, authorities, and the public by the apologists show how the Christians retaliated to the charges by hitting back. They therefore attacked their persecutors' religious thoughts and social and political

---

143. Justin, *First Apology*, 9, 11, 49.
144. Justin, 5.
145. Justin, *Second Apology*, 1.
146. Justin, 3.
147. Tertullian, *Apologeticum*, 7, 11.15, 27, 5.4, 50.12.
148. Tertullian, 41.1.
149. Tertullian, 1.1, 27.3, 41.1.
150. Tertullian, *Ad Scapulam*, 2, 3, 4, 5.

ideas. It can further be argued that these attacks are more against the Roman gods and social order and also equally against the public. The attacks on the authorities by the apologies are by comparison more restrained. Justin's major attack on the authorities is found in *First Apology* where he describes them as irrational, specifically in their dealings with Christians – but this was a specific irrationality that contrasted with general rationality.[151]

Tertullian on his part launches various attacks in *Apologeticum* and *Ad Scapulam* by suggesting that the authorities are haters of the truth, that they are "cruel" and "ignorant," that they are marked by "cunning ruse" and "cruel," and that they are fighting against God.[152] On the other hand, the heaviest attacks in the apologies to the authorities are directed at the public, possibly because they initiated the entire process of the hostilities by acting as the accusers.

Strategy

It is important to bring to light how the apologists tried to defend the Christian cause. Interestingly, they did not adopt a particular method but a mixed method in defending the Christian faith. To convince the audience of the text, Justin used the Christian idea of the apocalypse as well as rhetoric by employing sarcasm and questions.[153] Skarsaune affirms Justin's use of philosophy, rationalization, and ridicule in his apology.[154] In general, Justin uses two major argumentative strategies. In the first place, he uses what is termed "argument from prophecy" to show that Christianity is not a new religion but has existed since time immemorial and so suggests that Christianity is even greater than the Roman culture.[155] He does this by showing that Moses was older than Homer and that some great philosophers like Socrates and Plato were kind of proto-Christians even before the advent of Christ.

In the second place, Justin tries to show that Christianity is a philosophy of truth that appeals more to reasoning. Therefore, at the end of *First Apology*, he argues that "And if our account seems to you reasonable and true, respect it; but if it seems foolish to you, despise it as nonsense. And do not decree

---

151. Justin, *First Apology*, 9.
152. Tertullian, *Apologeticum*, 1.1, 27.3, 41.1; *Ad Scapulam*, 1.
153. Justin, *First Apology*, 2, 6, 11, 53; *Second Apology*, 2, 9.
154. Skarsaune, "Justin and The Apologists," 125.
155. Justin, *First Apology*, 15, 20, 22, 23, 30–53, 59–60; *Second Apology*, 4, 13.

death against those who have done no wrong as against enemies."[156] He shows in *Second Apology* that what is being perpetuated against the Christians is "unreasonable" and so he is writing to appeal to the authorities.[157]

Tertullian also uses irony, appeals to conscience, logic, rhetoric, and argument from prophecy including the Christian doctrine of the apocalypse to defend the Christian course. In the *Apologeticum*, he categorically states his argumentative strategy, which can be termed polemic-apology, when he says: "I will not only refute the charges brought against us but will turn them against those who bring them."[158] Therefore, he uses this strategy a lot in this text. Again, in *Ad Scapulam*, he uses a unique strategy that can be described as a rebuttal of the hostilities on the authorities.[159] He recounts the evils and pains that have come to some of the authorities who were hostile to the martyrs and the blessings that came upon some of the authorities for being friendly to the Christians. This strategy was to appeal to the governor Scapula to think through these issues and stop his hostilities against the Christians.

It can therefore be argued that the apologists adopted various strategies in dealing with the charges that were leveled against the Christians. They predominantly used rhetorical, philosophical, and religious methods in advancing the case of the Christians.

Sources

It is certainly important to look into the basis of the argument used by the apologists. This is important because the basis of the sources used will help the apology to achieve its aim of stopping the hostilities and converting the audience to Christianity. Therefore, it would be very useful for the apologists to use sources that are familiar and appeal to the audience to attain the purpose of the text.

Justin in *First Apology* among other sources uses pagan, Jewish, and scriptural sources.[160] What is even more interesting is that Justin cites Emperor Hadrian's rescript to Minucius Fundanus to back his argument as a conclusion.[161]

---

156. Justin, *First Apology*, 68.
157. Justin, *Second Apology*, 1.
158. Tertullian *Apologeticum*, 4:1.
159. Tertullian, *Ad Scapulam*, 3.
160. Justin, *First Apology*, 8, 20–21, 26, 30–64.
161. Justin, 68.

In *Second Apology*, he still depends on pagan and scriptural sources as the basis of his defense to address the emperor.[162] Tertullian interestingly does not use as many different sources as Justin does though he also uses pagan, Jewish texts (especially those from Josephus), Roman history, and the scriptural sources in *Apologeticum*.[163] In his address to Scapula, Tertullian makes references to recent historical events of the Roman Empire and uses scriptural sources to present his defense of Christianity in North Africa.[164]

The apologists use both Christian and non-Christian sources to support the arguments addressed to the authorities of the Roman Empire. The use of pagan sources is very important because it builds on the idea of arguing from the "known to the unknown." In this way, the authors begin with or spice up what they intend to tell their readers with what the audience already knows before teaching them what they may not know. The apologists, therefore, adopt either a new interpretation of the non-Christian source or use the pagans' understanding but twist it a little to get their readers to appreciate the texts. The apologists carefully considered their sources especially the texts from the pagan sources as well as Scripture to be able to drive home their points.

Themes

A few themes can be gathered from these apologies, and it is important to understand the purpose of the texts. Justin touches a lot on Christology and Christian practices, as well as philosophers like Socrates and Plato. He also mentions more briefly Christian heresies especially those of Marcion in *First Apology*.[165] In *Second Apology*, he speaks about the theology of God, Christian obstinacy, Christian virtues, Christian superiority over Plato and Socrates, and again, there is a brief mention of Simon as the instigator of heresy.[166] Tertullian also builds on themes such as injustice against the Christians, Christian practices, truth, and the Christian apocalypse in *Apologeticum*.[167] In *Ad Scapulam*, some of the major themes are on the doctrine of God, the

---

162. Justin, *Second Apology*, 4–13.
163. Tertullian, *Apologeticum*, 4.3, 14.2, 14.6, 31.1–3.
164. Tertullian, *Ad Scapulam*, 2, 3, 4, 5.
165. Justin, *First Apology*, 8, 21, 50, 54, 58–60.
166. Justin, *Second Apology*, 7, 11, 12, 13, 15.
167. Tertullian, *Apologeticum*, 1–2, 34, 47, 49.

transformation that Christianity brings to its converts, and the blessings and bane of the persecutors or emperors.[168]

To this extent, it can be said that the prominent themes or topics that the apologists discuss in their apologies are issues of injustice, Christian doctrine, Christology, truth, and Christian identity (against heresies) as well as themes of the apocalypse. These topics show that the apologists were interested in defending the Christian course by explaining what Christianity is all about by using the major themes that were used against Christianity.

In arguing the case of the Christians, the apologists attack the Jews, the Roman gods, authorities, and the general public polemically. They use multifaceted arguments while using both Christian and non-Christian sources in their argument. They also discuss major Christian themes in their defense against the accusations of the Christians.

Other Peculiar Features

It is interesting that in each apology, this group of apologists have some peculiarities which other apologists do not necessarily touch on, possibly due to the audience of the texts. Justin in *First Apology* is seemingly sermonic and educative, which is often termed kerygmatic and didactic. He touches on Christian practices such as baptism, the Eucharist, and Sunday meetings.[169] His *Second Apology* builds extensively on the logos theology by Roman philosophers.[170] In *Apologeticum*, Tertullian is briefer in his treatment of logos theology but has a passage where he explains Christian prayer practices and themes, in particular, that they pray for the emperors' long life, secure rule, safe home, brave armies, a faithful senate, honest people, and a quiet world. Tertullian also describes the spread of Christianity and the Eucharist.[171] His *Ad Scapulam* is peculiar in the way he recounts especially recent issues and the blessings or bane of emperors or magistrates who have either supported or resisted the hostility against the Christians.

These particular aspects of the texts show the purpose and intended audiences. The apologies addressed to the authorities raise issues on the

---

168. Tertullian, *Ad Scapulam*, 2, 3, 4, 5.
169. Justin, *First Apology*, 61–67.
170. Justin, *Second Apology*, 6–10.
171. Tertullian, *Apologeticum*, 30.4, 37.4, 39.5–6.

persecution and martyrdom of the early Christians in the first to about the third centuries of the Roman Empire.

Apologies to the Public

The second category of apologetic texts, those addressed to the public, will be analyzed using the comparative elements in this chapter. The text addressed to the public was largely to explain the Christian faith to the public. It was therefore anticipated that when the public start to appreciate Christianity, they might stop hunting down the Christians and ultimately become Christians themselves.

Account

This major comparative category has three main issues to harmonize for the apologies addressed to the public. In the first place, their narrative content will be discussed; second, the character of the martyrs as portrayed by the apologists, and finally, the character of the persecutors will also be evaluated. The aim is to understand how the apologists present the characters involved in or subjected to the persecution. Additionally, the forms of the suffering of Christians are similarly compared here.

Narrative

This class of texts does not focus on storytelling as a feature of what they seek to tell their audience. Tertullian's *Ad Nationes* has a little sketch of the story of the martyrs[172] while Tatian's *Oratio ad Graecos* does not look into the accounts of the martyrs at all. They are very much concerned with defending the charges against the Christians rather than narrating the passion of individual Christians.

Character of the Martyrs

Tertullian projects the Christians and, indeed, the martyrs as courageous, innocent, loving, just, and upright,[173] while Tatian projects them as courageous and chaste.[174] These positive characters as created by these apologists was intended to feed the minds of the audience such that they would be prompted

---

172. Tertullian, "Ad Nationes," l.1.
173. Tertullian, I.18.
174. Tatian, *Oratio Ad Graecos*, 4.1.

to see that the martyrs did not deserve persecution or death. Even more, this positive picture tries to show Christians as the most just and useful members of society, but that they had to suffer the wrath of the wicked. According to the apologists, the martyrs and the Christians, in general, were hunted heroes rather than offenders against Roman culture.

Identity of the Persecutors

Tatian does not present much about the identity of the persecutors; he identifies Crescens, a fellow philosopher who was likely to have reported Justin.[175] Tertullian suggests instances of a father and slave masters being the accusers of the Christians.[176] These identities are interesting because the accusers were people from the same household where it is a father against his Christian son and a slave master against his slave(s). This "strife" in the household setup is interesting because, by these identifications, it seems that there were struggles or discord in the household.[177] Usually it would be assumed that a father should have some authority in the religious convictions of a ward especially a son and a slave master should control the religious expression of his/her slave; yet these authority figures had lost this authority to the extent that they may have to publicly "give-up" on their "subordinates" by personally reporting them for persecution and martyrdom.

The identities of those involved in the persecution and martyrdom indicate that the accusers were the public. This shows that the public was not passive in this process since they played significant roles in initiating the entire process, hence the need to address them in an apology to defend against the allegations and convictions that might have pushed them to accuse the Christians. It is significant to note that the emphasis placed on the public did not imply the absence of the authorities in these hostilities since the proceedings were cast in legal framework and presided over by the authorities of the provinces and the empire.

---

175. Tatian, 19.1.

176. Tertullian, "Ad Nationes," I.4.

177. "This seems to affirm Jesus's words in Matthew 10:34–35: "Do not assume that I have come to bring peace to the earth; I have not come to bring peace, but a sword. For I have come to turn 'a man against his father, a daughter against her mother, a daughter-in-law against her mother-in-law.'" (Berean Study Bible)

Form of Suffering

This aspect of the comparative element considers what was done to the Christians by the persecutors according to the image projected by the apologists. Tertullian talks about torture, beasts, swords, fire, and the martyrdom of Christians by execution or crucifixion.[178] Tatian does not provide an in-depth list of the pains the Christians suffered.

These forms show that several activities were used, according to Tertullian, to intensify the pains of the Christians. They were tortured with various instruments and animals as well as bruised by fire and eventually crucified like Jesus, their leader.

In essence, the account and narrative aspects of the apologies point to the fact that they are not very interested in narrating a story out of the persecution and martyrdom of the early Christians. The character of the Christians and the martyrs are painted in heroic terms. The persecutors included family members and slave-masters of Christian slaves. Therefore, the nature of the persecution and martyrdom of the Christians included various means of torture and, eventually, death by crucifixion.

Accusation

The comparative elements in this category seek to investigate the legal framework of the persecution and martyrdom of the early Christians. It embraces four main issues: legal procedure, charges, and allegations as well as motives including the demands to sacrifice.

Legal Procedure

The central issue for these apologists is the question of injustice and the apologists argue that the Christians were not allowed to defend themselves in the trials.[179] The entire proceedings are described in a way that still points to *cognitio extra ordinem* – where the authority is both the interrogator and arbitrator in the process of prosecution against the Christians. The public acted as the accusers, and the authorities acted as arbiters of the legal process.

---

178. Tertullian, "Ad Nationes," I.3, 6.
179. Tertullian, I.2.

Charges and Allegations

Various allegations were leveled against the Christians by the public in the legal system. *Ad Nationes* identifies infanticide, incest, shameful acts, and presents that the Christians were accused of being responsible for the natural disasters.[180] The Christians, therefore, faced charges which projected them as destroyers of the state, atheists, and obstinate.[181] They were also saddled with the charge of the name Christian. Tatian also relates that outsiders alleged that Christians were foreign and cannibalistic.[182] Tatian predominantly focuses on the charges of atheism and obstinacy in his refutation.[183]

The accusations were a mixture of ethical, political, social, and religious allegations. This indicates that according to the apologists, there were multiple charges against the Christians. Tertullian suggests that to the public these crimes were "more atrocious and numerous."[184]

Motive

Because of the charges, persecutors, and the form of hostility, it can be strongly suggested that in this subgenre too, the persecutors sought to preserve the Roman peace, thus *pax deorum*. Tertullian captures this idea very well with his famous statement that "if the Tiber has overflowed its bank, if the Nile has remained in its bed, if the sky has been still or the earth been in commotion, if death has made its devastations or famine its afflictions, your cry immediately is 'This is the fault of the Christians!'"[185] Therefore, since the Christians had offended the gods of the non-Christians by not worshiping the gods, it led to such disasters breaking out on the society. There is therefore no doubt that the perceived Christian atheism and the resultant perceived threat to the *pax deorum* were presented as the first motivating factor which provoked the persecution of the Christians.

---

180. Tertullian, l.2, 5, 9.
181. Tertullian, l.1, 3, 10, 11, 17.
182. Tatian, *Oratio Ad Graecos*, 1.1; 25.3.
183. Tatian, 4.1–2, 5.1–3, 32.1.
184. Tertullian, "Ad Nationes," I. 2.
185. Tertullian, l.9.

Demand

The martyrs, according to the apologists, were allowed to sacrifice to the gods of the empire using the image of the emperor, to clear themselves of the accusations. In both apologetic texts, the authorities demanded the Christians to make the sacrifice, but the Christians refused.[186] The Christians, to a large extent, felt that the gods of the Romans were man-made who were contemptible[187] and so they could not worship such gods.

In the light of this legal framework as portrayed by the apologies addressed to the Roman public, the legal procedure was likely to be *cognitio extra ordinem*, while the accusations against the Christians ranged from social, religious, political to ethical, and these accusations were affirmed in the unpreparedness of the Christians to sacrifice using the *genius* of the emperor. The motivation of the persecutors, as presented by the apologists, can be attributed to their desire to see the preservation or restoration of peace with the gods.

Argumentation

The comparative elements under this heading seek to look into how the apologists defended the Christians from the charges and allegations. The possible presence of polemics is discussed and the argumentative strategy adopted by the apologies is also evaluated. Furthermore, the sources used in these defenses as well as the central themes that are discussed by the apologists are also explored. These elements will help understand the defense approach adopted by the apologists who wrote to the public to protect Christianity.

Polemic

It is normal for apologists to adopt the polemic approach in defending their course. Tertullian charges the persecutors as "unjust," "ignorant," "absurd," blind, and haters.[188] He says to the people: "You are ashamed, I suppose, to worship unadorned and simple crosses."[189] Tatian describes the gods as "demons" and the persecutors as mad, and fools.[190] He describes the public's

---

186. Tertullian, I.12; Tatian, *Oratio Ad Graecos*, 13.3, 14.1, 27.2.
187. Tertullian, I.10; Tatian, 18.2.
188. Tertullian, I. 1, 6, 7, ll.2, 7.
189. Tertullian, I.12.
190. Tatian, *Oratio Ad Graecos*, 14, 21.1, 22.1, 33.1.

action on several instances as "non-sense"[191] and refers to the hostilities in strong words by admonishing them to "drop all their nonsense and be done with this criminal hatred of us."[192]

These polemic attacks were against the Roman gods, and even more so the general public. It must be stressed that there are no direct attacks on the authorities in this category of apologies to the public. The attacks, especially Tatian's, are mostly against the public and the Roman system or practices. Tatian's apology is strongly marked by his dislike for the Greek culture and its practices.[193] Hence, the apologists direct the attacks at the public to solicit a change in their attitudes against the Christian faith and to win them to Christianity.[194]

Strategy

The authors of these apologetic texts adopted various methods in defending the Christian faith from the charges and allegations against them. Tertullian's *Ad Nationes* uses rhetoric which includes logic, questions, sarcasm, and the history of the Romans as well as the Christian idea of the apocalypse to defend and explain the Christian practices to the public.[195] He says, "It is quite uncertain whether I shall laugh at your absurdity or unbraid you for your blindness."[196] Tatian's strategy is similar to Tertullian's; he uses rhetoric, recent events, history, the apocalypse, and argument from prophecy.[197] He ridicules the Roman gods when he says, "Your official festivals are ridiculous, celebrated in honor of evil demons who disgrace human beings."[198] He also points out the double standards in the Roman system by suggesting, "You sacrifice animals to eat meat and you buy men to provide human slaughter for the soul, feeding it with bloodshed of the most impious kind."[199]

---

191. Tatian, 26.2, 33.1.
192. Tatian, 9.4.
193. Foster, "Tatian," 107; Hawthorne, "Tatian and His Discourse, "180–81.
194. Hawthorne, 187.
195. Tertullian, "Ad Nationes," l, 1–4, 6, 8, 9, 10, ll.1–2, 10, 14.
196. Tertullian, ll.12.
197. Tatian, *Oratio Ad Graecos*, 1.1, 3.1–4, 4.1–2, 6, 8, 11.2, 13.1, 17.1, 22, 31, 32.2.
198. Tatian, 22.1.
199. Tatian, 23.2.

The authors employed various strategies in defending and explaining the Christian practices to the general public who were involved in the persecution and martyrdom of the Christians. The authors of these apologies, therefore, adopt rhetorical, philosophical, and religious approaches in defending the Christian faith from their adversaries. The various approaches were adopted based on the different aims of the text. While the rhetorical, logical, and argument from prophecy aspects appeal more to philosophers and educated members of the society, the sarcastic and reasoning aspects appeal more to the non-educated members of the society. The apocalyptic strategy, without a doubt, seeks to attract the audience for conversion to Christianity. The strategy is therefore a mixture that has various motives to defend against the charges, explain the Christian practices, and convert the audience of the text.

Sources

To make the texts attractive to the audience, the authors depend on various sources in advancing their arguments. Tertullian depends on history, non-Christian sources, and scriptural materials to make his thoughts attractive to the audience.[200] Tatian similarly uses non-Christian sources, recent events, and scriptural sources.[201]

It is certainly interesting and important that the apologists chose to use both Christian and non-Christian sources as it helped them to bring the arguments to the doorstep of their audience. Tertullian categorically shows the usefulness of the non-Christian sources:

> Wishing, then, to follow step by step your own commentaries which you have drawn out of your theology of every sort (because the authority of learned men goes further with you in matters of this kind than the testimony of facts).[202]

The apologist used sources that the audiences were very familiar with but used them differently to meet the needs of the apologies. The non-Christians may have some awareness of the Christian Scriptures, so the apologist used this source to explain the Christian understandings and practices.

---

200. Tertullian, "Ad Nationes," l.2–4, 5–7, 10, ll.1–2, 7, 9–14.
201. Tatian, *Oratio Ad Graecos*, 1, 2, 13, 21–26, 31, 37–41.
202. Tertullian, "Ad Nationes," ll.1.

The use of both Christian and non-Christian sources by the apologists who wrote to the public in defense of the Christians is very important as this helps in making their arguments appealing and more effective.

Themes

Identification of the main themes discussed in these apologies also helps to understand better the texts of the apologies addressed to the public. The main theme of Tertullian's *Ad Nationes* is to build on the idea of injustice against the Christians, the status of the Roman gods, and the usefulness of Christian converts.[203] In *Oratio Ad Graecos*, Tatian builds more on non-Christian practices, the argument from prophecy, Christian identity, and his conversion.[204]

These themes as identified in these texts are mostly about Christian ideas aimed at attracting the audience to Christianity. They are aimed at projecting a good image of Christianity while making the Roman culture dark and unattractive. The authors suggest that the audience must look at the brighter side of Christianity by focusing on the positive impacts of Christianity on life and society in general.

The defense of Christianity from the charges as addressed in the apologies to the public was quite holistic. Various argumentative methods are used especially by way of presenting polemical charges against the Roman system and exalting Christianity above the Roman ways of doing things. The apologists used sources familiar to the public not to make new arguments but to give them the breath of freshness to convince the pagans. The argumentations in these apologies are therefore comprehensive and thoughtful.

Other Peculiar Features

The apologetic texts addressed to the public have their peculiar features. The second book of Tertullian, *Ad Nationes*, is devoted to Varro's theory of the classification of the gods.[205] Tertullian devotes this seventeen-chapter book to explore and argue against this theory. Another peculiar issue Tertullian brings to the table is concerning why the Christians pray facing the east.[206] Tatian on his part does not have other major issues in his texts apart from his defense

---

203. Tertullian, l.1, 2, 4, 6, 10, 14.
204. Tatian, *Oratio Ad Graecos*, 22–26, 29–30, 36–41.
205. Tertullian, "Ad Nationes," ll.1–17.
206. Tertullian, 13.

of the Christian positions; it is worth noting that other apologists do not provide information to their readers apart from laying stress on philosophy while attacking the Roman gods and social order.

In conclusion, it is argued that these classes of texts, while neglecting narrative elements, still paint comprehensive pictures of the persecution and martyrdom of the early Christians. They are useful for the understanding of the statutes and actions against the Christians and how the Christians defended themselves to the public, the initiators of the persecution and martyrdom. The fundamental aim of addressing this category of recipients can be classified as evangelistic rather than provoking an end to the hostilities.

The picture of the persecution and martyrdom against the Christians in the Roman Empire as portrayed by the apologists is to be compared with the apologies to the authorities to bring out the similarities and differences. This internal comparison of apologetic texts is necessary for two reasons. In the first place, it allows the developing of a synchronized picture of the persecution and martyrdom of the Christians as projected by the apologists. This single picture can then be compared to the picture of the persecution and martyrdom of the early Christians as portrayed in the martyr texts, to bring out the similarities and differences in the texts.

The second reason for this internal comparison is to address the question of the submission status of the apologies to the authorities. The similarities and differences that emerge from the synthesis of the two subgenres may be helpful in addressing this issue. This internal comparison is therefore crucial in the realization of the aims and significance of this book in all respects.

Similarities and Differences

This section seeks to synchronize the harmonized versions of the persecution and martyrdom of the early Christians as projected by the two different kinds of apologetic texts. The synchronized version of the similarities and differences between these two categories of the apologies is further in chapter five compared to the synchronized version of the persecution and martyrdom in the martyr texts from chapter three. The comparison is outlined based on the thirteen main comparative elements categorized into the four groups and their peculiarities.

Account

The three comparative elements under this subheading bring out the similarities and differences between the apologies addressed to the authorities and those addressed to the public in terms of the nature of the accounts of the hostilities against the Christians. The accounts' possible narrative content as well as the characterization of the accounts into persecutors and martyrs are compared. Again, the forms of the suffering of the Christians as portrayed by the two classes of the apologetic texts are also compared.

Narrative

It is evident from the texts addressed to the authorities that the narrative presented in this class of texts is very small. Apologies addressed to the public also do not have narrative contents. To a large extent, therefore, it can be argued that the apologetic texts, in general, have very little presence of narratives. The authors of these texts were more interested in defending and explaining the Christian course of action rather than telling stories about the plights of the Christians in the Roman Empire.

Character of the Martyrs

It is equally significant to look at how the martyrs and the Christians, in general, are presented in these texts. The accounts portray the Christians and martyrs as innocent, and the outsiders as amazed by the Christians' display of courage, composure, and even thankfulness when they were tortured and sentenced to death.

These martyrs followed the ways of their founder (Jesus) and were aware that they would have to die when they decided to be Christians.[207] They were ready to die also because they would be going to a perfect place of justice. The apologists, therefore, present the martyrs in glorious and heroic terms to make them attractive to the audience.

The texts are intended to be read by insiders (Christians) so the authors sought to portray these characters as people who stood unwaveringly against all odds. This courage of the martyrs as projected by the apologists was intended to encourage the Christians and also suggest that when charges are made against them, they should stand as the others had done. On the other

---

207. Tertullian, *Ad Scapulam*, 1, 3; Justin, *Second Apology*, 12; Tertullian, *Apologeticum*, 1.12, 21.3, 46.1, 49.14–15, 50.1; Tatian, *Oratio Ad Graecos*, 4.1.

hand, the texts appealed to the outsiders (non-Christians) to see in these characters glorious victims of injustice even to the point of death. This picture is used by the apologists as an evangelistic tool to attract others to the Christian faith. Indeed, Barnes, for instance, suggests that Tertullian's conversion to Christianity was a result of the impression made on him by the character of the martyrs because the martyrs showed no fear of death.[208] Both classes of apologetic texts projected the Christians in a positive light and utilized it as a tool to encourage other Christians and to impress non-Christians.

Identity of the Persecutors

The two classes of texts agree that the hostilities perpetrated against the Christians were carried out by both the authorities and the public. The public included family members, professional groups, and individuals who found the Christians detestable and hence reported them to the authorities and pursued the matter until the Christians were killed. Apart from the public who reported the Christians, the authorities of the empire sometimes including the emperor himself and the resources of the empire were committed to the persecution and martyrdom of the Christians. The resources are seen as being used since the charges were presented against the Christians in the courts. The agreement between these two classes of texts gives a coherent picture of the roles of the public and the authorities in the persecution and martyrdom against the early Christians in the Roman Empire.

Form of Suffering

The texts agree that the early Christians suffered physical torture of various forms before their execution. The agreement between these texts is very strong and conclusive.

Accusation

The four categories of comparative elements draw on the legal framework the Christians faced. The analysis will look at the harmony of the classes of texts concerning the legal procedure, charges, and allegations as well as the motive of the persecutors and the demand for the Christians to sacrifice.

---

208. Barnes, *Tertullian*, 2.

Legal Procedure

The texts point to *cognitio extra ordinem* as being the process/form used in cases against Christians. The apologists contend that the Christians were not allowed to defend themselves in long formal speeches. The authorities were unwilling to allow the Christians proper time to answer when cross-examined.[209] Tertullian says:

> Whatever you charge against us, when you so charge others, they use their own eloquence, they hire the advocacy of others, to prove their innocence. There is freedom to answer to cross-question, since in fact it is against the law for men to be condemned, undefended and unheard. But to Christians alone it is forbidden to say anything to clear their case, to defend the Truth, to save the judge from being unjust. No! One thing is looked for, one alone, the one thing needful for popular hatred – the confession of the name. Not investigation of the charge! Yet if you are trying any other criminal, it does not follow at once from his confession to the name of murderer, or temple-robber, or adulterer, or enemy of the state.[210]

Tertullian points to three major deviations from normal or more classical (republican) judicial process: first, personal defense without the support of advocate (lawyers); second, no investigation after the confession of being Christians, and; third, no opportunity for the accused Christian to give a proper defense against the foundation of the hatred for this name. To this extent, therefore, the addressees of these apologetic texts agree that the Christians were subjected to *cognitio extra ordinem*.

Charges and Allegations

The apologies identify political, social, religious, and ethical allegations. The texts addressed to the authorities stress the political (conspirators, treason, obstinacy), ethical (infanticide, incest, adultery), and religious charges (godless, impious, worshipers of ass and cross, sacrilegious, magic). On the other hand, apologies addressed to the public stress the ethical (incest, infanticide,

---

209. Tertullian, *Apologeticum*, 1.1; Tatian, *Oratio Ad Graecos*, 27.1.
210. Tertullian, 2.2–4.

shameful sect, and cannibalism), religious (atheist), and social issues (natural disaster). It is argued that the charges were inter-related.

When the Christians were arraigned before the courts, the allegations changed officially to charges. The apologies addressed to the authorities present that the charges against the Christian were political, ethical, and religious. Meanwhile, the apologies addressed to the public focus on religious, social, and political charges.

There is a little twist between the texts here; while the apologies addressed to the public tone down on the political charges, the texts to the authorities stress and try to prove that the Christians were neither conspirators (Justin),[211] nor traitors (Tertullian).[212] These little twists in the allegations that are refuted in the texts addressed to the general public compared to the allegations that are refuted in the texts addressed to the authorities, show that the content of the texts is influenced by the addressee and not only by the common context of the two types of texts.

The twist in the charges here is the silence on the ethical issues regarding the charges against the Christians as addressed to the public. This does not imply that they were absent, rather that relatively little mention of them is made. Most of the defenses in this class of the apologetic texts are concerned with the religious charges such as atheism and the name of "Christian.". This is important although the charge of the name may suggest some ethical behaviors which do not align with the Roman worldview.

Motive

Given the charges and allegations as well as the form of hostilities against the Christians as described in the apologies to the authorities and those to the public, it is logical to argue that the persecutors were motivated by the need to reinstate or maintain the peace between the Romans and the gods. The two classes of texts agree on this point – that the *pax deorum* was seen by outsiders as important, that the Christians were perceived to be a threat to this peace with the gods, and that this prompted the persecutions.

---

211. Justin, *First Apology*, 12.
212. Tertullian, *Apologeticum*, 2.6.

Demand

All the texts in the apologetic category agree that the accused Christians were asked to offer sacrifice. This demand may have been influenced by the correspondence between Pliny and Trajan, which Tertullian refers to.[213]

Argumentation

The comparative elements seek to look into the methods and forms of defense of the Christians adopted by the apologists. Four main issues are compared in this group; polemic content, argumentative strategy, sources of the arguments, and the major themes of the various classes of the apologetic texts.

Polemic

An apology may contain both offensive and defensive elements,[214] where the offensive elements may be described as polemics since they turn the charges against the accusers. The apologies to the authorities attack the Jews, the Roman gods, the authorities, and the public. Most of the direct attacks can hierarchically be arranged – first the public, then the gods and only then against the authorities.

On the other hand, the apologies to the public also attack the gods as well as the Roman systems and practices including the general public. The only distinction between the two classes is that in the apologies to the authorities, the Jews are attacked due to their interpretation and use of Scriptures.[215] Both kinds of apologetic texts attack the Roman religious system, especially the gods, in very strong terms. Hawthorne suggests that Justin's and Tatian's texts are not apologies because of their depth of attacks on the Greeks, and are harangues instead.[216] Tatian launches a strong attack against the Roman religious system, and Tertullian attacks the system even more in *Apologeticum*. What is true and most significant in synthesizing the two classes of apologies is the attacks on the public and the authorities.

Most of the direct attacks in the apologies addressed to the authorities are against the public. There are about twenty direct attacks against the public while there are only about seven direct attacks against the authorities. The

---

213. Tertullian, *Apologeticum*, 2.6-9.
214. Edward, Goodman, and Price, *Apologetics in the Roman Empire*, xi, 106.
215. Tertullian, *Apologeticum*, 21.15.
216. Hawthorne, "Tatian and His Discourse," 188.

apologies to the public do not lay direct attacks on the authorities. This is a major difference between these two classes of texts, which must be further investigated.

Strategy

It is crucial to explore the ways the apologists in the various classes of texts defend the Christian cause. The apologies to the authorities predominantly used arguments from prophecy and rhetoric which encompassed philosophy, logic, reasoning, sarcasm, and irony. The apologies to the authorities primarily depended on rhetorical, philosophical, and religious methods in dealing with the charges against the Christians. The apologies to the public equally used the same methods like those to the authorities.

Although these texts agree in terms of the strategies there are slight differences with regard to the predominant strategy used. Whereas the apologies to the authorities depended more on rhetorical and philosophical methods, the apologies to the public depended more on philosophical and religious strategies. This means that philosophical strategy was key to both classes and apologies to the authorities also depended more on rhetorical tools while texts addressed to the public depended on religious strategies.

The two classes of texts used philosophical strategies because Roman society was philosophically inclined. However, owing to the aims of the text especially with the addressees, those to the authorities used rhetorical forms that were not much different from the philosophical strategy but texts addressed to the public preferred religious strategy to aid conversion and speak against the Roman religious and social order. Therefore, in terms of the strategy, there are great similarities but nuanced differences in terms of what they emphasize.

Sources

The authors of the various texts depended on two main sources. They used both Christian and non-Christian sources. Apologies to the authorities and those to the public together used pagan and Jewish sources, scriptures, history, and events in the empire as the basis of their argument. These sources as used by the authors were applied forcefully. However, the major issue here is emphasis. Whereas the apologies to the authorities depended a lot on the non-Christian sources especially the pagan sources, the apologies to the public depended on Christian sources especially the Christian Scriptures. A cursory count of scriptural usage from Tatian's apology has about thirty-five quotations; thirty-one from the Old Testament and four from the New Testament. The stress on the types of sources used shows that the authors had various aims and selected their sources according to the addressees of the texts.

Themes

It is without a doubt that the major themes developed by the various apologies were concerned with Christian themes. The apologists tried to explain issues about the Christian faith in terms of Christology, apocalypse, Christian ethics, conversion, and the transformation that Christianity brings to the entire society. Another major theme of the two types of apologies relates to Christian practices that mark the Christian identity such as the Eucharist, Sunday services, prayer topics, forms of prayer, and membership of Christians irrespective of age, sex, and social status.

Generally speaking, when comparing the two types of apologetic texts the argumentative forms overlap largely, but with a few nuanced differences. This indicates that the texts responded to the same context (persecution), had overlapping aims (bringing the hostility to an end, impressing outside readers positively, and building the identity of Christian readers), but were intended for partly different audiences reflecting the addressing of the texts to authorities and general public respectively.

Submission Status

In attending to scholarly debate on the possibility of the Roman authorities reading the content of the apologetic texts, particularly those addressed to them, the internal comparison of the two subgenres helps to address some aspects of the quest. The argumentative forms or the comparative elements of these two classes based on the addressees relate to how the defenses were presented. This can point to either an intended submission or otherwise of the apologetic texts, especially those addressed to the authorities.

The following is a list of polemic attacks found in the various texts and to whom they were directed.

The assumption is that the apologies addressed to the general public may have a strong polemic approach compared to those addressed to the authorities. Furthermore, the sources of the argument in the apologies presented

Table 3.1 Polemic attacks in the apologetic texts

	Gods/ Roman System	Authorities	Public
First Apology	*Evil *Demons	*Irrational	*Unreasonable *Stupidity *Dissolute
Second Apology			*Wicked *Against Crescens
Apologeticum	*Are not gods *Profane idols and deification of human names *Perjury, *Catastrophe *Contempt *Misfortune	*Haters of truth *Cunning ruse and cruel rage	*Unjust, *Dogs *Impious, *Foul *Foul charges *Danger, *Cruel
Ad Scapulam	*Demons	*Cruel *Ignorant *Fighting the god	
Oratio Ad Scapulam	*Demon *System *Madmen *Ridicule *Non-sense		*Non-sense *Criminal hatred
Ad Nationes	*Dead *Absurd		*Ashamed *Incest *Absurdity *Blindness

to the general public may use both Christian and non-Christian sources while those addressed to the authorities may depend more on non-Christian sources, and philosophy, logic, and legal arguments, apart from the Christian and non-Christian sources.

Given the synthesis analyzed above, it is clear that both classes of the apologetic texts raised serious polemics against the public; next in the line of fire were the gods and Roman social-religious systems, followed by the authorities. Most of the attacks among the apologies addressed to the public were against the pagans and did not directly attack the authorities. Direct attacks against the Roman gods were more frequent than attacks against the authorities in the apologies to the authorities. It can therefore sufficiently be argued that owing to the fewer number of direct polemics against those in authority, it is logical to conclude that the apologies were at the very least intended to receive the attention of those in authority in the Roman Empire. In terms of the intensity of the polemics too, the authorities were charged as being "ignorant," "haters of truth," "cunning," and "cruel."[217] Meanwhile, some of the charges against the public were "unreasonable," "stupid," "dissolute," "wicked," "cruel," "unjust," "impious," "foul," "criminal," "non-sense," "ashamed," "absurd," "blind," etc.[218] Those directed against the gods and the Roman system were harsh. The gods were described as dead, "absurd," "demons," "contemptuous", "no god", "profane" etc.[219] These examples show that the intensity or the heat was less on the authorities compared to the public and the gods. Therefore, it can be suggested that the authors indeed wanted the authorities to read their petitions to possibly stop the hostilities and to convert them to Christianity.

In terms of the sources used in the arguments and the argumentative strategies, though similar, they show a little difference. Although both the apologies to the authorities and those to the public used Christian and non-Christian sources, those addressed to the authorities used more of the non-Christian sources, particularly pagan sources. This strategy was important for conviction because it used the "known to the unknown" approach to lure the reader. It is not very likely that the authorities knew so much of the Christian sources, but it is highly possible that they were hands-on with the pagan sources. To make them understand the arguments, therefore, the apologists in both classes of apologies, used texts that were familiar to outsiders and thus brought the arguments to their doorstep. Justin copies a whole rescript of the emperor as a conclusion of his *First Apology*.[220] It can therefore be inferred from this that his targeted audience was not the emperor or the authorities.

---

217. Justin, *First Apology*, 9; Tertullian, *Apologeticum*, 1.1, 27.3; *Ad Scapulam*, 1.

218. Justin, *First Apology*, 5, 11; *Second Apology*, 3, Tertullian, *Apologeticum*, 5.4, 7.1, 21.27, 41.1, 50.12; "Ad Nationes," I.12, II.7; Tatian, *Oratio Ad Graecos*, 26.2.

219. Tertullian, *Apologeticum*, 9.2, 11.15-16, 28.3, 40.6, 41.1; *Ad Scapulam*, 2; "Ad Nationes," I.14, II.2; Tatian, *Oratio Ad Graecos*, 8.1.

220. Justin, *First Apology*, 68.

Again, in terms of argumentative strategy, both classes of apologies used a lot of philosophical argumentative strategies to defend the Christians and to explain the Christian practices. This strategy was very important to the apologists when writing to the authorities and even to the public since the Roman society valued philosophy. Justin in *First Apology* shows the inclination of the emperor to philosophy when he says, "To the Emperor Titus Aelius Hadrianus Antoninus Pius Augustus Caesar and his philosopher son Verissimus, and Lucius the philosopher"[221]; the principal characteristic of the members of the imperial family listed here is their affinity to philosophy. The apologist was aware that these authorities were interested in philosophy so he needed to dance to the tune of his audience. Kahlos suggests that the best form of argumentation is to build on the premise of common mutual grounds, which Christian apologists do very well within many cases.[222] It will therefore be out of place to assume that the apologies did not want such persons to read them, after making such efforts to use arguments and sources which the authorities were known to respect and relate to.

Consequently, based on the internal comparison in this chapter, it is logical and suggestive that the apologists who addressed apologies to the authorities also wanted these authorities to read their apologies. There were relatively fewer polemic attacks directed against the authorities and the few that were targeted at them were not couched in very strong language compared to those targeted at the gods and the public. Furthermore, the argumentative strategy and sources of arguments too are suggestive that the apologies did their works in the manner designed to be attractive to the authorities by depending more on pagan sources and adopting a heavy philosophical approach. At the very least, therefore, the apologists certainly wanted the authorities to read their apologies.

Conclusion

The analysis of the apologetic texts in this chapter has demonstrated that this subgenre of texts is useful in the exploration of the persecution and martyrdom of the early Christians. Many of the comparative elements in this internal

---

221. Justin, 1.
222. Kahlos, *Debate and Dialogue*, 67.

comparison affirm and corroborate what each other suggest in most of the cases. They talk about the same things although they are not perfectly united because there are a few nuances based on the addressees and where the stress is placed. The most important aspect of the nuances is that they do not contradict each other but supplement what the other sources are quite indistinct about, probably due to the addressees of the text. This, therefore, suggests that in using the apologetic texts to understand the persecution and martyrdom of the early Christians, the two categories of the texts must be used side by side for a comprehensive picture of the hostilities. On the other hand, these little divergences help with the discussion of the submission status of the apologetic texts addressed to the authorities. This chapter argues that, based on the nuances particularly relating to the accusations and argumentative forms, the authors of the texts certainly wanted the authorities to read them.

It is therefore important to compare the synchronized picture of the persecution and martyrdom of the early Christians in the Roman Empire as suggested by the apologists to the synchronized version of the martyr texts from the previous chapter. The next chapter brings the two pictures together to identify their similarities (supplement or corroborate) and differences (contradict) concerning the hostilities against the Christians in the Roman Empire from the second to around the third century.

CHAPTER FIVE

A Two Genre Sources Approaches and Reception by the Authorities – Martyr and Apologetic Texts

The persecution and martyrdom of the early Christians in the Roman Empire made their mark on emerging Christianity; Christians reacted to them and felt the need to remember them in writing. Two prominent types of written responses composed from a Christian perspective were the martyr accounts and the apologetic texts. However, these two broad genres of texts have been rarely used together by scholars in their pursuit to understand the subject of the persecution and martyrdom of the early Christians. It is therefore important to compare them to identify their corroborative, supplementary, or possibly contradictory aspects on the subject of the persecution and martyrdom. For the understanding of the character of the persecution and the motives of the persecutors, the texts that are used the most, along with texts written by non-Christian authors about the Christians, are the martyr texts, while the apologies have not been exploited. The apologetic texts sought to complain about unjust treatment, to defend Christianity, and to target, at least on the level of rhetoric, out-group recipients. The apologetic and the martyr texts were however written around the same time. They were, therefore, different reactions to persecution and martyrdom.[1]

To this end, I argue that it is needful as a preliminary step toward exploiting the texts as sources to other questions – a prominent example being the

---

1. Lieu, "Audience of Apologetics," 210.

questions concerning the character of these hostilities and the motives of the persecutors – to systematically and comprehensively compare the two types of texts. Further, such a comparison should have both an internal dimension (where the different kinds of apologetic texts are compared with each other and the different kinds of martyr texts with each other) and an external dimension (where the different kinds of apologetic texts are compared to the different kinds of martyr texts).

In this chapter, the two separate pictures of the persecution and martyrdom as projected by the martyr texts (synthesis) and that which is painted by the apologetic texts (synthesis) are compared externally to develop a comprehensive picture of the image projected by the early Christians of the persecution and martyrdom they were subjected to. The comparisons stress the similarities and differences between the two types of texts and to ascertain whether the image of the persecution and martyrdom of the early Christians as presented in the two genres of texts corroborate, supplement, or contradict each other.

This comparison will pave the way for a discussion of the submission status of the apologies addressed to the authorities, that is, whether they were submitted, intended for submission, or not. I assume that if the external comparison brings out some slight differences in content, then it will be agreed that they were meant to be read by the different addressees. If, for example, the apologetic texts (addressed to outsiders) need to argue or explain Christian habits or rituals, such as calling each other brother or sister, the Eucharist, and baptism, since Christians did not need to be convinced that they were not incestuous or cannibalistic, then it will be agreed that they were meant to be read by outsiders, that is the addressees. On the other hand, if there are similar levels of explanation in martyr texts that were aimed at insiders and apologetic texts that were rhetorically aimed at outsiders, then the apologies may not have been intended for submission to the addressees by the apologists, especially those addressed to the authorities.

On another line, if the differences are significant concerning descriptions of the character of the persecution, the identity of the persecutors, the motives of the persecutors etc, then it would be just to suggest that such differences would pose a problem for how we may use the texts as sources for such questions. Such major differences will show that either one or the other of the two types of texts, or indeed both of them, are projecting distorted images of the persecution. If so, the entire phenomena of the persecution and martyrdom of the early Christians could be argued to be largely imaginary as was the practice in antiquity.[2] It would also question whether the apologies were ever intended for submission since they may be fictional.

Before undertaking the comparison in this chapter, the audience and purpose of the two categories of the texts are discussed to determine the motivation for writing the texts. This is followed by analysis of the synthesized images of persecution and martyrdom portrayed by the two classes of texts. These emerging similarities and differences are then highlighted to determine the contours of their corroborating, supplementing, or contradicting each other. Eventually, the submission status of the apologies is discussed.

Fusion of the Martyr and Apologetic Texts

This section of the discussion tries to bring together the synthesized pictures of the persecution and martyrdom of the Christians in the martyr and apologetic texts. The comparison between the martyr and apologetic texts concerning the persecution and martyrdom of the early Christians in the Roman Empire from the second century reveals many similarities. The analysis here is about the fusion of the harmony of the texts done in chapters three and four.

Similarities

In the first place, the two classes of texts agree that the martyrs were courageous, heroic, and worthy as examples not just for the Christians but also for the Roman public and the authorities. The authors of the apologetic texts present the martyrs in glorious terms even in the apologies to the authorities. These positive depictions of the martyrs were intended to solicit the sympathy of the audience because even when they were unjustly sentenced, the martyrs gave thanks. The glorious characterization of the martyrs by the Christian authors in the martyr and apologetic texts emphasize the texts as evangelistic tools.

The two classes of texts again agree on the identity of the persecutors as being the public and the authorities. Both the martyr texts and the apologetic texts identified on the narrative level the significant role of the public

---

2. Engberg, "Truth Begs No Favours," 178.

as those who brought the allegations. The category of the public may include the pagans, Jews, and even family members of the Christian martyrs. The texts further point out that there were different authorities involved. It is clear from the two classes of texts (martyr texts and apologetic texts) that the leaders of the empire and the provinces played significant roles in perpetuating hostilities against the Christians. Some of these authorities included the emperors, governors, and prefects. The second category of the authorities which included institutions and infrastructure of the empire and the local authorities were equally committed to the persecution and martyrdom of the early Christians. This category may include the local police-like forces, soldiers, amphitheaters, tribunals, arenas, forums, dungeons among many other facilities of the empire. The argument here is that these facilities could not have been committed to the persecution and martyrdom of the Christians without the permission of the authorities. The martyr texts and the apologetic texts equally paint the picture of a spectrum of authorities involved in the persecutions, which can therefore be labeled as permeating and comprehensive.

Additionally, regarding the legal procedure used against the Christians, the two classes of the martyr and apologetic texts agree on this strongly. The Christians were presented in trials where the *cognitio extra ordinem* procedure was employed. Urch has argued that based on Cicero's *Orations*, the Romans had two main legal procedures: the accusatorial and the inquisitorial systems.[3] The accusatorial procedure was done in public, where enough time for defense was allowed and the judgment was based on testimony. Meanwhile, the inquisitorial procedure was where the prosecutor was the judge sitting on the bench, the testimony was made in secret, with little time for defense and the whole procedure was based on questions. *Cognitio extra ordinem* was a blend of these two processes. Most scholars attribute the *cognitio extra ordinem* to Augustus;[4] it combined the normal preliminary and trial sessions of the Roman judicial system into one, usually under the magistrate.[5] This early Roman judicial system was where a charge was brought against a person and

---

3. Urch, "Procedure in the Courts," 93–94.

4. Turpin, "Formula, Cognitio, and Proceedings," 501; Johnston, *Roman Law in Context*, 121; Borkwoski and du Plessis, *Textbook on Roman Law* (Oxford: Oxford University Press, 2005), 80.

5. Borkwoski, *Textbook on Roman Law*, 81; Johnston, *Roman Law in Context*, 121–22.

the magistrate interrogated the defendant.⁶ In this system, a private person brought the accusation acting as *delator* while the magistrate or the governor acted as the interrogator and judge at the same time.

Furthermore, the two classes of texts agree to the degree that the martyrs were allowed to save their lives by sacrificing to the Roman gods. The opportunity to sacrifice to the Roman gods or the *genius* of the emperor was offered to the martyrs but they refused. The Christians refused to recant because it would be tantamount to idolatry from a Christian perspective since it was against the first two commands of the Decalogue. The agreement of the texts to this proof is significant because this formula is largely traced to Pliny since he applied this from Bithynia. The fact that the authors of the martyr and apologetic texts agree on this formula shows the relationship between them.

In the same light, the texts agree mostly on the terms of the form of the persecution and martyrdom. Both the martyr and apologetic texts identified physical torture of various kinds and added that the martyrs were eventually executed, although the narrative martyr texts, being mostly narrative, included some psychological pressure in what they describe. There is no shred of doubt concerning the form of the persecution of the early Christians in the Roman Empire. The agreement in the martyr and apologetic texts here show the level of suffering of the Christians in these hostilities. They suffered at the hands of metallic instruments such as sword and racks, and at the hands of animals such as lions, beasts, a heifer, and a bear; they faced fire and beheading, and all because they were Christians. Both types of texts agree that the Christian martyrs faced physical torture and executions.

What is more, the martyr texts and the apologetic texts agree about what motivated the persecutors in the persecution and martyrdom of the early Christians. Christopher Haas argues strongly that the motivation of the persecutors in the persecution and martyrdom of the Christians was largely religious.⁷ The texts are in harmony that the persecutors were largely influenced by the need to maintain the peace of the empire, the *pax Romana*. This peace is, to the Romans, guaranteed when the relationship with the gods is intact, the *pax deorum*. The non-Christians were pushed by this responsibility toward a fervent relationship between the people and the gods. The Romans, to a

---

6. Turpin, "Formula, Cognitio and Proceedings," 544–54; Boamah, *Christian Magic*, 55.
7. Haas, "Imperial Religious Policy," 133–44; Walsh, "On Christian Atheism," 256.

large extent, held a worldview of religious influence on almost every event in society. Roman society was a highly religious society, which believed that religion controlled the political, economic, and social life, and therefore a destabilization of the religious sphere would mean a destabilization of the society. To this end, since the Christians refrained from offering sacrifice to the gods, it was believed that they would anger the gods and that such anger would bring about natural disasters, famine, pestilence, invasions, or civil war. The perpetrators, therefore, sought to appease the gods by persecuting the Christians. The perceived need to preserve or restore the *pax deorum* in the face of a perceived Christian threat to this relationship with the gods was thus a motivating factor for the persecutions as evident in the martyr texts and the apologetic texts.

Finally, the two types of texts predominantly tried to develop Christian ideologies. The central themes of the martyr texts and the apologetic texts were issues connected to the Christian identity. The texts deal with misconceptions the persecutors had against the Christians that motivated hostilities. The authors of the apologetic texts dealt with Christian beliefs and practices, such as the Eucharist, baptism, Sunday services, conversion, and ethics. They described these beliefs and practices in ways that downplayed the allegations of outsiders and in ways that presented Christianity as attractive.

Nuances

Despite these close similarities between the martyr texts and the apologetic texts, there are nuances in a few instances. These cannot be described as differences but rather similarities with different emphasis. Although they agree about these issues, the different texts put emphasis on one part which the others touch on sparingly.

In the first place, in terms of the allegations leveled against the Christians by the public, the two types of texts agree but with a little divergence. Although the allegations in both texts can be categorized into religious, political, social, and ethical categories, the martyr texts do not emphasize the social allegations, while the apologists do.

Second, the charges in both classes of texts were classified into religious, social, ethical, and political. Among the categories of charges identified in the martyr and apologetic texts; the martyr texts especially stressed the religious and ethical charges but were relatively silent in relation to the social and even political charges. Meanwhile, the apologists confronted all the charges with a little more stress on the political. This seeming twist can be described as a result of the addressees of the texts. Since the martyr texts were predominantly written with a Christian audience in mind, the religious factor must be stressed. On the other hand, since the apologies had a non-Christian audience in mind, the other holistic aspects were stressed with the motive to convert as well as stop the persecution and martyrdom of the early Christians.

Third, concerning the presence of polemics in the texts, both types of texts attacked the public and the authorities. However, there was a stronger and higher number of attacks in the martyr texts. Thus, many of the counterattacks in the texts were directly aimed at the authorities. On the other hand, the apologists attacked the most the Roman gods and the customs or worldview of the Romans. After the Roman gods, many of the attacks were directed toward the public and then the authorities. This slight shift between the texts can best be explained as a result of the intended recipients. This is because it is logical to be less aggressive to a reader of a text especially when the text is in anticipation of something. What it implies is that since the authors of the martyr texts had their fellow Christians in mind, it was right to attack the authorities. Yet the apologists were less blunt in their attacks on the authorities because the aim was for the authorities to be converted and to stop the hostilities – this restraint was most pronounced in the apologies addressed to the authorities. Here, the authors preferred to attack the gods or the customs and the public. The little shift in the direction of the strength of polemics in the martyr and apologetic texts was thus influenced by the intended audiences of the texts.

The martyr texts and the apologetic texts painted a coherent and consistent picture of the plight of the Christians in the Roman Empire in the early years. The comparative elements used in this book have shown that the similarities, apart from corroborating the stories, also have little twists that supplement the accounts in one way or another. The comparative elements shown in these similarities make it clear that to have a comprehensive understanding of the persecution and martyrdom of the Christians, the martyr and apologetic texts should be used in the comparison. When these sources are combined, a comprehensive and conclusive picture of the persecution and martyrdom can be drawn in future studies.

Differences

The account of the persecution and martyrdom of the early Christians as portrayed in the martyr and apologetic texts, when compared, bring to light a few differences which however cannot be described as contradictory but supplementary.

First, while the narrative of the martyr texts was purely narrative, those written in the protocol form focused on the dialogue between the magistrates and martyrs. The narrative martyr texts presented the story of the martyrs following a structure of pre-trial, trial, and post-trial, while the texts of the protocol form focused almost exclusively on the trial. The apologies to the authorities were written in the form of petitions following a well-known pattern and tradition in the Roman Empire for writing such petitions on all kinds of subjects and directing them to the authorities. This slight difference between the texts shows that the intended recipients of the texts influenced the form of the texts and that both the intended recipients and the form influenced the content. While the authors of the martyr texts recorded stories of the martyrs with Christians in mind, the apologists wrote a plea to the non-Christians as their primary audience.

Second, the strategies in these texts were different. Since the narrative martyr texts were mostly narrative in form, the strategy was storytelling. The authors of these texts informed their readers by telling the story of the Christians to the Christian community. However, this is not the case in the apologies. They instead adopted multifaceted approaches in arguing the Christian case. They used philosophical, rhetorical, and religious strategies to convince the authorities and public about Christianity. The methods used by the apologies were well-known and recognized in the Roman Empire and therefore potentially able to convince outside readers. Therefore, there is a divergence between these two classes of texts; while the narrative martyr texts largely used storytelling and the protocol texts dialogue as strategies, the apologists used philosophical and rhetorical strategies to convince their readers.

Finally, there is some divergence, although with a little intersection, between the martyr texts and the apologetic texts in terms of the sources used by these authors. The authors of the martyr texts used Christian sources especially Scriptures. They depended a lot on Scriptures and Christian-authored materials in conveying the Christian stories to the Christians. However, the apologists used both Christian and non-Christian sources. The Christian apologists used Christian sources such as Scriptures and a few other Christian materials but they depended more on non-Christian sources. It was very useful for the apologists to use sources that appealed to the non-Christian Roman public with imperial documents such as Emperor Hadrian's rescript and Trajan's rescript to Pliny. It was also useful for them to appeal to the history of the Romans and philosophy. Their rhetoric finally included references to some recent social occurrences such as eclipses and floods. The approaches used by the apologists were not visibly used by the authors of the martyr texts, showing some divergence of the two classes of texts.

To this end, the form of the texts in terms of the narrative and defense forms, as well as the argumentations of the texts based on their strategy and sources, bring some divergence between the two classes of texts. This implies that although the texts have some similarities, yet there are a few unique aspects that show their originality and boundaries. Irrespective of the fact that these two classes of texts were influenced by the same social circumstance, yet they were influenced by the purpose and addressees of the texts. The various texts talk about the circumstance in different ways. Whereas the writers of the narrative martyr texts used narration and depended on Christian sources to write the story of the martyrs, the apologists wrote a plea using both Christian and non-Christian sources with multifaceted approaches. These differences, instead of contradicting each other, rather supplement one another.

Submission Status of the Apologetic Texts

The question of the submission status of the apologetic texts to the authorities has engaged the minds of many scholars in the study of the Christian apologetic texts. While some scholars believe the authors intended their texts to be read by their addressees, others maintain that the apologies were not intended for submission. These polarized arguments have been going back and forth, while other scholars do not intend to take sides.

Using the systematic comparative method, I attempt to bring to rest these arguments. The major objective of this section is to find out if the authors of the text intended their texts to be read by their addressees especially those addressed to the authorities. The premise of this book is to address this question which is extensively based on the external comparisons of the martyr and apologetic texts. The premise is based on the explicit addresses of the texts since the martyr texts were addressed to a Christian audience while the apologies were addressed to a non-Christian audience. Therefore, if both texts were talking about the same phenomena of the persecution and martyrdom of the Christians, there may be some similarities and differences in the texts. Hence, if the accounts were nearly very similar, then the apologists likely did not intend their non-Christian addressees to read their texts but applied such addresses to heighten interest in the texts, as the scholars who believe they were not meant to be submitted maintain. On the other hand, if there is substantial agreement on the main picture of how, why and by whom the Christians were persecuted, but with some important differences in how and why this was described and in how the authors argued and presented their case, then it would be logical to argue that the authors had different aims and audiences in mind, that the apologies addressed to outsiders wanted to reach this outside audience (hence the nuanced differences). It will be equally logical to argue that the two kinds of texts reflected the same context of persecution (hence the major overlap and agreement in the picture the two kinds of texts painted of these persecutions). This premise as adopted in this book is already answered in the external comparison of the martyr and apologetic texts with the persecution and martyrdom of the early Christians in the mid-second to the early third centuries of the Roman Empire.

The premise that near-total similarity in these texts would suggest a non-submission while overlaps with a few nuanced but telling differences would suggest a possible submission, is applied in this section of the study. It is clear from the discussions above that the apologies were intended to be submitted to the non-Christian audience, especially those to the authorities. The apologies were intended to be read by the addressees, particularly those addressed to the authorities, and they were analyzed in four elements: the form of the texts, accusations, sources of the texts, and the polemic contents of the texts. The comparison of the martyr and apologetic texts through these elements suggest that the apologetic texts were meant to receive the attention of their addressees, particularly the authorities, to stop the hostilities against the Christians and to convert the addressees.

First and foremost, based on the form and explicit addressees of the texts being different yet influenced by the same time and context, it seems that the apologists wanted outsiders to read their texts. Comparing the apologetic texts with the martyr texts, it is clear that the authors were members of the same communities and witnessed the same kinds of persecutions, but they chose different forms and addressees in their texts. The narrative forms appealed to the Christians and their needs because the authors wanted to encourage and have a record of Christian history. These purposes are very much attained by using stories to show the agonies of the martyrs to encourage the other Christians and to know why there is a need to celebrate such heroic characters of the faith.

However, to convert and stop the persecutions, the non-Christians were not likely to be influenced much by stories but rather a method appealing to their sensibilities in their own ways. The apologies were aimed at influencing outsiders. The authors knew Roman society and culture and argued philosophically, rhetorically, and legally especially to those in authority. These forms are typical examples of the saying: "when you go to Rome, do as the Romans do." Therefore, the apologists who wanted their texts to be read by their addressees adopted means that were familiar and highly appealing to the non-Christians, different from the forms used by the authors of the martyr texts. The apologists that addressed their texts to emperors or magistrates, therefore, submitted these apologies and intended them to be read.

Second, based on the twists in the accusations and thus the allegations and charges, there is every reason to suggest that the apologists hoped that their texts were going to be read by their addressees. The martyr texts stressed the religious accusations while the apologies were rather systematic in stressing both religious and political accusations which have ethical as well as sociological consequences. The emphases show the interest of the authors and their intention regarding readership. Since the martyr texts were targeted toward Christian readers, the religious aspects of the charges were of utmost importance, and indeed, the Christians were primarily killed for being Christians. Therefore, their aim was to encourage Christian readers to religiously keep the Christian faith. However, the apologists wrote to the authorities and public who were more interested, apart from the religious situation, in the political, social, and ethical fabric of the society. The apologists, therefore, met the demand of the addressees by clearing the Christians of the political, social, and ethical accusations apart from the religious accusations which the narratives also deal with. This differentiation between the martyr texts and the apologetic texts in terms of the accusations shows that the apologists were influenced by the thoughts of the non-Christians. The comprehensive nature of the accusations on the apologetic materials would have been not only to generate interest in the texts but also so that their addressees would read them and be influenced.

Third, it can be argued that the apologies were intended for submission based on the sources used in the two classes of texts. Owing to the variety of purposes and factors which pushed for the writing of these texts, multiple and various sources were employed by the authors of these texts. The martyr texts relied deeply on Christian sources especially Scripture, which was well known to the Christians besides being the source of their ideology. It would certainly be interesting if the apologies also used more scriptural materials in their texts. In this case, it would be plain that the apologists did not intend their texts to be read by the addressees because those Scriptures were not as relevant to the non-Christians as to the Christians. However, although being Christians, the Christian apologists certainly made some scriptural references but these were not dominant compared to their usage in the martyr texts. The apologetic texts rather depended more on texts that appealed to the non-Christians such as imperial documents like Emperor Hadrian's rescript, Tertullian's reference to Pliny and Trajan, as well as philosophical and Roman historical materials. All this was intended to make an impact on the addressees. This difference between the martyr texts and the apologetic texts can best be explained if we take seriously that the authors of the martyr texts had Christian readers in mind, whereas the apologists aimed at non-Christian readers.

Last but not least, the elements in the external comparison of the martyr and apologetic texts which show that the apologies were hopeful that they would be read by the addressees are based on the polemic content of the texts. Although Evans suggests strongly that the texts intended to be read by non-Christians employ more polemics compared to those to be read by Christians,[8] it is rather more logical in this class of texts to argue that if the authors intended the readers to appreciate the text, the authors were less likely to attack the readers. This was influenced by the aim of the text. Since the apologists wished that the hostilities were halted, when they wrote to those who could stop it (the authorities), the text must appeal to their conscience rather than being aggressive toward them. In comparing the level of apologies

---

8. Evans, "On the Problem of Church," 21–36.

in the martyr and apologetic texts, it is clear that the martyr texts heavily attacked the authorities of the empire. Meanwhile, the apologies attacked the gods and the Roman system, especially their customs and worldview before attacking the public and only after which they attacked the authorities who could stop the persecutions. It was the intention of the apologies to have their audience read them and that was why the apologists did not attack the authorities more in their texts, but since the authorities were less likely to read the martyr texts, the polemic attacks against the authorities abound.

Given the form of the texts, accusations, sources, and the polemic aspects of the martyr and apologetic texts, it is evident that the addressees were expected to read these texts. The authors of the apologetic texts consciously employed elements that were appealing and attractive to the non-Christians. It suggests strongly that the apologists looked forward to reaching the non-Christians, principally the authorities, with these texts. They made use of the standard practice of the time by writing such texts not just addressed to the non-Christians. Because of the foregoing analysis, I find that the authors did not apply the addressees to these texts to create significance for the texts but consciously adopted elements that were more Roman than Christian in the content to meet the standard of the audience they addressed.

Conclusion

The martyr and apologetic texts certainly represented different reactions and reflections on the persecution and martyrdom of the early Christians in the Roman Empire. Although they had strong appeal to different audiences, the martyr texts mostly aimed at Christians and the apologies most clearly aimed at non-Christians, they had overlaps in terms of the authors' perspectives, and these may have been intended overlaps.[9]

Finally, the authors may have intended Christian readers to use the arguments provided in the apologetic texts in debates with outsiders. Thus, there were also overlapping purposes between the martyr texts and apologetic texts: to encourage the Christians, establish their identity and history while equipping them to debate with outsiders using the texts, their arguments, or their stories as evangelistic tools to convert the non-Christians and stop the

---

9. Boamah, "Apologetic and Martyr Text," 46–48.

hostilities against the Christians. Many scholars over the years have mostly depended on the martyr texts to explore the persecution of the Christians. However, I have shown the usefulness of the apologetic texts in understanding the plight of the early Christians in the second and third centuries of the Roman Empire. The two classes of texts corroborate and supplement each other on the persecution and martyrdom of the early Christians.

This conclusion affirms Judith Lieu's thesis that since the martyr and apologetic texts were influenced by the same social setting, they were very similar in many respects and seldom contradicted each other.[10] The external comparisons of the texts which are derived from the internal comparison show that the texts were very similar in most ways but with little differentiation when compared to each other. The twists and differences in the texts did not contradict each other but rather emphasized the blinded or blurred sides of each other, thereby providing a comprehensive picture of the hostilities when used together.

This systematic comparison has also helped to address the submission status of the apologetic texts, particularly those addressed to the authorities. The submission status of the texts is tackled using the few twists and differences between the texts, as clear evidence that the authors intended to have their texts read by their addressees to stop the hostilities and, even more importantly, convert them to Christianity. All in all, the martyr and apologetic texts are both useful for a comprehensive picture of the persecution and martyrdom of the early Christians in the Roman Empire during the late-second to the mid-third centuries as they corroborate and supplement each other.

---

10. Lieu, "Audience of Apologetics," 208–23.

CHAPTER SIX

Epilogue

The early Christians suffered a great deal in the Roman Empire. Though a religious group, they were perceived to be a threat to the political sect. These hostilities influenced the writing of two sets of texts by the Christians: martyr and apologetic texts. These texts have their targeted audiences and specific aims. However, a majority of scholars studying the persecutions have largely depended on the martyr texts and the texts written by pagans about the Christians. However, to a limited degree, the apologetic texts have also been used in this context, but Sherwin-White has criticized their use as distorting.[1] The apologetic texts have mainly been analyzed with other questions in mind, for example, the development of Christian theology, canon-formation, the relationship between Christianity and philosophy, argumentative strategies, etc.[2] Yet, since these two types of texts are influenced by the context of the hostilities, it is prudent to compare the picture that the two types of texts project. A comparison of the picture emerging from a class of texts with the other will also help appreciate the usefulness of the two classes of texts as sources for the study of the persecution and martyrdom of the early Christians.

The martyr texts gave either narrative depictions or they focused on the dialogue between martyrs and magistrates in court. No martyr texts leave room for elaborate apologetic discussions, where the charges were refuted or where Christian habits, rituals, or doctrines were explained. In contrast, the last two aspects were the focus of the apologetic texts. The martyr texts focused mostly on the procedure and charges against the victim but did

---

1. Sherwin-White, "Why Were the Early Christians?" 23.
2. Ulrich, "Apologists and Apologetics," 1–34.

not contain reflective and comprehensive responses of the victim, which the apologies largely provided. Generally, most scholars have analyzed the plight of Christians in the Roman Empire, especially in terms of the persecution and martyrdom, by largely depending on the martyr and pagan texts as well as New Testament sources, and using apologetic texts very minimally. This has left gaps in the picture of the persecution and martyrdom of the early Christians since this approach focuses little attention on the apologetic texts. The gap is created because the martyr texts do not reflect the reaction of the Christians to the charges, although natural law makes provision to listen to the reaction of the accused, which the apologetic texts do. Again, scholars have not attempted to systematically compare the hostilities against the Christians as portrayed in the martyr texts to that which the apologists present to evaluate the usefulness of the apologetic texts to the phenomena of the hostilities. Such a comparison could reveal whether the picture emerging from the study of the martyr texts is corroborated, supplemented, or even contradicted.

With regard to the recipients and readership of the apologetic texts, some scholars argue that some apologists addressed their texts to the authorities for literary purposes such as making the texts seem more interesting. Other scholars do not agree with this but maintain that writing such notes to the authorities at the time was a standard way to communicate with them.

The objective of the book was to examine the image of the persecution and martyrdom of the early Christians as portrayed in the martyr and apologetic texts as well as the relevance of these texts to Ghanaian Christianity. This was segmented as:

1. To weigh against each other, the portrait of the hostilities presented in the apologetic texts as corroborative, supplementary, or contradictive to the martyr narratives.
2. To establish the submission status of the apologies.
3. To explore some examples of persecution and martyrdom in Ghanaian Christian history especially during the missionary period.
4. To assess if lessons from the martyr and apologetic texts are relevant for the Ghanaian Christians in dealing with suffering today.

Epilogue

This concluding chapter of the project summarizes the issues raised in this book guided by the objectives and research questions. In the first place, the discussion of the purpose and audiences of the texts is summarized, and then the similarities and differences between the two classes of texts are highlighted. The attention of this chapter is to further bring together the various arguments on the submission status of the apologies and eventually, lessons from the various texts to help African Christians deal with current predicaments of suffering are reflected upon. Finally, this chapter concludes by putting forward a few recommendations for future studies.

Purpose and Audience of the Martyr and Apologetic Texts

The purpose and audience of the texts certainly helped to appreciate the motivation of the authors of the texts.[3] In this light, it is concluded that the martyr texts were directed toward the Christians but with some attention on the non-Christians. The martyr texts were predominantly directed toward the Christian audience to encourage them in the faith, construct their communal identity, and recollect their history, apart from serving as an evangelistic tool to win the non-Christians. The apologetic texts, though inherently useful to the Christian community, were directly addressed to the non-Christian community. The intentions were to dispel allegations, correct misunderstandings and false rumors, explain Christian rituals, practices, and beliefs, and most ambitiously, to make outside readers favorably disposed toward the Christians, even perhaps converting them. Therefore, both texts were written to a predominantly different category of readers; the martyr texts generally to Christians while the apologetic texts appealed more to non-Christians (implying those in authority and the broad-spectrum of the public) but with a strong Christian community readership in mind. This in essence implies that the two classes of texts, despite their appeals, met at an intersection of Christian readers.

There were differences and similarities in the purposes and intended audiences of the two kinds of texts. They sought to encourage the Christian community (apologetic texts and martyr texts), to make converts of the

---

3. Boamah, "Apologetic and Martyr Text," 30–53.

non-Christians (apologetic texts), construct the Christian identity (apologetic texts and martyr texts), and ultimately halt the hostilities against the Christians in the Roman Empire (apologetic texts). These similarities in the motivations and purposes of the texts suggest their contents may be corroborative and supplementary, while the differences in motivations, intended audiences, and purposes suggest supplementary depictions of the persecution and martyrdom of the early Christians.

The comparisons of the depictions in the two kinds of texts are mostly similar, which is ascribed to the similar context out of which the texts grew and their overlapping purposes, and so lend credence to the general trustworthiness of their depictions. On the other hand, the differences in the pictures are found based on the different audiences (the martyr texts aimed almost exclusively at a Christian audience, the apologetic texts at both a Christian and an outside audience). In essence, the general permeating similarities seasoned by nuanced differences between the depictions in martyr texts compared to the apologetic texts, point to the trustworthiness of the pictures. This suggestion is built on the logical inquisitiveness that there are some similarities and possible differences between the two classes of texts.

Findings – Martyr and Apologetic Texts Compared

My findings in this book are generated based on the objectives and research questions of the study, influenced by the methodological approach in attaining the goals of the study.

The Usefulness of Apologetic Texts

In addressing the first objective and research question regarding the usefulness of the apologetic texts as corroborative, supplementary, or even contradictory to the martyr texts, the systematic comparison helps to arrive at an answer. It is clear from the analysis that the apologetic texts are corroborative and supplementary to the martyr texts rather than contradictory on the subject of the persecution and martyrdom of the early Christians in the Roman mid-second to early third Roman centuries.

Internally, a comparison of the narrative martyr texts to the protocol accounts clearly shows that the two styles of martyr texts are greatly corroborative with permeating similarities seasoned by nuanced differences related to the styles in which the two types of martyr texts were written. The similarities are evident in terms of the identity and motives of the persecutors, the legal process used, the allegations, charges and the demands of the authorities and the forms of persecution. This general agreement lends credence to their depictions as reflecting a historical reality.

Notwithstanding these similarities, there are few nuances. Some of the few peculiarities are because of the order of events, the character of the persecutors, and the apologetic contents of the texts. It is argued that these nuances do not contradict but rather supplement each other. The peculiarities show the influence of the style of the text on what should go into the content of the text. Thus, a protocol form does not have the time to include what happened before the arrest of the martyrs or the events after the martyrs are killed but rather focuses more on the interaction between the authorities and the martyrs.

Internal comparison of the apologetic texts addressed to the authorities and those addressed to the public equally shows some major similarities. These similarities include the narrative content, character of the martyrs, identity of the persecutor, motives, procedure, demand, form of the persecution, among others. These major unities concerning the depiction of the persecution and martyrdom again lend credence to the idea that the texts have grown out of and do reflect real persecutions. However, there are a few important nuanced differences between the two categories of apologetic texts that are influenced by the intended readers of the texts. The peculiarities are in the areas of accusations, defense strategies, sources, and polemics among others. The interesting issue is that the nuances or peculiarities do not contradict each other but rather supplement one another.

It has been argued that the peculiarities are a result of the addressees of the texts, thus those addressed to the public built more on social accusations while those aimed at the authorities dealt with political accusations. That is not to suggest the apologetic texts addressed to the authorities did not deal with social charges but that the emphasis or most of the accusations were captured in political terms and vice versa. This is why they are called nuances or peculiarities in this book. These nuances are seen to be of supplementary value because if scholars depend on a text that is addressed toward the authorities, the conclusions are likely to be skewed; therefore, collaborative use of the two types of the apologetic texts will offer a holistic picture as projected by the apologetic texts. Additionally, the few peculiarities also help to address the submission status of the apologetic texts addressed to the authorities which will be discussed after this subtopic. Therefore, the two types of apologetic texts equally present a corroborative and supplementary picture to each other regarding the persecution and martyrdom of the early Christians.

Externally, the martyr and apologetic texts develop a coherent and consistent picture of the predicaments of the early Christians in the Roman Empire. The comparative elements have shown that while the similarities between the texts corroborate their accounts, the nuances are of supplementary value. The corroborative similarities point to the usefulness of the apologetic texts as sources to the study of the persecution and martyrdom of the early Christians. This implies that, to a large extent, Sherwin-White is wrong to suggest that the apologetic texts are not useful in a discussion on the persecution and martyrdom of the early Christians. On the other hand, the supplementary nuances between the martyr and apologetic texts point to the fact that not only are the apologetic texts useful but imply that the two texts need to be synchronized for a comprehensive picture of the hostilities against the Christians to emerge.

Further studies of the persecution and martyrdom of the early Christians should of course still pay diligent attention to the texts written by non-Christians about the Christians. There is a gap in scholarship because of the failure to adequately appreciate the importance of also studying the elaborate and reflected defense offered for Christianity in the martyr narratives and apologetic texts, thereby making the picture of the hostilities incomplete. However, when the apologetic sources are included in these traditional sources, a comprehensive picture of the persecution and martyrdom may emerge.

Submission Status of the Apologetic Texts

The second objective and research question seeks to ascertain the possibility or otherwise of the submission status of the apologies. As suggested in the introductory chapter, the similarities and differences or nuances in the texts are likely to help address the submission status of the apologies to the authorities. The comparative elements used in this systematic comparison of the texts internally and externally help to define that at the very least, the texts were intended for the authorities' consumption.

The internal comparison of the apologetic texts addressed to the authorities and those addressed to the public suggests that the apologists certainly wanted the authorities to read their works. The texts addressed to the authorities dealt with more legal matters as compared to the texts addressed to the public. The authorities were likely to be more interested in legal issues rather than the public. Further, there is a strong polemic content in both categories of apologetic texts. There are however nuanced differences in the priority or focus of the polemic. Those addressed to the authorities did not attack the authorities much, instead they attacked the Roman gods and system as well as the public more. This is crucial because the apologists wanted to be more favorable to the authorities who can stop the hostilities when they read their texts, therefore the need to attack them less.

The external comparison of the martyr and apologetic texts equally concludes that the apologists intended their texts to be read by the authorities. The principle is that if the martyr and apologetic texts were similar in every way, then the texts addressed to the authorities were not intended for submission but if there were differences in certain specified nuances, then the texts were intended to receive the attention of the authorities. The basis of this principle suggests that since the readers of the martyr texts were expected to be different from the apologetic texts, the content and style of the texts when compared must exhibit some differences even if they were both talking about the same thing. The comparative elements in the first place show that apart from the form and addresses of the texts being different, the accusations were also different. Thus, while the martyr texts dealt more with religious accusations, the apologetic texts focused more on political and ethical accusations.

Second, the sources cited by the various authors in the different texts also show some differences. The martyr texts largely depended on Christian sources especially Scriptures while the apologetic texts used both Christian (although not many scriptural texts) and even more importantly non-Christian Roman sources.

A third important difference between the martyr and apologetic texts is the argumentative strategy employed in the text. This is interesting because while the apologetic texts used philosophical, rhetorical, and religious strategies, the martyr texts used storytelling or dialogue form as their strategy to portray the story of the hostilities against the early Christians.

Finally, the level and direction of polemics in the martyr and apologetic texts are different. While the apologetic texts abound in polemic and largely direct these attacks to the Roman gods and system as well as the public, the few attacks in the martyr texts were largely directed toward the authorities. This is fascinating because the explicit addressees of the martyr texts were the Christians so the authors were free to attack the authorities.

Therefore, the form of the texts, accusations, source, and the polemic aspects of the martyr and apologetic texts suggest that the apologies were intended to be read by their outside addressees. The authors of the apologetic texts intentionally adopted elements that were appealing to the non-Christians because of their explicit readers. To a large extent therefore, unlike what some scholars maintain, the apologists did not apply the addressees to these texts to heighten the significance of the texts. They rather consciously chose elements that were more Roman than Christian in content to meet the standard of their audience, particularly the authorities. It is therefore argued that the texts were strongly intended to receive the attention of the authorities especially by addressing the texts to them.

In view of the conclusion on the usefulness of the apologetic texts to the subject of the persecution and martyrdom of the early Christians in the Roman Empire, it is evident that they are of corroborative and supplementary value. This usefulness has also helped to define the submission status of the apologies. It is therefore imperative to review the significance of the subject of the persecution and martyrdom of the early Christians to how the modern African Christians can deal with suffering based on how the early Christians sustained the situation. The link between the two contexts is necessary because they both exhibit the beginning of Christianity in a new environment where there was an already established religious worldview of the people. The historic reality of the contexts provides a basis for contemporary Christians because there cannot be experience without history so that history will serve as a guide for contemporary followers of the faith. On the subject of the persecution and martyrdom of the early Christians, it is without doubt that suffering is indeed a universal element and a composite part of the Christian calling. Therefore, since the founder of the faith suffered and the early apostles including the church fathers suffered, contemporary Christians are also likely to suffer. Yet, the most important part of the issue of suffering is how a person will be able to endure it. In most cases, examples of how others have overcome similar predicaments will serve as precedence for contemporary Christians, thus helping them to understand how others have faced the same thing. Therefore, how the early Christians endured those predicaments will help the Christians today who continuously face similar challenges to adopt those same strategies to overcome current challenges.

The Texts and Contemporary Ghanaian Christianity

The third and fourth objectives and research questions that seek to show the relevance of the subject of the persecution and martyrdom as well as the relevance of these texts to African Christianity today are explored in chapter two.

The subject of the persecution and martyrdom of the early Christians is not only a Roman or European ideology but African too. In the first instance, the Roman Empire encompassed some African territories where some of the accounts used in this book were recorded on Roman African soils. The account of the persecution and martyrdom of Perpetua and Felicity as well as the accounts of the Scillitan martyrs were both recorded in African societies. Additionally, Tertullian was an African from Carthage who wrote extensively about some of the predicaments against the early Christians.

Furthermore, the modern African environment is not insulated from various sufferings and discomforts suffered by Christians as a result of their faith. Examples of the subject of the persecution and martyrdom of the early Christians can be found in the modern African era, most especially during the missionary times. Many of the European missionaries accepted to come to the African region knowing very well that they might not survive. They suffered due to the environment including the weather, therefore only a few survived more than two years. On the other hand, it was not only the European missionaries who suffered but also the African missionaries and agents equally suffered a great deal for the sake of the gospel. The examples from Mamfe, and Samuel Otu and his wife of the Presbyterian Church of Ghana are widely known. There are other examples such as William deGraft who suffered imprisonment and loss of privileges for the sake of their Christian convictions. The Christians even today including Ghanaians suffer various degrees of excruciating pain because of their Christian beliefs. It is therefore prudent to learn from the examples of the early church in dealing with similar challenges today. The Ghanaian today can learn a great deal from how the early church was able to contain those challenging periods of its growth to deal with contemporary hostilities against the Christian faith.

The church today and the Ghanaian Christians, for that matter, must accept the inevitability of suffering as part of the Christian calling. The martyr and apologetic texts teach the Christians today to learn to record their history to help succeeding generations remember their heroes. Furthermore, the early Christians did not see the hostilities as an individual predicament but a collective challenge and therefore stood in solidarity with those suffering, knowing it was an attack on the entire Christian community. The courage of the early Christians in the face of death is worthy of emulation by the African Christians. They did not run away in the face of death but rather stood their ground in defense of their faith. These Christians enviably did not cling to "action begets reaction" but restrained themselves, even though they could have retaliated in equal measure by committing the same kind of violence against their persecutors. These are commendable steps that the African Christians can learn from these texts concerning dealing with suffering today.

The texts are therefore very significant to help Ghanaians deal with current predicaments of suffering as the Christians faced in the Roman Empire. The Ghanaian Christians today can learn a great deal from these texts to deal with current challenges such as social justice. Since the questions are answered by the systematic comparative approach, it is crucial to make a few recommendations for scholarly considerations. These recommendations are made based on the texts and are aimed toward the future of scholarship on the persecution and martyrdom of the Christians.

Lessons for Contemporary Ghanaian Christianity

The incidences of the persecution and martyrdom of the early Christians as presented in the martyr and the apologetic texts have important lessons for Christians today with regard to dealing with suffering. Christians today are faced with some form of persecution or discomfort as a result of their faith; these texts are useful in dealing with such issues. Although international organizations will not sanction horrific punishment such as condemning people to die at the hands of carnivorous animals even if those victims are notorious criminals, the subject of the persecution and martyrdom is ongoing. Many Christians today suffer discomfort, discrimination, and abuse as a result of their faith. As Jesus told his disciples in John 15:18–25, the world will persecute Christians because the world does not know them for Christians are not of this world. And so, he encouraged them to take heart and stand firm. It is therefore prudent to learn from those who have suffered and overcame.

It implies adopting the strategies used by the forerunners in dealing with current and similar predicaments. Romans 15:4 (RSV) says, "For whatever was written in former days was written for our instruction, that by steadfastness and by the encouragement of the scriptures, we might have hope." Paul's words here make analysis of the relevance of the texts to Christian situations imperative. Although he made this statement about Scripture, it is not limited to Scripture because of the beginning statement "For whatever was written in former days was written for our instruction." I have argued elsewhere that scriptures in most cases are generated from a group of texts and possibly from scripture which may find its place in a canon.[4] It can also be argued that to some extent, particularly based on the account of the martyrdom of Polycarp, these martyr texts were used as scriptures to encourage other Christians.[5]

Christians today the world over, including Ghanaians, can learn a great deal from the accounts of these martyrs which were recorded by the apologists and the martyrologists. Christians today must learn to record their histories, stand in solidarity with fellow Christians in their sufferings, recount the histories to succeeding generations from time to time, and also show courage in the face of adversities. These and many other lessons come out clearly from the martyr and apologetic texts which Christians today can emulate, in their bid to deal with situations of suffering.

Recording History

It is prudent for Christians today to learn to document their history for the benefit of succeeding generations. It has already been argued in chapters three and four that the martyr and apologetic texts are a record of history. The apologetic texts are described as historical since they describe things that happened at a particular time during the reign of a particular emperor. This is clearly evident in Tertullian's apology to Scapula, in chapters four and five which present the history of how some emperors treated the Christians and the consequences it had on their lives.[6]

These accounts record the happenings and plights of Christians who lived in the Roman Empire from the first to about the third centuries. Furthermore,

---

4. Boamah, "Making of a Canon," 8–11.
5. Martyrdom of Polycarp, 1; Martyrdom of Perpetua, 1:2.
6. Tertullian, *Ad Scapulam*, 3, 4.

the account of the martyrdom of Polycarp opens with the statement: "We are writing to you, dear brothers, the story of the martyrs."[7] Eventually, the authors of the account stated that the writing of this history was prompted by the recipients' request for recording the account of what happened.[8] This suggests that the account was a pure recounting of the history of the Christians to fellow Christians. The accounts of the martyrdom of Justin and his companions as well as the Scillitan martyrs, can similarly be described as historical documents because they both situate the accounts on a particular date by identifying the authority at the time of their writing.[9] The account of Perpetua and Felicity is not any less a historical account, as it contains the personal memoirs of martyrs in chapters three to thirteen while the others were added by an editor.[10] What would have encouraged martyrs to personally record their plights, if not to record their histories? What would encourage an editor to pick someone's memoir and provide a framework of introduction and conclusion, if not to compose it as a historical work for fellow Christians? The martyr and apologetic texts are, to a large extent, historical accounts of the pains of the Christians in the early church.

Christians today must learn to record their history for future generations to benefit from what happened to their predecessors. This is very important particularly to the African Christians because very few records are kept by Ghanaian Christians about their past.[11]

The church today must learn from the recording of the plight of the Christians in the Roman Empire. It is not to say that these two texts are sacrosanct historical records, because the texts have some challenges. They are nevertheless useful records of past events which could have been

---

7. Martyrdom of Polycarp, 1:1.
8. Martyrdom of Polycarp, 20.
9. Martyrdom of Justin, 1 (all recensions); Scillitan Martyrs, 1.
10. Musurillo, *Acts of the Christian Martyrs*, xxv.
11. As a part of our studies when I was a student, we were to write a term paper of the history of churches in Ghana which are about a hundred years old using sources such as old preaching journals and announcement books. Students faced a lot of problems because the few churches which are in this range do not either have the documents to write their history or what they have is shallow and inadequate. There was a church where a minister had committed to flames old preachers' diaries kept by the church, cradle roll, announcement books and other past documents because they were past records considered no longer useful today. In another church, the archival room was in shambles because the documents were heaped on the floor in a room under lock and key. Interestingly, no one knew who had the keys.

lost completely if they had not been written down. The church today and Ghanaian Christians must learn to record their history for generations yet unborn to know what happened. This will provide encouragement and a blueprint for actions tomorrow.

Communalism/Solidarity

There is an Akan adage, "sɛ wokɔto sɛ abowa bi te wo nuaso a, nka sɛ sɔre ne so, na mmom sɔreyɛn so," which can be translated as, "if you see a beast on your brother, don't say get off him, but rather get off us." This idea is built on the principle of communalism or solidarity. There is a need to see the threat of suffering against other Christians as a threat against the entire Christian fraternity and therefore the need to stand in solidarity against a common enemy. It can be inferred from the martyr and apologetic texts that the early Christians stood in solidarity with the martyrs in their most difficult moments. The apologists wrote to their addressees to defend the case of the Christians. At the time of writing, the apologists did not suffer the pains themselves but they took the pain in all solidarity to stand with their fellow Christians who were suffering. The apologists used pronouns such as "we, me, I" showing their identification with the martyrs.[12] They showed their solidarity by identifying themselves with the martyrs without fear of being arrested and martyred too. Tertullian was very fascinated with identifying himself with the smeared Christians. He preferred to be associated with the martyrs to the extent that he encouraged voluntary martyrs.[13] He even threatened the emperor that if the oppressors were not careful, the surviving Christians would give themselves up for martyrdom in solidarity because there were many more Christians than the emperor might think.[14]

In the account of the martyrdom of Polycarp, the church did not desert him. When he fled into exile, there were still some Christians with him in his place of exile[15] and when he died from the fire, the Christians wanted to take his body for burial.[16] The church was so eager to bury him that even

---

12. Tatian, *Ad Graecos*, 10:1; 11:1.
13. Tertullian, *Ad Scapulam*, 5:2.
14. Tertullian, 5:3–4.
15. Martyrdom of Polycarp, 7:2–3.
16. Martyrdom of Polycarp, 17:1–2.

when he was cremated, the church in solidarity still wanted to bury his ashes remarking that "collecting the remains that were dearer to us than precious stones and finer than gold, we buried them in a fitting spot."[17] It can be argued that based on the style of writing, especially by quoting the direct words of Polycarp and the governor, the authors and possibly many other Christians walked with him to witness the entire trial from his arrest to cremation and did not betray him. The church showed solidarity, reverence, and support for Polycarp in his difficult moments. In the case of the Scillitan martyrs, the way the account is written shows that the other Christians did not desert the martyrs when they were arrested. In the account of the martyrdom of Perpetua and her companions, the Christians visited them in prison[18] and celebrated a Christian ceremony called a love feast with them.[19] The church was in solidarity with these martyrs every step of the way. In the account of the martyrdom of Justin and his companions, the Christians even had to secretly steal the corpse for burial.[20]

Christians today in their workplaces, homes, and other places need to stand in solidarity with fellow Christians who go through difficulties as a result of their faith. Sometimes owing to denominationalism, when Christians are struggling because of their faith, the others would rather disassociate themselves because their faith traditions are different. Christians should see the persecution of other Christians as an enemy that requires concerted and communal efforts from all in-group members. It is quite possible to find Christians putting up solidarity messages on social media such as Facebook, WhatsApp, and other platforms such as these, but they will not show this solidarity in person. Many Christians today are likely to be quiet when other Christians are maltreated in the workplace for fear of being victimized but that was not the way the early church faced the persecution and martyrdom. If such solidarity could come in the way of the hostilities, it could encourage the victims to face their difficulties while getting some motivation to endure. The early church stood by the martyrs in solidarity affirming that the attack on their personhood was an attack on the whole Christian faith, hence like

---

17. Martyrdom of Polycarp, 18.
18. Martyrdom of Perpetua, 9:1.
19. Martyrdom of Perpetua, 17:1.
20. Martyrdom of Justin, 6 (recension B and C).

the Akan adage, the other Christians must show solidarity in fighting the common enemy.

Recount History to the Generations

Just like the account of the martyrdom of Polycarp which was requested by the church,[21] Christians today must know about what others have suffered to establish the church today. The Philomilium church certainly wanted others to know and remember such characters and celebrate them; the recorders of the account therefore included the exact date of the martyrdom as 23rd February and the specific time as "two o'clock in the afternoon" on a Sabbath day.[22] These details were recorded to help the churches set aside such days for the celebration of these heroes and heroines of the church. This is very crucial for the growth of the church because future generations must be told of what earlier church heroes and heroines have done for the growth of the faith.

The account of persecution and martyrdom faced by the early church is a great lesson for the church today to reminisce so that the flames of yesteryears will continue to glow knowing where the church has come from. Among the various church traditions, the Catholic and Anglican churches are quite focused on celebrating heroes and heroines of the early church. There are celebration days for some of these martyrs and even more, 1st November is celebrated as "All Saints Day" to reminisce the canonical saints while 2nd November is "All Souls Day" to commemorate dead family members. However, some Methodists and Presbyterians celebrate only "All Saints Day." In some Methodist traditions, the early church fathers are not even mentioned, members of the church bring in names of their dead family members and these names are mentioned during the All Saints Day worship service as a way to remember them.[23] This is why only the ministers know the names of church heroes and heroines because they study about them at the seminary but they do not educate the congregation about them. The leadership of

---

21. Martyrdom of Polycarp, 20.
22. Martyrdom of Polycarp, 21.
23. We named our first son Polycarp owing to the inspiration from the account of the martyrdom of Polycarp. Many friends and family members kept asking what the name means and where we got that name from. It is interesting that apart from my Catholic friends and Methodist reverend ministers, all other persons had never heard the name Polycarp. This case in point shows how little the African Christian today knows about the early Christians.

the churches must celebrate heroes/heroines of the church similarly to the Catholic Church and teach congregations about the contributions of these early Christians who gave their lives and blood for the sake of the church. The church can do well to honor such great persons who planted the church with their blood, for they deserve to be remembered and commemorated.

The Courage of the Martyrs

The most easily identifiable character trait of the martyrs was their courage. The martyrs showed a lot of courage and were without fear even in the face of death. They were not afraid to die and even in the presence of the authorities of the Roman Emperor, they did not hesitate to speak in the face of death. The courage of the martyrs in many respects has been labeled as obstinacy which was one of the major reasons for their persecution and martyrdom.[24] When they were threatened with death, the martyrs stood resolute. For instance, when Polycarp was asked to swear by the emperor's genius, he responded: "if you delude yourself into thinking that I will swear by the emperor's genius as you say, and if you pretend not to know who I am, listen and I will tell you plainly: I am a Christian."[25] Tertullian threatened the governor that the emperor would not stand it if all the other Christians came forward to declare their faith because they were not afraid of death.[26] The early Christians would not recant their faith just to escape death but stood prepared, ready to die.

Christians must stand resolute in the face of temptation or during suffering. Many Christians may want to avoid some uncomfortable situation by denying their faith so that they may escape suffering. There are many Christians who have chosen to compromise their faith on anything that came against it in their workplaces, families, etc. In contrast, the early Christians, instead of recanting to save themselves, stood strong in the faith for what they believed in without giving up.

Restrain over Reaction

The courage of the early Christians is a crucial lesson to learn because it shows how Christians should respond in the face of suffering. Christians in

---

24. Boamah, *Magic and Obstinacy*, 16; Engberg, *Impulsore Chresto*, 191–93.
25. Martyrdom of Polycarp, 10:1.
26. Tertullian, *Ad Scapulam*, 5:2–5.

the face of suffering have to decide between restraint and reaction. This is a critical decision to make because when a person is hit, it is natural for the person to retaliate especially when he or she feels they are not treated justly. Many African countries including Ghana are now multireligious societies and African Christians face the increasing need to defend their faith well in the face of opposition and persecution from people of other religions.

The accounts of the martyr narratives and the apologetic texts show that the early Christians did not respond to the violence against them with an equal measure of violence. They rather resorted to writing to restrain other believers from taking to the streets to deal vengefully against the non-Christians. They also wrote to the authorities and the general public to plead the case of the Christians. The early Christians restrained themselves when they were persecuted and martyred by the non-Christians. The African Christians today need to learn from this example by restraining and not reacting in like manner when responding to their persecutors.

Commendations

Based on the findings of this study, I want to take the opportunity to make a few commendations for scholarly consideration. These appraisals are organized under academic and pastoral levels in addressing the issues.

Academically, scholarship on the persecution and martyrdom of the early Christians must employ both martyr and apologetic text sources – along, of course, with the texts written by non-Christian authors about the Christians. As evident from the systematic comparison of the martyr and apologetic texts, the two classes of texts do not only corroborate but, more significantly, supplement each other on the hostilities against the early Christians. This conclusion suggests that if the martyr texts are used alone, the defense of the martyrs would be lost, whereas where the apologetics is used alone, the development of the accusations and their maltreatment would be lost. However, when the two are used together, a fuller story of the Christian perspective on the persecution and martyrdom of the early Christians will be captured, thus making the approach more satisfactory from a scholarly perspective. To this end, it is prudent to use both classes of texts for a comprehensive picture of the plight of the Christians in the Roman early second to mid-third centuries as presented by the Christians.

Furthermore, I strongly suggest that African scholars must, among other areas of specialty, champion the study of the history of the early church. Although many African scholars are engaged in various aspects of religious studies and theology such as biblical studies, history, and Pentecostal studies among others, scholars in the area of early church history are lacking. It is interesting that the few African scholars who specialize in the history of religions only focus on the epochs from the medieval period to the present, and not the early periods from about the first to around the sixth centuries. The lack of scholarly work in this period leaves a great gap in the study of religions in capturing the early developments of the faith. To this end, religious and theological institutions must have a patristic section of their faculty where issues of church history are taught and not as supplementary to the main courses. This will generate interest for students and hence introduce scholars to the area.

On the pastoral front, I recommend that preachers educate the congregation on the subject of the development of the Christian faith. When preachers do this, members of the church will become familiar with their roots and have a comprehensive understanding of the faith they profess. An appreciation of where the faith has come from and the circumstances around it will deepen the faith and expressions of the practitioners.

When preachers teach on the subject of the early beginnings of the faith, members will appreciate well the relationship between the persecution and martyrdom of the early Christians and contemporary sufferings of Christians. This will help members to pick up lessons on how the early Christians stood firm during this period and it will serve as fertile ground to accommodate better current predicaments. This will imply that the prosperity gospel ideologies will be minimized, if not eliminated, from the worldview of the contemporary Christian expression. Members will appreciate that the Christian calling includes suffering since Christians are pilgrims on this earth.

I, therefore, commend that a study of the persecution and martyrdom of the early Christians must encompass the martyr and apologetic texts. Furthermore, African scholars must show an interest in the study of the early church by including patrology in the academic field of religion and theology institutions. At the pastoral level, the teaching on the early developments of the faith will deepen the faith of the members while it will help members handle suffering better.

Future Studies

An important development which the martyr and apologetic texts point to, which is suggested for further studies in the study of the persecution and martyrdom of the early Christians is a study of the relationship between the early Christian hostilities and conversion. The analysis of the martyr and apologetic texts, brings to the fore the theme of conversion or evangelism which must be investigated by scholars. Tertullian, for instance, threatens that "We multiply when we are mown down by you."[27] Many scholars including Frend support the position that the persecution and martyrdom increased the membership of the Christians.[28] Dunn also suggests that the purpose of Tertullian's *Apologeticum* was not intended to acquit the Christians from the charges but rather to convert the non-Christians.[29] This theme is strategically placed in these texts to show how other non-Christians have come to accept the Christian faith based on the martyrdom of one Christian or the other. This subject deserves attention since an analysis of the texts show they were written in a context where the persecuted church also grew and eventually became the most important institution in society. It would be interesting to discuss the relationship between persecution and growth since the rise and persecution of Christians in the global south has also been linked to examples from the patristic period.

Conclusion

The major contributions of this book to knowledge are realized largely through the methodological approach of the study. The martyr and apologetic texts grew out of the same predicament of the early Christians in the Roman Empire. I have shown the usefulness of combining both texts for a comprehensive image of the persecution and martyrdom. While the martyr texts describe the events for a Christian audience with the perlocutory effect of stimulating admiration and determination to follow the martyr's example, the apologetic texts were addressed mainly to a non-Christian audience to

---

27. Tertullian, *Apologeticum*, 50:3.
28. Engberg, "Martyrdom and Persecution," 95; Frend, *Martyrdom and Persecution*, 257–58.
29. Dunn, "Rhetorical Structure," 49–51.

explain the Christian faith, answer questions about the rites and traditions of the Christians by demonstrating the fallacy and prejudicial nature of the accusations against the Christians. The perlocutory effect of the apologies is to contribute to ending the hostilities and to integrate Christianity into the socioreligious landscape of the Roman Empire and to win people to Christianity. Therefore, the main finding of the research is the proposal to integrate the apologetic texts to corroborate and supplement the martyr texts on the subject of the persecution and martyrdom of the early Christians in the Roman Empire.

The external comparisons of the texts which are derived from the internal comparison show that the texts are very similar in most ways but with a little differentiation when compared to each other. The twists and differences in the texts do not contradict each other but rather emphasize the blinded or blurred sides of both and thereby provide a comprehensive picture of the Christian image of the hostilities when used together. This systematic comparison has also helped to address the submission status of the apologetic texts, particularly those addressed to the authorities.

The submission status of the texts is tackled using the few twists and differences between the texts. Scholars are divided on the submission status of the apologies, while a good majority considers the apologies to be a pure literary fiction, others maintain they were factual incidents that happened in the Roman Empire. The literary critical approach based on Kennedy's rhetorical critical model and systematic comparison method shows that the authors of the apologies intended to submit their texts to their addressees to stop the hostilities and even more importantly, convert them to Christianity. This conclusion affirms Judith Lieu's thesis which suggests that the martyr and apologetic texts being influenced by the same social setting are very similar in many respects.[30]

Finally, the study rediscovers the history of Ghanaian martyrs (both European and African missionaries), a history that is still not largely written but deserves to be known. A comparative study between the inceptions of Christianity in the early Roman and Ghanaian contexts offers a new perspective to Ghanaian Christianity. The blood of the Ghanaian martyrs can therefore be the "seed" of a true Ghanaian and biblically founded Christianity. The

---

30. Lieu, "Audience of Apologetics," 208–23.

examples of these martyrs can help curb the effect of the prevalent prosperity preaching and mould Christians who can stand up for their values against Ghana's developmental agenda that is marked by rampant corruption and money-centric attitude.

Bibliography

Agbeti, Kofi J. *West African Church History: Christian Mission and Church Foundations (1482–1919)*. Leiden: W. J. Brill, 1986.

Agyeman, Fred. *Ghana's First Christian Martyr: Samuel Otu, 1870–1900*. Accra: Waterville Publishing House, 1989.

Alexander, Loveday. "The Acts of the Apostles as an Apologetic Text." In *Apologetics in the Roman Empire: Pagan, Jews and Christians*, edited by Mark Edwards, Martin Goodman, Simon Price, and Christopher Rowland, 15–44. Oxford: Oxford University Press, 1999.

Arbesmann, Rudolph. "Tertullian to Scapula." In *Tertullian Apologetical Works and Minucius Felix Octavius, The Fathers of the Church: A New Translation*, edited by Rudolph Arbesmann, Emily J. Daly, and Edwin A. Quain. Washington: The Catholic University of America Press, 1950.

Asamoah-Gyadu, Kwabena J. *African Charismatics: Current Developments within Independent Indigenous Pentecostalism in Ghana*. Edited by Paul Gifford, Marc R. Spindler, and Ingrid Lawrie. Leiden-Boston: Brill, 2005.

———. *Contemporary Pentecostal Christianity: Interpretations from an African Context*. Oxford: Regnum Books International, 2013.

Barnard, Leslie W. *Justin Martyr: His Life and Thought*. Cambridge: The University Press, 1967.

———. *St. Justin Martyr: The First and Second Apologies*. New York: Paulist Press, 1997.

———. *Studies in the Apostolic Fathers and Their Background*. Oxford: Basil Blackwell, 1966.

Barnes, Timothy D. "A Note on Polycarp." *The Journal of Theological Studies* 18, no. 2 (1967): 433–37.

Barnes, Timothy D. "Legislation against the Christians." *Journal of Religious Studies* 58 (1968): 32–50.

Barnes, Timothy D. "Pre-Decian Act Martyrs." *Journal of Theological Studies* 9 (1968): 509–31.

———. *Tertullian. A Historical and Literary Study*. Oxford: Clarendon Press, 1971.

———. "Legislation against the Christians." *Journal of Religious Studies* 58 (1968): 32–50.

Bartels, Francis L. *The Roots of Ghana Methodism*. Cambridge: Cambridge University Press, 1965.

Beard, M., J. North, and Price Simon. *Religion of Rome*. Vol. 1. Cambridge: Cambridge University Press, 1998.

Bediako, Kwame. *Christianity in Africa: The Renewal of a Non-Western Religion*. Accra: Regnum Africa, 2014.

———. *Jesus in Africa: The Christian Gospel in African History and Experience*. Akropong-Akuapem: Regnum Africa, 2013.

———. *Theology and Identity: The Impact of Culture upon Christian Thought in the Second Century and in Modern Africa*. 2nd ed. Oxford: Regnum, 1999.

Benko, Stephen. *Pagan Rome and Early Christians*. Bloomington: Indiana University Press, 1986.

Bingham, Jeffrey D., ed. *The Routledge Companion to Early Christian Thought*. London: Routledge, 2010.

Birtwhistle, Allen. *Thomas Birch Freeman: West African Pioneer*. London: The Cargate Press, 1950.

Bisbee, Gray A. *Pre-Decian Acts of Martyrs and Commentarii*. Philadelphia: Fortress Press, 1988.

Bisbee, Gray A. "The Acts of Justin Martyr: A Form-Critical Study." *Journal of Early Christian Studies* 3, no. 3 (1983): 129–57.

Boamah, Kwaku. "Apologetic and Martyr Texts: A Christian Response to the Persecutions and Martyrdoms in the Roman Empire." *Trinity Journal of Church and Theology* 20 (2020) 30–53.

———. *Magic and Obstinacy of the Early Christians: Persecutions and Martyrdoms in the Roman Empire*. Saarbrucken: Lambert Academic Publishing, 2011.

———. "The Making of a Canon: Impact of the Old Testament Scriptures in the Chrisitan Canon Development." *International Letters of Social and Humanistic Science* 80 (2018): 8–11.

———. "The Persecution and Martyrdom of the Early Christians and the Prosperity Theology Today." *E-Journal for Religious and Theological Studies* 3, vol. 1 (2019): 32–41.

Bonner, Gerald. "The Scillitan Saints and the Pauline Epistles." *Journal of Ecclesiastical History* 4, no. 1 (1953): 141–46.

Borkowski, Andrew, and Paul du Plessis. *Textbook on Roman Law*. Oxford: Oxford University Press, 2005.

Bowersock, G. W. *Martyrdom and Rome*. Cambridge: Cambridge University Press, 1995.

Boyarin, Daniel. *Dying for God: Martyrdom and the Making of Christianity and Judaism*. Stanford: Stanford University Press, 1999.

Carrington, Philip. *The Early Christian Church*. Vol. 2: The Second Christian Century. Cambridge: The University Press, 1957.
Cook, John G. *Roman Attitude towards the Christians: From Claudius to Hadrian*. Tubingen: Mohr Siebeck, 2010.
Dankwa, Serena O. "'Shameless Maidens': Women's Agency and the Mission Project in Akuapem." *Agenda: Empowering Women for Gender Equity* 63 (2005): 104–16.
de Smith, S. A. *Judicial Review of Administrative Action*. London: Stevens and Sons Limited, 1968.
Debrunner, Hans W. *A History of Christianity in Ghana*. Accra: Waterville Publishing House, 1967.
Dehandschutter, Boudewijn. "The New Testament and the Martyrdom of Polycarp." In *Trajectories through the New Testament and the Apostolic Fathers*, edited by Andrew F. Gregory and Christopher M. Tuckett, 395–406. Oxford: Oxford University Press, 2005.
Dorvlo, Kofi. "The Contributions of German Missionary Evangelism and Education in German Togoland." In *Germany and Its West African Colonies*, edited by Bea Lundt Wazi Apoh, 119–34. Berlin: Lit Verlag dr. W. Hopf, 2013.
Dunn, Geoffrey D. "Rhetorical Structure in Tertullian's Ad Scapulam." *Vigiliae Christianae* 56, no. 1 (2002): 47–55.
Edward, Mark, Martin Goodman, and Simon Price. *Apologetics in the Roman Empire. Pagan, Jews, and Christians*. Oxford: Oxford University Press, 1999.
Ekem, John D. K. *Priesthood in Context. A Study of Priesthood in Some Christian and Primal Communities of Ghana and Its Relevance for Mother-Tongue Biblical Interpretation*. Accra: Sonlife Press, 2009.
Engberg, Jakob. "'From among You Are We. Made, Not Born Are Christians': Apologists' Accounts of Conversion before 310 A. D." In *Continuity and Discontinuity in Early Christian Apologetics*, edited by Jörg Ulrich, Anders-Christian Jacobsen, and Maijastina Kahlos, 49–78. Frankfurt am Main: Peter Lang, 2009.
Engberg, Jakob. "Condemnation, Criticism and Consternation: Contemporary Pagan Authors' Assessment of Christians and Christianity." In *In Defence of Christianity: Early Christian Apologists*, edited by Jakob Engberg, Anders-Christian Jacobsen, and Jörg Ulrich, 201–28. Frankfurt am Main: Peter Lang, 2014.
———. *Impulsore Chresto*. Frankfurt am Main: Peter Lang, 2007.
———. "Martyrdom and Persecution – Pagan Perspectives on the Prosecution and Execution of Christians c. 110–210 AD." In *Contextualising Early Christian Martyrdom*, edited by Jakob Engberg, Uffe H. Eriksen, and Anders K. Petersen, 93–118. Frankfurt am Main: Peter Lang, 2011.

———. "Truth Begs No Favours – Martyr-Literature and Apologetics." In *Critique and Apologetics. Jews, Christians and Pagans in Antiquity*, edited by Anders-Christian Jacobsen, Jörg Ulrich, and David Brakke, 177–208. Frankfurt am Main: Peter Lang, 2009.

Esler, Philip F., ed. *The Early Christian World*. Vol. 2. London: Routledge, 2006.

Essamuah, Caseley B. *Genuinely Ghanaian: A History of the Methodist Church Ghana, 1961–2000*. Trenton: African Word Press, 2010.

Evangelical Presbyterian Church, Anyako. "150th Anniversary Celebration Brochure." Anyako: Evangelical Presbyterian Church, Anyako, 2007.

Evans, E. "Tertullian Ad Nationes." *Vigiliae Christianae* 9, no. 1 (1955): 37–44.

Evans, Robert F. "On the Problem of Church and Empire in Tertullians Apologeticum." *Studia Patristica* 14, no. 3 (1976): 21–36.

Falkenberg, Rene. "Tatian." In *In Defence of Christianity: Early Christian Apologists*, edited by Jakob Engberg, Anders-Christian Jacobsen, and Jörg Ulrich, 67–80. Frankfurt am Main: Peter Lang, 2014.

Falls, Thomas B. *The First Apology, Second Apology, Dialogue with Trypho, Exhortation to the Greeks, Discourse to the Greeks, The Monarchy or The Rule of God*. Washington D.C: The Catholic University of America Press, 1977.

Fowler, Warder. *The Religious Experience of the Roman People*. London: Macmillan, 1933.

Frend, W. H. C. *The Donatist Church. A Movement of Protest in Roman North Africa*. Oxford: The Clarendon Press, 1952.

———. *Martyrdom and Persecution in the Early Church: A Study of a Conflict from the Maccabees to Donatus*. New York: New York University Press, 1967.

Frosini, Vittorio. "A Theory on Natural Justice." *Archives for Philosophy of Law and Social Philosophy* 82, no. 1 (1996): 102–9.

GhanaWeb. "I'm Expensive Pastor – Duncan Williams." 1 November 2011. Accessed 25 August 2020, https://www.ghanaweb.com/GhanaHomePage/NewsArchive/I-m-expensive-pastor-Duncan-Williams-222742.

Gifford, Paul. "The Prosperity Theology of David Oyedepo, Founder of Winners' Chapel." In *Pleasures of Plenty: Tracing Religio-Scapes of Prosperity Gospel in Africa and Beyond*, edited by Andreas Heuser, 83–100. Frankfurt am Main: Peter Lang, 2015.

Gilkey, Langdon. "The Christian Understanding of Suffering." *Buddhist-Christian Studies* 5 (1985): 49–65.

Grant, Robert M. *Greek Apologists of the Second Century*. Philadelphia: The Westminster Press, 1988.

Guerra, Anthony J. *Romans and the Apologetic Tradition. The Purpose, Genre and Audience of Paul's Letter*. Cambridge: Cambridge University Press, 1995.

Gyekye, Kwame. *African Cultural Values: An Introduction*. Accra: Sankofa Publishing Company, 1996.

Haas, Christopher. "Imperial Religious Policy and Valerian's Persecution of the Church, A.D. 257–260." *Church History* 52, no. 2 (1983): 133–44.

Hartog, Paul. *Polycarp's* Epistle to the Philippians *and the* Martyrdom of Polycarp. *Introduction, Text, and Commentary.* Oxford: Oxford University Press, 2013.

Hawthorne, Gerald F. "Tatian and His Discourse to the Greeks." *The Harvard Theological Review* (Cambridge University Press) 57, no. 3 (1964): 161–88.

Hayes, John H., and Carl Holladay. *Biblical Exegesis.* 2nd ed. London: John Knox, 1987.

Headland, T. N., K. L. Pike, and M. Harris. *Emic and Etic.* Newbury Park: Sage, 1990.

Heffernan, Thomas J. *The Passion of Perpetua and Felicity.* Oxford: Oxford University Press, 2012.

Heuser, Andreas, ed. *Pleasures of Plenty: Tracing Religio-Scapes of Prosperity Gospel in Africa and Beyond.* Vol. 161. Frankfurt am Main: Peter Lang, 2015.

Hinnells, John R. "Why Study Religions?" In *The Routledge Companion to the Study of Religion*, edited by John R. Hinnells, 5–20. London: Routledge, 2010.

Holmes, W. Michael, trans. *The Apostolic Fathers in English.* Grand Rapids: Baker Academic, 2006.

Holmes, W. Michael. "The Martyrdom of Polycarp and the New Testament Passion Narratives." In *Trajectories through the New Testament and the Apostolic Fathers*, edited by Andrew F. Gregory and Christopher M. Tuckett, 407–32. Oxford: Oxford University Press, 2005.

Hunt, Emily J. *Christianity in the Second Century. The Case of Tatian.* London: Routledge, 2003.

Jacobsen, Anders-Christian. "Apologetics and Apologies – Some Definitions." In *Continuity and Discontinuity in Early Christian Apologetics*, edited by Jörg Ulrich, Anders-Christian Jacobsen, and Maijastina Kahlos, 5–22. Frankfurt am Main: Peter Lang, 2009.

———. "Main Topics in Early Christian Apologetics." In *Critique and Apologetics: Jews, Christians and Pagans in Antiquity*, edited by Anders-Christian Jacobsen, Jörg Ulrich, and David Brakke, 85–110. Frankfurt am Main: Peter Lang, 2009.

Janssen, L. F. "'Superstitio' and the Persecution of the Christians." *Vigiliae Christianae* 33 (1979): 131–59.

Johnson, Luke T. *Among the Gentiles: Greco-Roman Religion and Christianity.* New Haven: Yale University Press, 2009.

Johnston, David. *Roman Law in Context.* Cambridge: Cambridge University Press, 1999.

Kahlos, Maijastina. *Debate and Dialogue: Christian and Pagan Cultures c. 360–430.* Aldershot: Ashgate, 2007.

Kennedy, George A. *New Testament Interpretation through Rhetorical Criticism.* Chapel Hill: University of North Carolina Press, 1984.

Keresztes, Paul. *Imperial Rome and the Christians: From Herod the Great to about 200 AD.* Lanham: University Press of America, 1989.

———. "Law and Arbitrariness in the Persecution of the Christians and Justin's First Apology." *Vigilae Christianae* 18, no. 4 (1964): 204–14.

———. "Paul and the Christian Church." In *Aufstieg und Niedergang der Römischen Welt*, edited by Temporini Hildegard and Haase Wolfgang, 273–87. Vol. 2. Berlin: Walter de Gruyter, 1979.

———. "Tertullian's Apologeticus: A Historical and Literary Survey." *Latomus* 25 (1966): 124–33.

Krentz, Edgar. *The Historical-Critical Method.* Philadelphia: Fortress Press, 1975.

Kwateng-Yeboah, James. *The Social Effect of Prosperity Gospel on Poverty Reduction in Ghana.* Saarbrucken: Scholar's Press, 2016.

Langmuir, Gavin I. *History, Religion, and Antisemitism.* Berkeley: University of California Press, 1990.

Lee, Shayne. "Prosperity Theology: T. D. Jakes and the Gospel of the Almighty Dollar." *CrossCurrents* 57, no. 2 (2007): 227–36.

Lieu, Judith. "The Audience of Apologetics: The Problem of the Martyr Acts." In *Contextualising Early Christian Martyrdom*, edited by Jakob Engberg, Uffe H. Eriksen, and Anders K. Petersen, 205–24. Frankfurt am Main: Peter Lang, 2011.

Lloyd, A. C. "Natural Justice." *The Philosophical Quarterly* 12, no. 48 (1962): 218–27.

Lynch, Joseph H. *Early Christianity: A Brief History.* New York: Oxford University Press, 2010.

Marjanen, Antti, and Petri Luomanen. *A Companion to Second-Century Christian 'Heretics.'* Leiden: Brill, 2005.

Martyr, Justin. *Dialogue avec Trypho.* Translated by Philippe Bobichon. Fribourg: Academic Press Fribourg, 2003.

Mbiti, John S. *African Religious Philosophy.* Oxford: Heinemann Educational Publishers, 1969.

McCracken, George E. "Critical Notes to Arnobius' Adversus Nationes." *Vigiliae Christianae* 3, no. 1 (1949): 37–47.

Millar, Fergus. "The Imperial Cult and the Persecution." In *Le culte des souverains dans l'Empire Romaine*, edited by Willem den Boer, 145–75. Geneva: Foundation Aardt, 1972.

Moss, Candida R. *Ancient Christian Martyrdom: Diverse Practices, Theologies, and Traditions.* New Haven: Yale University Press, 2012.

Moss, Candida R. "On the Dating of Polycarp: Rethinking the Place of the Martyr of Polycarp in the History of Christianity." *Early Christianity* 1 (2010): 539–74.

Musurillo, Herbert, trans. *The Acts of the Christian Martyrs*. Edited by Henry Chadwick. London: Oxford University Press, 1972.

Oden, Thomas C. *How Africa Shaped the Christian Mind: Rediscovering the African Seedbed of Western Christianity*. Illinois: InterVarsity Press, 2007.

Oehler, Franciscus, ed. *Tertulliani Quae Supersunt Omnia*. Lipsiae: Lipsiae T. O. Weigel, 1857.

Opoku, Kofi A. *West African Traditional Religion*. Accra: FEP International Private Limited, 1978.

Opoku, Theophilus. *Mamfe: Missionary Report*, 1891, 15.02.

Origen. *Origen Contra Celsum*. Translated by Henry Chadrick. Cambridge: Cambridge University Press, 1953.

Paden, William E. "Comparative Religion." In *The Routledge Companion to the Study of Religion*, edited by John R. Hinnells, 225–42. London: Routledge, 2010.

Parvis, Sara, and Paul Foster. *Justin Martyr and His Worlds*. Minneapolis: Fortress Press, 2007.

Paul, Foster. "Tatian." *The Expository Times* (2008): 105–18.

Petersen, Anders K. "The Diversity of Apologetics: From Genre to a Mode of Thinking." In *Critique and Apologetics: Jews, Christians and Pagan in Antiquity*, edited by Anders-Christian Jacobsen, Jörg Ulrich, and David Brakke, 15–42. Frankfurt an Main: Peter Lang, 2009.

Pliny. *Pliny to the Emperor Trajan*. Vol. 2, chap. 96–97. In *Pliny. Letters and Panegyricus*, translated by Betty Radice, 284–93. London: William Heinemann, 1969.

Pobee, John S. *Persecution and Martyrdom in the Theology of Paul*. Sheffield: JSOT Press, 1985.

Presbyterian Church of Ghana. *Biography of the Late Samuel Otu (1870–1900), Ghana's First Christian Martyr*. Tachimantia: Godson Printing and Multimedia Centre, 2000.

Prior, Joseph G. *The Historical Critical Method in Catholic Exegesis*. Roma: Editrice Pontificia Universita Gregoriana, 2001.

Quarcoopome, T. N. O. *West African Traditional Religion*. Ibadan: African University Press, 1987.

Reicke, Bo. "The Epistles, James, Peter, and Jude: Introduction, Translation and Notes." In *The Anchor Bible*, edited by Foxwell W. Albright and David N. Freedman, 69–185. Garden City: Doubleday, 1964.

Rendall, Gerald H., trans. *Minucius Felix*. London: William Heinemann, 1977.

Roberts, Alexander and James Donaldson, eds. Latin Christianity: *Its Founder, Tertullian*. Vol 3 in The Ante Nicene Fathers: *Translations of the Writings of the Fathers down to AD325 Chronologically Arranged, with Brief Notes and Prefaces by A Cleveland Coxe*. New York: The Christian Literature Company, 1887.

Rutherfurd, Andrew. "The Passion of the Scillitan Martyrs." Vol. 9. In *The Ante-Nicene Fathers: Translations of The Writings of the Fathers down to AD 325*. Edited by Allan Menzies. Translated by J. A. Robinson, 283–90. New York: The Christian Literature Company, 1896.

Sanneh, Lamin. *West African Christianity: The Religious Impact*. Maryknoll: Orbis Books, 1983.

Sharpe, Eric J. "The Study of Religion in Historical Perspective." In *The Routledge Companion to the Study of Religion*, edited by John R. Hinnells, 21–38. London: Routledge, 2010.

Shaw, Eric K. "Pennies from Haven: An Integration of Cognitive Dissonance and Spiritual Frames in a Prosperity Church." *Sociological Focus* 34, no. 2 (2001): 213–29.

Sherwin-White, A. N. "Early Persecutions and Roman Law Again." *Journal of Theological Studies* 3 (1952): 772–87.

———. *The Letters of Pliny. A Historical and Social Commentary*. Oxford: Oxford University Press, 1966.

———. "Why Were the Early Christians Persecuted? An Amendment." *Past and Present* 27 (April 1964): 23–27.

Sill, Ulrike. *Encounters in Quest of Christian Womanhood: The Basel Mission in Pre- and Early Colonial Ghana*. Leiden: Brill, 2010.

Skarsaune, Oskar. "Justin and the Apologists." In *The Routledge Companion to Early Christian Thought*, edited by D. Jeffrey Bingham. London: Routledge, 2010.

Stark, Rodney. *The Rise of Christianity: How the Obscure, Marginal Jesus Movement Became the Dominant Religious Force in the Western World in a Few Centuries*. New York: Princeton University Press, 1996.

Ste. Croix, G. E. M. de. "Why Were the Christians Persecuted?" *Past and Present* 26 (1963): 6–38.

———. "Why Were the Early Christians Persecuted? A Rejoinder." *Past and Present* 27 (1964): 28–33.

Tacitus. *The Annals*. Leob Classical Library. Translated by John Jackson. Vol. 5. London: Harvard University Press, 1969.

Tate, Randolph. *Biblical Interpretation: An Integrated Approach*. 3rd ed. Peabody: Hendrickson, 2008.

Tatian. *Oratio ad Graecos*. Edited by Molly Whittaker. Oxford: Clarendon Press, 1982.

Tertullian. "Ad Nationes." In *Ante-Nicene Fathers: Translations of the Writings of the Fathers down to A.D. 325*. Edited by Alexander Roberts and James Donaldson.

Translated by Peter Homes, 3–15, 109–717. Edinburgh: T&T Clark, 1866–72, 1997 reprint.

Tertulliani, Quinti Septimi Florentis. *Ad Nationes Libri Duo.* Edited by Janus Guilielmus Philippus Borleffs. Leiden: Brill, 1929.

Tertullian. *Apology. De Spectaculis.* Translated by T. R. Glover. Cambridge: Harvard University Press, 1977.

Tilley, Maureen A., trans. *Donatist Martyr Stories: The Church in Conflict in Roman North Africa.* Vol. 24. Liverpool: Liverpool University Press, 1996.

Tull, Patrick K. "Rhetorical Criticism and Intertextuality." In *To Each Its Own Meaning: An Introduction to Biblical Criticism and Their Application*, edited by Steven L. McKenzie and Stephen R. Haynes, 156–79. Westminster: John Knox Press, 1999.

Turcan, Robert. *The Gods of Ancient Rome, Religion in Everyday Life from Archaic to Imperial Times.* Cambridge: Edinburgh University Press, 2000.

Turpin, William. "Formula, Cognitio and Proceedings Extra Ordinem." *Revue Internaltionale des droits l'Antiquite* (1990): 499–574.

Ulrich, Jörg. "Apologists and Apologetics in the Second Century." In *In Defence of Christianity: Early Christian Apologists*, edited by Jakob Engberg, Anders-Christian Jacobsen, and Jörg Ulrich, 1–34. Frankfurt am Main: Peter Lang, 2014.

Ulrich, Jörg. "Justin Martyr." In *In Defence of Christianity: Early Christian Apologists*, edited by Jakob Engberg, Anders-Christian Jacobsen, and Jörg Ulrich, 51–66. Frankfurt am Main: Peter Lang, 2014.

Urch, Erwin J. "Procedure in the Courts of the Roman Provincial Governors." *The Classical Journal* (1929): 93–101.

Walls, Andrews. *The Cross Cultural Process in Christian History: Studies in the Transmission and Appropriation of Faith.* Maryknoll: Orbis Books, 2002.

———. *The Missionary Movement in Christian History: Studies in the Transmission of Faith.* Maryknoll: Orbis Books, 1996.

Walsh, Joseph. "On Christian Atheism." *Vigiliae Christianae* 45 (1991): 255–77.

Wilken, Robert L. *The Christians as the Romans Saw Them.* London: Yale University Press, 2003.

Willert, Niels. "Tertullian.". In *In Defence of Christianity: Early Christian Apologists*, edited by Jakob Engberg, Anders-Christian Jacobsen, and Jörg Ulrich, 159–84. Frankfurt am Main: Peter Lang, 2014.

Witgen, Ralf. *Gold Coast Mission History.* Techny: Divine Word, 1956.

Young, Frances. "Greek Apologists of the Second Century." In *Apologetics in the Roman Empire. Pagans, Jews, and Christians*, edited by Mark Edwards, 81-104. Martin Goodman and Simon Price, Oxford: Oxford University Press, 1999.

Index

A

Ad Graecos 29, 30, 33, 99, 100, 104–107, 127, 128, 130–134, 136, 138, 144, 173
Ad Nationes 29, 30, 33, 42, 101, 110, 111, 113, 127–134, 144
Ad Scapulam 30, 33, 63, 98, 101, 102, 110, 113, 117–122, 124–126, 136, 144, 171, 173, 176, 179
Anlo 42
Apologeticum 29, 30, 33, 101, 102, 110, 111, 113, 117–126, 136, 138, 139, 140, 144, 147, 179
Augustinian Catholic Fathers 4

C

cannibalism 10, 11, 22, 73, 85, 139
celebrity pastors 2
cognitio extra ordinem 14, 84, 91, 121, 129, 131, 150
contradict x–xii, 3, 6, 35, 36, 55, 65, 67, 90, 94–96, 146, 148, 160, 165, 180
corroborate x–xii, 3, 6, 35, 36, 65, 67, 90, 95, 96, 146, 148, 160, 166, 177, 180

D

delator 84, 151

E

Engberg 3, 4, 7, 10, 11, 14, 15, 17, 21, 22, 24, 30, 33, 57, 60, 63, 85, 91, 95–97, 100, 149, 176, 179
eschatological 19, 81
Eucharist 23, 103–105, 126, 142, 148, 152

F

Felicity 44, 64–66, 69, 70, 73, 169, 172
Freeman 41, 45, 47–49, 52
fusion xii, 34, 56, 149

G

genius 70, 76
Ghanaian Christian 6, 7, 38
Ghanaian Christianity 162, 180
Ghanaian Christians 5, 169, 170, 172
Gyamea 44

H

harmony xiv, 34, 56, 66, 82, 137, 149, 151

I

immoral 10
incest 10, 22, 73, 85, 119, 130, 138

J

Justin 20, 22, 24, 25, 29, 30, 32, 33, 44, 56, 57, 60–63, 66, 82–89, 97, 99–104, 106, 116–119, 121–126, 128, 136, 139, 140, 144, 145, 172, 174

K

Kade 44
Komenda and Efutu 4

L

Lieu 23
Literary Critical approach 31

M

Mamfe 4, 42, 43, 44, 169
Martyrdom of Justin and his Companions 30, 56, 57, 82–89, 174
Martyrdom of Perpetua and Companions 56
Martyrdom of Perpetua and Felicitas 30
Martyrdom of Polycarp 29, 30, 32, 44, 49, 56, 57, 59, 60, 66–69, 71–73, 75–81, 91, 93, 171–173, 175, 176

N

name 7, 10, 11, 22, 25, 39, 46, 59, 65, 73, 79, 84, 91, 101, 114, 119, 120, 130, 138, 139, 175
narrative 30, 56, 66, 67, 69, 72, 73, 75, 78–82, 90, 92, 116, 127, 129, 136
nomen 13

O

obstinacy 10, 11, 14, 22, 43, 44, 48, 87, 93, 113, 115, 120, 121, 125, 130, 138, 176

P

pax deorum 75, 76, 86, 120, 130, 139, 151
pax Romana 74, 75, 87, 151
Perpetua 9, 24, 29, 30, 32, 33, 43, 44, 56–58, 63–81, 93, 111, 169, 171, 172, 174
Polemic 78, 88, 92, 131, 140, 143
Polycarp 24, 29, 44, 49, 58–60, 67–71, 73, 75–78, 80, 81, 92, 171–173, 175, 176
prosperity gospel 4, 6, 7, 26–28, 178
prosperity theology 2, 6, 25
protocol 30, 56, 82–84, 87, 88, 90, 92

R

Ramseyer 46, 49
religio 7, 20
Riis 46

S

Samuel Otu 4, 46, 49–51, 169
Scillitan Martyrs 29, 30, 32, 56–58, 62, 63, 66, 82–89, 108, 172
submission status xii–xiv, 4, 21, 35, 36, 96, 135, 146, 148, 149, 155, 160, 162, 163, 166, 168, 180
suffering xi, xii, 1–5, 7, 8, 25, 28, 29, 34, 35, 37, 53, 66, 76, 77, 87, 92, 115, 127, 136, 148, 151, 162, 163, 168–171, 173, 176, 178
superstitio 7, 10, 11, 74, 86, 91
supplement xii–xiv, 3, 6, 35, 36, 65, 67, 90, 94–96, 146, 148, 153, 155, 160, 162, 165, 177, 180
synthesis xii, 34, 56, 93, 135, 143, 148

T

Tatian 22, 25, 29, 30, 33, 99, 100, 102, 104–107, 127–134, 136, 138, 140, 142, 144, 173
Tertullian 2, 13, 25, 29, 30, 33, 42, 48, 49, 58, 59, 63, 98, 100,

102, 105, 107–113, 117–134, 136–140, 144, 158, 169, 171, 173, 176, 179
Theophilous Opoku 42

U
ungodly 9, 10, 11

V
visions 81, 93

W
Wilhelmina. Gyamea 43

Y
Yaa Kade 43

Langham Literature, with its publishing work, is a ministry of Langham Partnership.

Langham Partnership is a global fellowship working in pursuit of the vision God entrusted to its founder John Stott –

> *to facilitate the growth of the church in maturity and Christ-likeness through raising the standards of biblical preaching and teaching.*

Our vision is to see churches in the Majority World equipped for mission and growing to maturity in Christ through the ministry of pastors and leaders who believe, teach and live by the word of God.

Our mission is to strengthen the ministry of the word of God through:
- nurturing national movements for biblical preaching
- fostering the creation and distribution of evangelical literature
- enhancing evangelical theological education

especially in countries where churches are under-resourced.

Our ministry

Langham Preaching partners with national leaders to nurture indigenous biblical preaching movements for pastors and lay preachers all around the world. With the support of a team of trainers from many countries, a multi-level programme of seminars provides practical training, and is followed by a programme for training local facilitators. Local preachers' groups and national and regional networks ensure continuity and ongoing development, seeking to build vigorous movements committed to Bible exposition.

Langham Literature provides Majority World preachers, scholars and seminary libraries with evangelical books and electronic resources through publishing and distribution, grants and discounts. The programme also fosters the creation of indigenous evangelical books in many languages, through writer's grants, strengthening local evangelical publishing houses, and investment in major regional literature projects, such as one volume Bible commentaries like the *Africa Bible Commentary* and the *South Asia Bible Commentary*.

Langham Scholars provides financial support for evangelical doctoral students from the Majority World so that, when they return home, they may train pastors and other Christian leaders with sound, biblical and theological teaching. This programme equips those who equip others. Langham Scholars also works in partnership with Majority World seminaries in strengthening evangelical theological education. A growing number of Langham Scholars study in high quality doctoral programmes in the Majority World itself. As well as teaching the next generation of pastors, graduated Langham Scholars exercise significant influence through their writing and leadership.

To learn more about Langham Partnership and the work we do visit **langham.org**

www.ingramcontent.com/pod-product-compliance
Lightning Source LLC
Chambersburg PA
CBHW070805230426
43665CB00017B/2492